PUPPY BIBLE

The ultimate week-by-week guide
to raising your puppy

PUPPY BIBLE

The ultimate week-by-week guide
to raising your puppy

Claire Arrowsmith & Alison Smith

FIREFLY BOOKS

A FIREFLY BOOK

Published by Firefly Books Ltd. 2013

Second printing, 2013

Publisher Cataloging-in-Publication Data (U.S.)

Arrowsmith, Claire.
    Puppy bible : the ultimate week-by-week guide to raising your puppy / Claire Arrowsmith and Alison Smith.
[288] p. : col. photos. ;   cm.
Includes index.
Summary: A week-by-week planner starting before a puppy arrives until it is six months old. Includes their development, health, diet, socialization and first aid, as well as guidance for the owners.
ISBN-13: 978-1-77085-193-1 (pbk.)
1. Puppies. I. Smith, Allison. II. Title.
636.707 dc23   SF427.A7769 2013

Library and Archives Canada Cataloguing in Publication

Arrowsmith, Claire
    Puppy bible : the ultimate week-by-week guide to raising your puppy / Claire Arrowsmith & Alison Smith.
Includes index.
ISBN 978-1-77085-193-1
        1. Puppies. 2. Puppies—Training. I. Smith, Alison II. Title.
SF427.A77 2013   636.7'07   C2012-907506-X

Published in the United States by
Firefly Books (U.S.) Inc.
P.O. Box 1338, Ellicott Station
Buffalo, New York 14205

Published in Canada by
Firefly Books Ltd.
50 Staples Avenue, Unit 1
Richmond Hill, Ontario L4B 0A7

Printed in China

This title was developed by:
Hamlyn, a division of
Octopus Publishing Group Ltd
Endeavour House
189 Shaftesbury Avenue
London, WC2H 8JY

CONTENTS

INTRODUCTION

Comprehensive and simple to use, this is the ultimate reference book on how to raise a happy, healthy dog, whether you are an experienced owner or a complete novice. It is uniquely designed to guide you on a week-by-week basis from the all-important planning stages up to those first exciting days when you collect your new puppy and bring him home, right through to the first 6 months of his life and beyond. It's so easy – you can find out exactly how your puppy is developing, from birth to adulthood, and discover what needs to be done and the ideal time to do it.

This fresh new approach features natural, gentle and positive training methods and socialization techniques, which are based on kindness and rewarding good behavior. By following the expert guidance in this book, you can learn how to have a friendly, well-behaved puppy that is healthy, happy and a pleasure to own.

How this book works

This practical book works in two parts, each of which complements the other, and together they cover all your everyday puppy care needs.

Part 1: Week-by-week planner

The first part of this book contains a week-by-week planner, which tells you what to do, when to do it and what to look out for in the first 6 months of your dog's life. There is also a weekly countdown before your puppy is born as well as information on caring for older puppies from 6 months onward.

This section shows you how your puppy is developing and what you should be doing as a responsible owner. It also alerts you to any significant calendar events that you should look out for and be aware of. There is expert advice on:

• Your puppy's physical and mental development
• What to expect from his behavior
• What you should do at every stage
• Common problems that might occur.

The week-by-week planner is cross-referenced throughout to the second part of the book, giving you easy access to a more comprehensive resource when you require a more analytical approach.

Part 2: The puppy encyclopedia

The second part of this book provides you with detailed information that will help to answer any questions you might have about looking after your puppy. It features in-depth insight into every aspect of puppy care, including the following:

• Choosing the right puppy for you
• Settling him into your home
• Socialization and habituation
• Everyday care
• Housebreaking
• Diet and feeding
• Exercise and playing games
• Reward-based obedience training
• Body language and recognizing the signs
• Solving common behavior problems
• Keeping your puppy safe
• Health and canine first aid.

There are also handy checklists and tables for quick and easy reference when you are in a hurry. Useful tips and pet care essentials are highlighted throughout in box panels.

Training your puppy from his first few weeks with you will help you achieve a happy, well-behaved adult dog.

Expert advice

Owning a puppy can be daunting, especially if you are a first-time novice, but the expert advice in this book will give you the confidence to train, socialize and care for your puppy as well as setting your mind at rest as you encounter new experiences and situations. It teaches you how to troubleshoot on a practical level and explains why puppies behave differently at key points in their development, taking the stress out of puppy ownership and making it more enjoyable for you and your family.

Responsible ownership

This book will not only help you to become a more responsible owner but also show you how to make quality time for your puppy – however busy you are, you need to create space in your day to spend with your canine friend. This will enable you to develop a good relationship, based on mutual respect, and promote better awareness of what you must do to meet your puppy's basic needs. By communicating effectively and caring for him responsibly, you can get to know and understand him better, making socialization and training easier for both of you. Like any good human parent, you are responsible for your puppy's education, and the habits and behaviors that you teach him now from the earliest possible age will endure into adulthood.

Consult your vet

The information and advice given in this book are not a substitute for consulting your veterinarian. If you have any concerns whatsoever about your puppy's health or behavior, you should seek professional advice and discuss them with your vet and/or a pet behavior counselor.

Good behavior

By teaching your puppy good manners and how to behave responsibly in his early formative period, you can avoid many of the behavior problems that can occur later on in a dog's life, damaging good canine-human relationships. Dogs behave badly when they are insufficiently socialized as puppies, are bored or treated unkindly by their owners. It is your duty as a responsible owner to care for your puppy and actively promote his physical and mental welfare. This book tells you how to take this even further by motivating and stimulating your puppy with exercise, games and obedience training, and by providing pleasant encounters with as many people, other animals and different situations and environments as possible.

A rewarding relationship

This book is the definitive guide for puppy owners everywhere and will enable you to get organized in advance and enjoy the exciting journey ahead as you build a rewarding and enjoyable relationship with your puppy. By fulfilling his physical and psychological needs, he will not only be more relaxed but also more likely to have a long and healthy life. You will be proud to own a happy, well-behaved dog that you can take anywhere.

Left: Owning a dog is a very rewarding experience and the lifelong companionship it brings will add a new dimension to your life.

All puppies are cute and fun-loving but they soon grow up into adults, so take care to choose the right breed of dog for you and your family.

PART 1
WEEK-BY-WEEK PLANNER

Countdown
to your new puppy: 1

Your lifestyle

Different breeds suit different owners, locations and living arrangements. A giant breed, such as a Great Dane, would not be suitable if you live in a tiny apartment but a small dog might adapt well. Similarly, a working dog with excess energy needs more space and a large yard. Consider your lifestyle when choosing a dog:

• Where do you live? If you live in the city or a small apartment, a small dog may be best for you.
• Do you have a yard or access to a nearby park? Your dog will need regular exercise.
• Are you fit and energetic? If you are disabled or sedentary, don't buy an active dog.
• Are you retired or work from home? If so, you can spend more time with your dog.
• Do you work full-time or are you out all day? If so, you may need a dog walker.
• Do you have the time and energy for a dog? He will need lots of attention and exercise.
• Do you have young children or a baby? Choose a breed with a good temperament.
• Do you have other pets? If so, think carefully about getting a dog and how he will fit in.

Your budget

In addition to the cost of buying a puppy, you need to consider the other initial expenses:

Initial expenses
• Puppy collar, ID tag and leash
• Puppy bed/bedding
• Food and water bowls and puppy food
• Grooming equipment
• Microchipping
• Vaccinations and worming/flea treatments
• Toys, chews and treats
• Socialization and training classes

Long-term costs
• Collars, leashes, bedding, toys and general equipment
• Everyday food and treats
• Health insurance
• Annual vaccination boosters
• Regular worming and flea treatments
• Veterinary bills
• Professional stripping and grooming parlor
• Boarding/pet-sitting costs

Write a list

How much spare time do you have?

How close do you live to open spaces?

How big is your house and yard?

Do you own other pets?

Why do you want a dog?

- Do you want a companion for yourself?

- Or a family dog for your children?

- Do you want to take part in activities with your dog?

- Do you want to keep fit and go walking or jogging with your dog?

- Would you feel safer and more protected if you owned a dog?

See pages 82-83

Pros and cons

Think about all the benefits of owning a dog and then consider the potential problems, so you can make an informed decision.

Pros

- A puppy will bring you lots of joy and fun.
- It is beneficial for children to have a dog.
- A dog is great for socializing and getting out.
- Owning a dog helps you stay fit and healthy.
- Dog owners tend to be healthier and suffer less stress than other people.

Cons

- If you are out at work all day, you need to arrange for someone to check on your dog.
- A dog can restrict your freedom to go away on vacation. See pages 252–255
- You need to pay for his food, equipment, health and expenses.
- It takes time and patience to train a puppy. See pages 182–203
- You have to set aside time every day for exercise, training, playing games and grooming a dog.

A puppy will be a wonderful addition to your family but the decision to get one should not be taken lightly – a dog is for life.

Countdown
to your new puppy: 2

What sort of dog?

You need to think about which dog is best for you and your lifestyle. You must consider a breed's temperament, size and exercise requirements as well as its appearance.

Temperament: If you are laid-back or are an inexperienced owner, choose a dog with a gentle temperament and easy-going nature. Don't opt for a challenging, powerful dog or one that will be difficult to train and control.

Size: All puppies are small and cute but they grow up into adults, some of which are very large indeed. Check out the eventual height and weight of the breeds you like.

Exercise: Some dogs need a lot of exercise – a quick walk, first thing in the morning and last thing at night, is not enough. Even small Toy breeds require a surprising amount of exercise. ◗ See pages 242–243

Family dog: Some breeds are happier with adults than children – do your research.

Pedigree or mixed-breed?

If you haven't decided on a pedigree dog or a mixed-breed, consider the following points:

Pedigree
- You will know exactly the size, shape and coat of the adult dog.
- You will have a good idea of temperament.
- A pedigree puppy costs more than a mixed-breed.
- Some pedigree dogs have hereditary health issues and will need to be tested. ◗ See pages 276–277
- A pedigree dog will be registered (with papers) and you can show him if you wish.

Mixed-breed
- Mixed-breed puppies look similar but their adult size and appearance can be uncertain.
- Ownership costs are same as for a pedigree.
- Mixed-breed dogs are often unique.
- They have hybrid vigor and tend to be healthier than many pedigree dogs.
- You don't know their temperament. ◗ See pages 100–101

How many?

It's best just to buy one puppy, especially for first-time owners.

A dog is as happy to have you as a companion as another dog.

Socializing and training two puppies is very challenging.

Companion dog or show dog?

Most people keep dogs as companions, but dog showing has become a very popular pastime. You need to own a pedigree dog that has been registered with the Kennel Club in your country. It is an absorbing hobby but, win or lose, you always take the best dog home with you.

Girl or boy?

Before you start looking for a puppy, decide whether you want a female dog (bitch) or a male one. There are important factors to consider when making this decision.

Female dogs: These tend to be more gentle and less dominant than males and are usually great with children, although they can suffer from mood swings. They are often easier to housebreak and exercise as they do not display the marking behaviors of many male dogs. They need to be spayed as puppies (unless you plan to show and breed from her). A female dog in season will receive a lot of interest from all the male dogs in the vicinity. ◗ See pages 272–273

Male dogs: These may need a firmer hand during their formative training and socialization. If they are not neutered, they tend to roam more, to mount almost anything and, in some cases, can be aggressive toward other dogs. A neutered dog is often quieter and easier to handle and less likely to have territorial marking issues. ◗ See pages 226–227; 272–273.

Labrador puppies are very affectionate and friendly, making them ideal pets for families and inexperienced owners.

Countdown
to your new puppy: 3

Find a puppy

The time has come to look for your ideal puppy. Do your research carefully and thoroughly.

Check advertisements: Look in local papers or online for Kennel Club registered puppies.

Contact the Kennel Club: Ask for a list of responsible breeders who have undergone vigorous checks on their kennels.

Talk to the breed society: The secretary of the local breed society should know of existing or forthcoming litters as well as any young dogs in breed rescue.

Local vet's office: Visit and ask the staff whether they know of any good local breeders who have litters of puppies for sale.

Talk to other dog owners: Go to your local park or training class and ask the owners of the breeds you like to recommend breeders.

Go to local dog shows: You can source good breeders and talk to owners about their dogs.

What to avoid

There are many traps you can fall into when buying a puppy and you must be circumspect. Selling puppies is a lucrative business and, inevitably, there are some unscrupulous breeders and dealers as well as puppy farms. Always adhere to the following guidelines:

- Never buy a puppy off the Internet without doing your research and due diligence first.
- Never buy a puppy without meeting the breeder and seeing the litter and mother.
- Never buy a puppy from any outlet or "breeder" selling many different breeds.
- Never buy a puppy if the seller wants to meet in a parking lot or gas station.
- Never buy a puppy from a pet shop or pet "superstore" – these puppies have nearly always been badly bred and sold for cash.
- Never buy a puppy because you feel sorry for it, especially if it has health problems.
- Never buy a puppy from a puppy farm – these puppies are bred with no consideration for their physical or mental health and welfare. They are bred purely for profit.

Good breeders

There has been a lot of controversy recently about irresponsible breeding and how this has contributed to inherited diseases in some popular breeds, especially Cavalier King Charles Spaniels, German Shepherds, Basset Hounds, Pugs and Bulldogs. Responsible breeders work with specialized canine health organizations to eradicate a wide range of genetic conditions from their breeding lines. Screening tests are available for some of these, including hip dysplasia and eye abnormalities, and you should check whether your preferred breeds are affected. A responsible breeder will:

- Breed from healthy dogs with no genetic defects and test the puppies and provide results. ◗ See pages 276–277
- Keep the puppies and their mother in a stress-free environment in their own home.
- Socialize their puppies to everyday sounds, smells, other dogs and people. ◗ See pages 136–139
- Play with the puppies and give them toys.
- Encourage them to relieve themselves away from their nest.

Young puppies look very cute, but choose a healthy one rather than the runt of the litter – don't let your heart rule your head.

Countdown
to your new puppy: 4

Choose a breeder

The best breeders health check their puppies, breed responsibly, raise healthy, well-socialized dogs with good temperaments in their own home, and have relatively few litters.

Observe the mother: A good breeder will keep the puppies in a safe, warm environment with their mother. Ask to see them, and if they have been separated, find out why. Insist on seeing the mother, so you can observe her temperament and gain insight into the adult size of the puppies. Make sure that they have been brought up with her.

See all the puppies: A good breeder will let you handle all the puppies rather than just the one they offer you. If a particular puppy approaches you boldly, examine it individually.
❯ See pages 256–259

Discount the runt: A good breeder is unlikely to offer a puppy at a "bargain" price because it has a "minor" problem. If a puppy is not healthy or appears stressed, just walk away.

What to ask

Don't be afraid to question the breeder about their puppies and breeding lines. You must be confident about your purchase – the puppy you buy will be your companion for many years to come. Ask the following questions:

• How long have you been breeding?
• What are the strengths and weaknesses of your bloodlines?
• Where was the litter whelped – in your house, garage or a kennel? (The puppies need to be raised in the house for good socialization.)
• Did you have any genetic health tests done on the parents before you bred from them?
• Have you tested the puppies?
• Can I see the results?
• Have the puppies been wormed and vaccinated? Do you have records?
• What kind of guarantee do you offer?
• Will the puppies be Kennel Club registered?
• Do you insure the puppies?
• Are the puppies microchipped?
• At what age do you let your puppies go? (Do not take a puppy before it is 8 weeks old.)

Choose a puppy

It is often the case that once you find the right breeder and meet the puppies, your puppy will choose you. A particular puppy in the litter will stand out from the rest or approach you and do something appealing, and your mind will be made up for you. Check out the following:

- Check that the puppies are healthy with no discharge from the eyes, nose or anus.
  ◗ See pages 256–259

- If you have small children (under 5 years old), pick a middle-of-the-road puppy. A dominant puppy could intimidate them.

- If you have never owned a dog before, choose an average or gentle puppy. A less dominant personality will make it easier for you to take control right from the start.

- If you are an experienced owner with a successful track record in training dogs, you can pick any puppy you like.

- Allow your heart some say in the matter! If you are attracted to a specific puppy from the start, this may be for a good reason.

When you go to the breeder's home to view the litter, you may find that one particular puppy approaches and bonds with you.

Countdown
to your new puppy: 5

Get ready

Even if your puppy is still very young, it is never too early to start preparing for his arrival – the sooner you begin planning the better as this will prevent last-minute problems and omissions. You need to get going on the following:

Buy the equipment your puppy will need: This will include all the items on the checklist
❯ See opposite and pages 108–109

Block off restricted areas: Invest in a child safety gate to prevent your puppy accessing rooms that are off limits or staircases and hallways.
❯ See pages 106–107

Dog-proof your home: Provide a secure environment for your puppy. Check out your house and yard for potential dangers.
❯ See pages 106–107; 110–111

Source a vet: Visit your local veterinary clinics and register with a vet who specializes in canine care and with whom you feel comfortable.
❯ See pages 262–263

Safety first

Not only must you make both your home and yard escape-proof but you must also protect your puppy from potential dangers.

Dog-proof your yard
- Check fences are secure and there are no gaps in hedges through which he can escape.
- Attach wire mesh to the bottom of gates at ground level.
- Cover ponds with wire mesh.
- Lock sheds and store pesticides on a high shelf out of reach.
- Check out any poisonous plants. ❯ See pages 110–111

Dog-proof your home
- Keep electric wires and cables out of reach.
- Switch off electric sockets at floor level.
- Raise curtain rods and blinds off the floor.
- Lock away household cleaners.
- Secure safety locks to cupboards at ground level.
- Put away all shoes and children's toys. ❯ See pages 106–107

House rules

Start thinking about the way you want your dog to behave and the rules you are going to set as soon as possible. Talk to the rest of the family about this and draw up a set of house rules between you that you can all agree on. Make sure everyone sticks to them – dogs like consistency and your puppy will become, understandably, confused if one family member encourages him to sit on the sofa with them while another scolds him for doing so.

- Decide on the house rules and follow them.
- Agree what is acceptable behavior, and what is not acceptable.
- Work out a routine for your puppy for feeding, exercising, playing and sleeping.
- Agree on how you are going to housebreak him and get everyone involved.
- Think about what he needs to feel safe.
- Get everyone to agree on where he will be allowed to go and what will be restricted areas. ▶ See pages 134–135

Consider buying a crate for your puppy – it will provide a bed where he can rest, sleep, play with his toys and feel secure.

Week 1
The newborn puppy

Anatomy

What is it? Whatever your chosen breed, don't be surprised if the newborn puppy bears little resemblance to the dog he will turn into. For the first few days, he will be blind, deaf and, like a newborn baby, will have no teeth.

Senses: The puppy's senses of smell and touch are so important at this stage, as he uses both to sniff and root around in order to find his mother's nipples, which are very heavily scented to help him find them.

Temperature: Your puppy is totally dependent on his mother and littermates to regulate his temperature. If separated from them, he could become very cold and even die. He relies on his mother for food and cannot relieve himself on his own (she will stimulate him to do this every so often). She will also wash him, which provides him with essential petting stimulation.

Behavior

Sleeping: At this age, most of a newborn puppy's time – on average, approximately 90 percent of his day – will be spent sleeping. The other 10 percent is reserved for feeding. This allows all of his energy to go into growing, and in the first week alone, a puppy's weight will usually double.

Instinct: A puppy's behavior in the first few days is based primarily on his instinct. He will cry and whimper if he is separated from his mother and littermates; this, in turn, alerts the dam (mother) to his distress and she will gently bring him back into the family.

Communication: Puppies at this age are not able to communicate very much at all. Their mother will feed and clean them and will immediately sense their distress. She may need monitoring in case she lies on them.

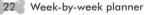

Things to do

Call some potential breeders.

Ask if they have puppies for sale.

Arrange a visit: Ask to view the puppies with their mother.

House rules

Talk to the family about the roles you will all play when your puppy arrives. Make sure that you include your children, in this process as they will form a lasting bond with him.

Draw up a provisional schedule in advance as to who will feed the puppy, housebreak him (this needs to be with the help of an adult) and be in charge of simple tasks, such as topping up his water bowl.

What you should do

Check your home: Get ready for your new puppy's arrival by taking a good look around your home. No matter how clean and clutter-free they are, most houses have some hidden dangers or problem areas for a new puppy and it's your responsibility to make it safe.

- Check for electric sockets plus chewable cables and wires at puppy height, and any gaps between furniture into which he might be able to crawl (and get stuck). ❯ See pages 106–107

- Ensure that your puppy cannot gain access to flights of stairs or hallways leading to external doors – use a child safety gate if this is the case. Buy a fire screen if there is an easily accessible fireplace. ❯ See pages 106–107

- Check that any painted surfaces are painted with nontoxic paint – puppies often find early on that these are good to chew. ❯ See pages 106–107

These young puppies are totally dependent on their mother who supplies all their essential needs.

Week 2
The dependent puppy

Anatomy

Eyes: Generally, week two of your puppy's life will see him take his first look at the world. A puppy's eyes don't spring open suddenly, but usually start opening at one side, then gradually open fully. The average age for this to happen is at 10 days old.

Weight: Your puppy is growing exceptionally fast and his body weight should now be just over double that of his birth weight. He will still look like a tiny ball of fur and he will bear little resemblance to the dog he will become.

Mobility: Your puppy will still be very unsteady on his feet, although he may well be trying to push himself up already. In addition, he is still totally dependent on his mother to provide all his feeding and general care.

Behavior

Dependency: Your puppy's behavior will not have changed very much at all from week one insofar as he is still dependent on others – his mother and also the breeder – for the provision of all his basic needs.

Vocalization: Some puppies may become a little more vocal at this early stage in their development, perhaps even "squeaking" at their littermates, or crying plaintively if they become separated from their mother and feel lost, cold or lonely.

Physical contact: Your puppy will still enjoy lots of physical contact from his littermates as well as his mother, and he may be happy to be petted very gently and handled by his breeder and you.

Things to do

Check out the local vets.

Find out which specialize in dogs.

Check which offices are closest.

Drive there and time the journey.

Inherited health problems

Research any hereditary diseases that are associated with the breed if you are looking at a pedigree puppy. Speak to the breeder about genetic tests and whether these will be done. Also check out your puppy's parents to ensure that they are both healthy dogs and free from problems.
▶ See pages 276–277

What you should do

Forums: If you have access to the Internet, go online and search for any relevant sites that include your breed. These are often groups of owners and breeders whose common interest leads to online discussions and chats, and you can pick up a plethora of useful information, advice and tips this way.

Research: Continue researching your breed and learning as much as possible. Whether it's a visit to a local dog show or a day out at a bigger event, it will be of great benefit to your growing knowledge of your dog, including his eventual size, characteristics, temperament, exercise and grooming requirements. ▶ See pages 86–99

Dog walking: It's never too soon to check out your local parks, countryside and woods. Look for interesting walks that are dog friendly and have dog waste bins along your route. Find out where you can let your dog off his leash safely when he is trained and has good recall.
▶ See pages 242–243

This Staffordshire Bull Terrier is suckling her 2-week-old puppies. At this age they are still dependent on their mother's milk and protection.

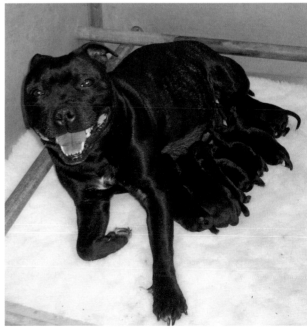

Week 3
The active puppy

Anatomy

Rapid changes: By the time your puppy reaches his third week of life, many physical and behavioral changes are taking place and these can happen quite quickly.

Scenting ability: Your puppy's sense of smell is developing rapidly now and he will sniff a variety of things he comes into contact with.

Hearing: He may also start to show signs of recognizing the sounds of individual voices, as well as responding to and being startled by loud noises. This all helps with the early socialization and habituation processes. ◑ See pages 136–141.

Vision: Although his eyes are now open, your puppy's outlook on the world will still be hazy. He will be able to follow movements now.

Behavior

Increasing independence: By now many puppies are starting to get active, moving around and taking a greater interest in their surroundings. Some become much more adventurous and want to do things more independently of their mother.

Feeding: Although the puppies are still dependent on their mother for food, many breeders may supplement this with puppy milk. Lots of puppies at this age will devour wet puppy food if it is offered.

Play: Puppies become more playful at this age, so responsible breeders will often add a selection of small, soft toys to their environment in an attempt to stimulate them as they grow more curious. ◑ See pages 158–159

Things to do

Check that the breeder has started worming your puppy.

Note down the dates of future worming in your diary.

Ask about flea treatments.

Parasite control

Speak to the breeder or your local veterinary clinic about a worming and flea prevention plan for when you bring your puppy home. Ask about suitable products and where you can obtain them. The brands sold by vets are sometimes more expensive but are often more effective than the ones available in some pet stores.

◗ See pages 268–271

What you should do

Toys: Shop around for some suitable toys and playthings for your puppy to have ready for when he arrives. Look for ones that are safe, nontoxic, sturdy and with nothing that he can chew off and swallow. He will need a selection not only for chewing while he is teething but also for playing with you, and to keep him busy and physically and mentally active.
◗ See pages 158–159; 206–207

Training classes: Find out about dog training classes in your area that offer weekly training sessions. These could be of benefit to you and your puppy, especially for his socialization.
◗ See pages 202–203

Grooming: If your puppy is a long-coated breed or one that needs professional clipping or stripping, why not check out your local grooming parlors? You may want to use these for bathing him as well as keeping his coat healthy and in good shape. ◗ See pages 228–231

These Cavalier King Charles Spaniel puppies stay close to their mother even though they are becoming more independent.

Week 4
The interactive puppy

Anatomy

Eyes: Your puppy may have blue eyes at this stage (much like human babies), but many breeds will experience a change in eye color as they grow older and mature.

Muscular strength: As he develops and moves around more, you will probably observe a change in your puppy's muscle tone and a growing strength, which can be noticeably different from day to day.

Coat: This may still be at the "fluffy" stage, but it will soon be changing to a more adult-looking coat. It may also change color, and in some breeds this can be quite drastic, such as in the case of Dalmatian puppies, whose coats are plain white at birth – the distinctive black or brown spots develop later on at around 3 to 4 weeks of age.

Behavior

Weaning: Puppies will still be getting their food from their mother, but by week four many will start the process of being weaned off her.

Movement: The puppies are still working hard on their movement, and they may have the occasional wobble or even a fall as they continue to find their feet.

Interaction: It's great to watch the puppies interact with each other now, as they play and socialize with each other. In fact, this early experience with their littermates is their very first taste of socialization with other dogs.

Handling: Young puppies at this age may be gently groomed, which is a good way to start socializing them and interacting with humans as well as bonding with people.

Things to do

Buy your puppy's first collar.

Get an ID tag engraved for it.

Purchase a leash as well.

Consider a harness for a small dog.

Food and diet

Have a word with the breeder about your puppy's diet and which foods he is being weaned on. Make sure that you can get hold of the correct food from your local supermarket or pet store and check out and compare the prices. Make a note to ask the breeder for a diet sheet, so you can buy some of the puppy's food in advance. Don't leave everything to the last minute.

What you should do

Safety checks: As the time for your puppy's arrival draws near do more household safety checks and make any essential changes. Start by looking at steep stairs, high steps and door security. If these are potential issues, buy and fit a child safety gate. ❯ See pages 106–107

Grooming: Your puppy will need regular grooming to keep his coat healthy, especially if he is a long-haired, high-maintenance breed. Find out which grooming tools you will need and buy them now. Many short-coated dogs will only require a brush and a comb, but you may also have to invest in specialty items, such as a stripping comb or slicker. Ask your breeder for advice on what to purchase. ❯ See pages 228–231

Dental care: At the same time, buy a canine toothbrush and specially formulated doggy toothpaste – some of these are meat flavored to make them more palatable to dogs. ❯ See pages 234–235

These Border Collie puppies enjoy playing together and, in the process, they learn some valuable socialization lessons.

Week 5
Socialization begins

Anatomy

Rapid development: By now the little bundle of "fluff" from just a couple of weeks ago will really be coming into his own physically and will be showing signs of rapid growth.

Senses: Your puppy's sight and hearing are functioning really well now, which will help him as he makes more concerted efforts to move around and to play.

Nervous system: This is more developed, too, which means that your puppy will no longer require his mother's stimulation in order to relieve himself.

Feeding: It is usually around now that his mother will start discouraging him from feeding from her, and she may even "evade" his advances with a gentle snap or low growl.

Behavior

Socialization: Weeks 5 to 12 in a puppy's life are known as the "socialization period." During much of this time, he will learn how to become a "dog." This often starts when his mother casts aside the role of care-giver and adopts a more dominant, teacher-like behavior toward her young. ◗ See pages 136–137

Good behavior: The mother will start to teach her babies what constitutes acceptable behavior by snarling, growling and even attacking them if they transgress. This tells a puppy very quickly – and in no uncertain terms – when he is doing something that is wrong. Many canine behaviorists believe that how a mother treats her puppies now can have a major effect on how they interact and behave with human beings as they grow older.

Things to do

Make a checklist of things to buy:

- Water and food bowls
- Puppy food
- Dog bed/crate/cage and bedding
- Toys and treats
- Puppy worming tablets.

Keep a record

Stay in touch with the breeder who will be happy to let you know how your puppy is progressing. Indeed, many will send you photographs or email digital images so you can keep track of his progress as he grows and develops. This will also help you and your family to begin the important process of bonding with him before you collect him and eventually bring him home.

What you should do

Sleeping arrangements: Decide where your puppy is going to sleep. Most puppies feel safe spending their first few weeks or months in a puppy crate or cage, as it gives them a secure place of their own to retreat to and relax in.

Choose a place where the floor is easy to clean – in case of accidents – and close to the door through which you will take the puppy into the yard to housebreak him. Also check out bedding. Types vary, from soft, sheepskin to larger cushions. Many are machine washable, so check the label.

Puppy pens and crates: Check these out on the Internet or visit your local pet store. Pens and crates range from soft canvas ones to sturdy metal versions. Both are acceptable, comfortable and safe, but you must make sure that the one you choose is big enough to accommodate a growing puppy. You may also want to invest in a pen to use in the house or outside in the yard.

At this age, if not earlier, the breeder will start weaning your puppy off his mother. This can be done using a creamy, easy-to-eat cereal.

Week 6
The energetic puppy

Anatomy

Vision: Your puppy's senses are now almost fully developed. At 6 weeks old, he can see nearly as well as an adult dog. Dogs have color vision equal to that of red/green color blindness in a human being, which means that he is unlikely to be able to see red and/or green as we can.

Sense of smell: Most of your puppy's interpretation of the world around him will come from the messages he receives from his nose. To put this into context, a dog uses an incredible 40 percent more of his brain on analyzing smells than humans do. We have only five million scent receptors, whereas a Bloodhound has up to 300 million.

Teeth: Your puppy's baby teeth may start to come through now, so he will chew more.
❍ See pages 206–207

Behavior

Space: Your puppy will now require much more space than he did at 5 weeks. This is because he will be more adventurous and will make a big effort to explore more of his surroundings. Many breeders have a puppy room, which is dedicated to this purpose, with sheets of newspaper covering the floor, and often the puppies are allowed to roam freely.

Sleep: Despite all this increased energy and activity, a 6-week-old puppy will still spend lots of time sleeping, which is essential to his continuing growth, health and well-being.

Playing: Puppies often "play" with their littermates around now. Pretend fighting is usually a favorite pastime and this is a valuable way of teaching good manners as well as how to interact with other dogs.
❍ See pages 148–151

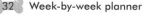

Things to do

Find out about grooming parlors.

Visit some in your area.

See what services they offer and how much they charge.

Decide which you like best.

Yard safety

Check all the fences, hedges and shrubs in your yard. Are there any gaps through which a small puppy could escape? If so, now is the time to fix them before you collect your puppy. You can use wire mesh or some cheap chicken wire to block holes. Also, check for anything dangerous or sharp, such as prickly plants, thorns or barbed wire.

▶ See pages 110-111

What you should do

Comfort blanket: If you go to visit your puppy at the breeder's home, take a blanket or an old piece of your clothing that is impregnated with your scent – just rub your hands on it. This will become a "comfort blanket" for him when he leaves the security of the litter and comes to live with you in 2 or 3 weeks' time.

Spread the word: Let all your friends and neighbors know that you will soon have a new puppy. If any have children or dogs who usually accompany them to your home, warn them that they may have to visit without them for a couple of weeks, or at least exercise caution around your new puppy for a while, as he settles in to his new home environment.
▶ See pages 144–147

Keep a record: Puppies grow up so quickly, so keep a record of your puppy's early weeks and development as he grows into an adult. Buy a photo album or a memory stick.

These black Labrador puppies still enjoy feeding from their mother, even though at this age they will be weaned onto solids.

Week 7
The curious puppy

Anatomy

Gaining weight: At 7 weeks of age, your puppy should be weaned fully from his mother and will be obtaining all the nourishment he needs from eating solid food and any liquids. This change in his eating habits will make him stronger and more active, and he will start to gain weight more rapidly.

Mobility: Your puppy will now be sure-footed enough to be taken into a secure yard area to relieve himself.

Teeth: These will still be appearing and your puppy will chew more to relieve the pain and discomfort. He will need plenty of toys and edible chews. Remember that a puppy's milk teeth, albeit small, are extremely sharp and can really hurt if he nips you, even in play.
❱ See pages 164–165

Behavior

Curiosity: Your puppy's main personality trait during this very important period of his development will be his inquisitiveness. At 7 weeks, puppies are now independent of their mother and littermates, and they want to start exploring their environment and are interested in new people and experiences.

Comprehension: Your puppy will gradually be becoming more receptive to simple commands and may respond to his name.

Play: Your puppy will play bite and growl now. However, be careful not to encourage this as it can lead to behavior problems later on in life. Have fun with him but never allow rough play to go too far or to get out of hand.
If this happens, stop the game immediately. He needs to learn good manners and respect.
❱ See pages 164–167

What you should do

Collecting your puppy: Speak with the breeder and arrange a mutually convenient date for you to collect your new puppy. Some breeders will let puppies go to their new homes at as early as 7 weeks as long as they are fully weaned. ❯ See pages 116–117

Final safety check: As the time of his arrival approaches, do a final safety check of your home. Check that low-level cupboard doors in your kitchen and laundry room close securely. Consider securing child-safety locks to deter the attentions of an inquisitive puppy. Secure trailing wires and cables out of reach and block or turn off electrical sockets at ground level. ❯ See pages 106–107

Socialization classes: Call your veterinary clinic and club and ask if they hold puppy socialization classes. Find out how old your puppy needs to be, what you need to take with you and what the sessions cost. ❯ See pages 136–139

These Parson Jack Russell Terrier puppies are exhibiting classic curiosity for their age, and are using their keen sense of smell to explore their environment.

Week 8
Bringing puppy home

Anatomy

Growth and development: Your puppy is still growing into himself and his bones are becoming increasingly strong. It's never a good idea to do too much physical activity with a puppy at 8 weeks, as this could have a lasting and detrimental effect on how well he matures physically, especially if he is one of the giant breeds whose bones and joints grow at a slower rate than small breeds.◗ See pages 260–261

Adult appearance: At this age, your puppy will start exhibiting the telltale signs of exactly what he will look like as an adult as well as what you can expect when he gets older. If you have bought a dog you intend to show or to compete with in agility or obedience, it will be more obvious to a trained eye how he is going to shape up in the future.

Behavior

Socialization: This is an incredibly important period in your puppy's life when his future character, behavior and habits are formed. However, even if his behavior during the first week of settling him in at home may cause you some concern initially, don't worry. It will take him time to adjust to his new environment and you need to be both patient and tolerant. ◗ See pages 118–119; 136–139

Initial nerves: When he is separated from his mother and familiar surroundings and encounters his new home, your puppy may appear introverted or even nervous at first. Don't worry – this is perfectly normal. He is in an unfamiliar place with new people and, possibly, other animals. Be patient and spend as much time as you can together, settling him in and starting his housebreaking. ◗ See pages 118–119; 122–127

Things to do

Book a visit to the vet for your puppy's first checkup.

Find out about any vaccinations he may need.

Ask your vet about microchipping.

Parasites

Many puppies, no matter how clean their living conditions, can be susceptible to fleas or other harmless skin conditions. Look out for excessive scratching or areas of skin that appear sore or where the hair is thin. Check for flea droppings in his coat – they look like sooty specks of coal. Treat them with an anti-flea preparation obtainable from the vet. Ask about preventative measures.
◗ See pages 268-269

What you should do

Rest: Allow as much human contact as you can, but respect your puppy's need for rest time and sleep – he is still very much a baby.

Housebreaking: Take him outside (in your yard is best) after each meal or when he wakes up to allow him to relieve himself. Repeat this exercise first thing in the morning and last thing at night, too. Obviously, this will not be enough, so watch for signs of him needing to relieve himself, such as sniffing the floor or walking in small circles. Praise and treat him each time he goes outside, but do not punish him if he has the odd "accident" in the house. ◗ See pages 122–127

Diet routine: Your puppy will probably be eating four small meals a day at the moment. Establish a regular routine and stick to it – he will thrive on this (dogs are creatures of habit). The breeder may give you a few days' supply of his food to take home with you. Make sure you have additional supplies in the cupboard. ◗ See pages 128–133

When you collect your puppy from the breeder, check that he is fit and healthy and examine him for any minor problems.

Week 9
The toddler

Anatomy

Physical development: Your puppy is now officially a toddler, and his physical development will be more obvious with each passing week as he continues to grow and put on weight during this important phase.

Male puppies: A few male puppies may start to lift their legs to urinate at about this time, as their muscle tone and coordination develop still further, but don't worry if this takes longer. It can take months or even up to a year or longer for some dogs.

Pads: The soft velvety pads on your puppy's feet will become harder as he starts walking on a variety of different surfaces. The pads need to toughen up to protect him on roads, pavements and rough, uneven surfaces when you start taking him out for walks after his final set of vaccinations.

Behavior

Habituation: Between 8 and 12 weeks your puppy will go through what is known as a general habituation or socialization period, and this is an extremely important phase in his behavioral development.

New experiences: You need to introduce him to as many new experiences as you can, including different people, sounds, objects, environments and other animals. Always stay with him when you do this, encouraging calm behavior and rewarding him with praise and a small treat when he responds well.

Confident or fearful: A puppy at 9 weeks can be erratic from a behavioral point of view. Many puppies will show great friendliness toward anyone and anything, whereas some experience a fear period.
❯ See opposite

Things to do

Give your puppy a basic health check.

Stroke him all over to look for any swelling.

Check his eyes and ears.

Look at his teeth and gums.

Sleepless nights

By now your puppy should have a more settled sleep pattern. If he is still restless at night, go over your evening routine again. Are you sticking to it or have you made some changes, however small? If it has become a little erratic, get back to the same procedure each night - this will soon settle him back down. Be patient ● See pages 118-119; 134-135

What you should do

Fear periods: Look out for and anticipate a "fear period." Any experience that induces anxiety at this time could have a lasting impression on your puppy for life. It is vitally important to avoid any form of punishment to try to correct this, and you must isolate him from the triggers that induce the fear.

Identify the noises, people or objects that cause him the most fear. When he is subjected to them, distract his attention immediately and reward him enthusiastically for a correct response – for example, if he comes to you when called – rather than rewarding his fear, which is counterproductive. ● See pages 154–155

Freedom: Allow your puppy more freedom and independence to explore inside your house and outside in the yard, but always continue to stay close to him, albeit in the background, at all times. ● See pages 134–135; 138–141

It is very important to give your puppy his own quiet space away from the hustle and bustle of everyday family life.

Week 10
The excited puppy

Anatomy

Teeth: Your puppy will have a mouth full of milk teeth by now, so make sure that he has plenty of hard toys to chew on, rather than your furniture, door frames and shoes. As with a human baby, teething can be painful for your puppy and he needs your help.

A great idea is to put a couple of hard, plastic dog chews in the refrigerator or freezer (baby teething chews are also acceptable). The cold chew will help with teething pain and distract him as well. ◑ See pages 206–207

Breed: If you have a pedigree puppy, he will now start to look recognizably similar to an adult dog of his breed. When puppies are very young and resemble fluffy balls of fur, it is often difficult to tell which breed they are.

Behavior

Excitement: It is natural for puppies to get very excitable about a wide range of things. Yours may have the occasional few minutes when he rushes madly around the house and then drops down exhausted.

Housebreaking accidents: Don't worry if your puppy has the occasional "accident" when he becomes very playful; instead of punishing him, firmly give the command "No" and take him right outside to relieve himself in the yard. ◑ See pages 122–127

Strong-willed puppies: Watch out for any emerging dominant behavior by your puppy toward his "pack" (your family). Some strong-willed puppies may display unwanted telltale signs, such as barking at you to get your attention, or even growling and snarling. Never, ever reward this behavior – ignore it.

Things to do

Check if any vaccinations are due.

Make sure your puppy's worming treatment is up to date.

Buy more puppy food if your supplies are running low.

Look out for

· Changes in his feces: These may be due to tummy upsets or if changes have been made to his usual diet.

· Cuts and abrasions: These can result from boisterous play.

· Biting and mouthing: Discourage "cute" puppy bites with a firm "No"; this can lead to problems later if they are not addressed at this age.
⊙ See pages 164-165

What you should do

Collar and leash: Introduce your puppy to his collar and leash on a daily basis. At first he may resist being walked around on a leash, but be patient and praise him each time he walks beside you without pulling or hanging back.

Practice recall: Use his name plus the word "Come" or "Here" to encourage him to return to you. You can do this either in the house or the yard, on or off the leash, or use a long training line to haul him in if necessary.
⊙ See pages 194–195

Health check: When you are grooming or cuddling your puppy, check him over for signs of fleas. Look in his ears, eyes and mouth.

• His eyes should be clear with no discharge.

• His ears should be clean and healthy looking and not smell unpleasant. ⊙ See pages 256–259

Appetite: Are you happy with his eating habits? He should display a healthy appetite but not overeat greedily or be too fussy.

To get your puppy accustomed to a leash, attach one to his collar and let him run around the yard, trailing it behind him.

Week 11
The anxious puppy

Anatomy

Bone growth: Your puppy's bones will still be growing significantly. Be careful and check that he does not become too boisterous on hard surfaces as he could injure himself.

Milk teeth: As your puppy continues to develop physically, he may start to lose a couple of his milk teeth to make way for his adult teeth. He has 28 milk teeth in total.

Growth and development: Several small walks a day are a good idea for puppies to keep them fit and active, but don't overdo any physical work while your puppy continues to develop and grow. This is especially important for large and giant breeds, such as Irish Wolfhounds and Great Danes, which grow more slowly than smaller dogs and need less exercise than you think.

Behavior

Anxiety: Watch out for anything that causes your puppy anxiety. You may identify noises or situations that are stressful for him, such as the vacuum cleaner, fireworks or children. Be reassuring and calm, but don't hide him away from these experiences as he needs to be de-sensitized to them. ❍ See pages 138–147

Rough play: At this age, puppies enjoy rough and tumble play, with either their family or other dogs. Allow your puppy to play, but don't let things get too rough and out of control.

Housebreaking: Continue to establish a good housebreaking routine. Put him outside first thing in the morning, immediately after every meal and at night before you settle him down. If you notice him circling or sniffing the floor, take him outside immediately. ❍ See pages 122–127

Things to do

Plan a socialization program.

Start when your puppy finishes his set of vaccinations.

Call friends with dogs to arrange walks and visits to their homes.

Bowel problems

Look out for changes in your puppy's bowel movements. These can happen when his feeding routine changes. Try offering a little bland cooked chicken and some plain boiled rice until his tummy settles down again, before gradually reintroducing his normal food over a period of about 4 to 5 days. ◗ See pages 128-131; 236-239

What you should do

Number of meals: If your puppy is still eating four small meals a day, start thinking about cutting him down to three meals now but providing slightly larger amounts. ◗ See pages 128–131; 236–239

Socialization: Introduce him to more people, including letter carriers and other tradespeople, your friends, neighbors and children. Allow them to pet your puppy under your supervision. ◗ See pages 144–147

Leash training: Intensify your leash training, too. By the time your puppy is 12–13 weeks old, he should have finished his set of vaccinations and will be allowed to go out on small walks around your neighborhood or in the local park. You need to make sure that he is accustomed to wearing his collar and can walk nicely on a leash without pulling. You can practice this in advance outside in your yard or even inside the house – it does not matter. ◗ See pages 196–197

Your puppy will need time to rest and sleep between meals, walks, playing games and bursts of physical activity – provide a quiet place for this.

Week 12
The fearful puppy

Anatomy

Mobility: Your puppy should be able to take his first walk outside now that he has had all his vaccinations. Several short walks a day on the leash are best initially, as his body is still growing, so do not give him too much intensive exercise during this important period in his physical development. ❍ See pages 196–197; 242–243

Motor skills: These are still developing but he will be able to walk and run like an adult dog. Some puppies look slightly gangly at this stage, but don't worry – this is normal.

Teeth: Your puppy will now be losing some of his milk teeth to make way for his set of permanent adult teeth – this usually happens between now and 16 weeks of age.

Behavior

Fear period: As your puppy takes his first steps outside the safety of his home, bear in mind that some dogs at this age are still in their "fear" period. Heavy traffic, loud cars, noisy buses and crowds of people may make him nervous. Reassure him, but remember never to praise him for his fear. ❍ See pages 142–143

Attention span: Your puppy's attention span is still relatively short, so limit your training sessions to a maximum of 10–15 minutes to keep him interested and motivated.

Motivation: He has begun to learn which behaviors are appropriate for which times, even if his attention span has remained short. Best of all, he has a strong desire to earn your attention and please you now you and your family have taken the place of his littermates.

Things to do

Book a puppy training class if you have not already done so.

Ask if you need special equipment.

Buy some treats and new toys as rewards for good behavior.

Teething Problems

Signs may vary, but puppies can develop diarrhea, "floppy" ears and a general demeanor of being out of sorts. Check your puppy's mouth regularly as he will start losing his teeth soon.

You can help by giving him an icy-cold chew that has been kept in the freezer, or even a rolled-up pair of old socks.
◐ See pages 206-207

What you should do

Further socialization: This is essential now that your puppy is being introduced to a host of new situations and people. You must continue to create new sights and sounds that will all add to his ability to mature mentally as well as take him to a range of new places.
◐ See pages 142–153

Separation anxiety: Some dogs suffer from this if they are left alone after being with people all the time. To avoid this happening, get your puppy accustomed to being left on his own for short periods of time. Always make sure that he is in a safe room with his bed and plenty of interesting toys. Turn the radio on.
◐ See pages 224–225

Nails: Check whether your puppy's nails need clipping. You should not be able to hear them tapping on a hard floor. Don't try to cut them yourself – if you cut into the "quick," it will bleed profusely. Ask your vet to show you what to do. ◐ See page 233

While your puppy is teething, he will enjoy chewing on hard toys and rubber balls as well as rawhide and commercially made chews.

Week 13
The teenager

Anatomy

Health and fitness: You should now be able to have a good indication as to how fit your puppy is and whether he is growing at a healthy rate by checking the following:

- Can you see and feel the outline of his ribs? He should have signs of a waist when you view him from above.
- He will begin to lose some of his "puppy fat" as a result of his increased exercise routine when you start taking him out for walks after his set of vaccinations has finished. If he is underweight, his ribs will be highly visible; if he is overweight, he will look as though he has a pot belly.

If you are concerned about his weight, you can adjust your puppy's food intake slightly and check him again in 2 weeks. Failing that, consult your vet. ❯ See pages 274–275

Behavior

Adolescent phase: You now have a teenager on your hands and, as with humans, this can be a problematic time of great transformation. Your puppy is ready to absorb more training and new experiences.

Challenging behavior: This is usually a time of great mental growth. Even an eager-to-please dog may start to test the boundaries as he gains confidence. He may challenge you and appear oblivious to your commands.

Setting boundaries: Identify the underlying causes of worrying behavior. Is it caused by separation? Is he tired or hungry? Does he need attention, a walk or more mental stimulation? Remember that this behavior is normal and it can be counteracted by sticking firmly to an established routine and setting clearly defined boundaries.

Things to do

Check out puppy health insurance:

- Does the policy need renewal?
- Does it cover breed-specific issues?
- Are there better options?
- Is it good value for the money?

Play biting

This is a common side effect of teething. It is acceptable as long as it is done on your terms. Never praise your puppy for this – a firm "No" repeated a few times should do the trick, or you can cry out exaggeratedly in pain. Your puppy will not want to hurt you and this should make him stop immediately. ◗ See pages 164–165

What you should do

Set limits: Reward those behaviors that you find acceptable or pleasing and ignore or redirect any that are unacceptable or annoying. Take care that you do not inadvertently "reward" bad behaviors by giving your puppy too much attention.

Obedience training: Continue with your basic obedience training, regularly practicing recall, "Sit" and "Down" on a daily basis. As well as making your dog more well behaved and reliable, training will keep him busy and exercise his mind. Make sure that it is fun for both of you – it should never be a chore.
◗ See pages 190–195

Rewards: Not all dogs are motivated by food treats and some respond better to games with a favorite toy or lots of praise and attention from you. If you do use treats when you are training your puppy, it's a good idea to keep them in a training pouch over your shoulder or around your waist on a belt.
◗ See pages 186–187

Play is a good way of reducing any "puppy fat" that your dog should begin to lose at this age.

Week 14
The exuberant puppy

Anatomy

Muscular and skeletal development: Your puppy is at a critical stage of his muscular and skeletal development at 14 weeks old, so it is important that he gets the right type and amount of exercise to grow properly. However, because puppies at this age can still lack judgment and coordination, injuries can occur if they are not exercised in the right way.
▶ See pages 242–243

Coat: Your puppy's coat should look shiny and healthy and feel soft. Puppies with a wiry coat should feel clean and crisp to the touch.
▶ See pages 228–231

Eyes and nose: Your puppy's eyes should be bright and inquisitive without any signs of tear staining. Healthy puppies often have the classic "wet nose" associated with dogs. However, there should be no discharge.

Behavior

Jumping up: As he gets bigger, your puppy may decide that he likes to jump up on visitors as well as you and his family. This may look like his way of extending a friendly greeting, but, in reality, when dogs jump on guests, they are not exhibiting unbridled joy and love toward them. They are actually committing a disrespectful act that would never be tolerated in the natural canine world.

To break your puppy's jumping habit, lean forward slightly and move into him when he jumps, literally taking space away from him. Alternatively, turn your back on him.

Ignore your puppy: You can prevent over-exuberant behavior now before he is fully grown and establishes bad habits by breaking your eye contact and ignoring him until he calms down. ▶ See pages 220–221

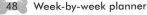

Things to do

Book an appointment with the vet.

Ask your vet about necessary upcoming checkups.

Note down further appointment dates.

Body language

By observing your puppy's body language carefully, you will have a better idea of what he is feeling. Look at his eyes especially:

· Half-closed eyes suggest contentment

· Wide-open ones mean that he is interested and enthusiastic

· An unblinking stare might signify that he feels dominant.
  ◐ See pages 168-171

What you should do

Training classes: Enroll your puppy in a course of training classes now if you have not already done so. You will both learn and benefit from the experience and will receive expert advice and useful tips. Do your research in advance and ensure that the instructors are well qualified and that they use kind, modern methods based on rewarding good behavior.
▶ See pages 202–203

Socialization: Continue to explore a wide variety of new situations and surroundings with your puppy. Always make sure that he is on his leash and that you are in control when you are out in public places. ▶ See pages 142–143

Use rewards: The best way to teach your puppy right from wrong is to consistently reward (with treats and/or praise) correct behavior. Ignore unwanted behavior and you will soon have an obedient and well-mannered puppy. ▶ See pages 186–187

Practice with your puppy what you learn at training classes in other situations and locations, such as the park or your yard.

Week 15
The challenging puppy

Anatomy

Growth spurts: Puppies have growth spurts and achieve physical maturity at different ages, depending on their breed and size. Smaller dogs grow far more quickly than puppies of large and giant breeds. For most puppies, their growth and essential caloric intake start to slow down by the time they reach 15 weeks of age. ◗ See pages 260–261

Appetite: Many puppies continue to have voracious appetites, even though they no longer need as much food, and this can lead to many owners unknowingly overfeeding their pets. Overfeeding a growing puppy can cause musculoskeletal disorders, particularly in large-breed dogs. If you are concerned about your puppy's weight, talk to your vet and seek expert advice. ◗ See pages 274–275

Behavior

Children: Fifteen weeks is a good time to start teaching your puppy and children how to play together. They should get along really well, as long as some basic ground rules are set and strictly observed. Always supervise these play sessions with very young children.

If your puppy gets overexcited during play or begins to nip, he will definitely need to take some time out. You or your children should tell him firmly "No," take away the toys and ignore him for at least 10 minutes.

Challenging behavior: Your puppy may begin to challenge your leadership at this age, and it is important that you establish yourself as the authority figure. Be firm and do not allow him to set the agenda and boundaries of what is considered acceptable behavior. ◗ See pages 134–135

Things to do

Write down all the training class contact details.

Note the dates and times.

Buy additional treats and special equipment for training.

Possessive behavior

Your puppy must give up his toys when you ask him. If he becomes possessive, attract his attention with something else, such as an interesting alternative toy or a tempting treat, and then remove the toy he is holding. Return it to him only when you decide to do so, not on demand. It is important to start teaching him good manners. ● See pages 166–167

What you should do

Encourage good behavior: Continue with your treat/reward training to reinforce your puppy's appropriate behavior. Use food treats or games as well as lavish praise to reward correct behavior. Never punish incorrect behavior – just ignore him instead.
● See pages 186–187

Jackpot: If your puppy behaves exceptionally well in training, he may deserve a bonus reward immediately after he performs the desired behavior. Give him a "jackpot" of extra tasty treats or a special game he enjoys to encourage him to work even harder next time.

Mental stimulation: Use a combination of games, interesting toys and light training to keep your dog mentally stimulated and busy. A bored puppy can easily become destructive and develop bad habits. It is your duty, as a responsible owner, to prevent this from happening by playing games together every day and providing regular walks and plenty of exercise. ● See pages 158–159; 214–215

Possessiveness can be an issue at this age so offer a more interesting toy to teach him to "Drop" or give up an object that you want to take from him.

Week 16
The dominant puppy

Anatomy

Weight gain: Puppies grow rapidly between birth and 6 months of age, and how much they grow or the amount of weight they put on will depend on their breed, diet and ultimate adult size. By 16 weeks of age, your puppy could be at least half of his adult weight.

Urination: Your puppy can generally hold his urine for about 5 hours now. This means that you will need to take him out at least once every 5 hours to continue his housebreaking and build on his success to date.

Senses: Your puppy will show fear, pain, pleasure and excitement. He can see and hear well and is learning to differentiate between various smells. His ear muscles are maturing as he learns to manipulate his ears to allow the entrance of sound waves, which adds to his keen sense of hearing.

Behavior

New places: At 4 months old, your puppy will be ready for new challenges all the time. Don't be nervous about providing him with daily challenges, such as vacuuming, loud music or the washing machine. If anything appears to bother him, don't use praise, just calm reassurance. ◗ See pages 140–141

Other pets: This can be a time when he will begin to react more with other household pets. He may find them fascinating, frightening or fun to play with. Monitor his behavior closely. It's not a good idea to let him play with the family's pet rabbit yet, but by all means let him observe it in a safe environment.

Dominance: Do let any form of dominant behavior go unnoticed at this stage. A firm "No" will put your puppy gently in his place.

Things to do

Check worming schedule.

Check flea prevention dates.

Buy antiparasitic preparations if you are running low.

Hazards

As your puppy goes through this stage in his development, make sure there is nothing at his level or within his reach that he can break as he runs around the house or wags his tail vigorously. Vases of flowers, ornaments, cups and glasses on coffee tables are all vulnerable. Make his environment as safe as possible. Do not leave inviting food or items that he can chew on low surfaces.
◗ See pages 210–211

What you should do

Socialization: Allow more people to handle your puppy to further his socialization. Actively seek out more opportunities to introduce him, under your supervision, to new people and experiences. Take him to a range of new places: the countryside, the beach, outdoor cafés, on buses and trains. The more you do now, the less problems you are likely to experience later on when he is an adult.
◗ See pages 144–147

Grooming: Make this a regular feature of your puppy's day. Grooming will not only maintain his coat and keep it healthy and shiny, but it will also give you an opportunity to spend some quality time together and bond. You can take advantage of this special time to carry out a quick health check and look for the early telltale signs of potential future problems. Check your puppy's eyes, ears, mouth, nose, teeth, nails and anal area. Part the fur around his neck and head and near the tail to look for signs of flea droppings. ◗ See pages 228–231; 233; 256–259; 268–269

A treat dispenser toy can keep your puppy occupied for long periods, especially when you are out or too busy to play.

Week 17
The explorer

Anatomy

Teeth: This week is a very active teething stage in your dog's development. As his new teeth come through, he will enjoy chewing, so have a good supply of appropriate chew toys. However, don't leave too many toys out at once – hide some of them and reintroduce them when he seems bored.

Coordination: Your puppy is still a little awkward but he is getting stronger and more coordinated with each week that passes. He can play, jump and run with a high degree of accuracy. This is a period when he will have lots of excess energy; making time to play together with a variety of "fetch type" toys can be a good release and will also help to stimulate him mentally and prevent boredom.
❍ See pages 158–165

Behavior

Exploration: Your puppy is still extremely interested in his environment, and this could put him at a higher risk of "getting into trouble" as he explores your home, yard, local park and the places he visits. Make sure that there are no opportunities for him to get hurt. Do not leave him unattended in public spaces.
❍ See pages 106–107; 110–111

Fear phase: Some puppies undergo a second brief phase of fear at this time in their life as they respond to unexpected noises or new phenomena and unfamiliar experiences. Don't try to protect and shield your puppy from these. Instead, continue to deliberately expose him to a wide range of unfamiliar objects, and allow him to investigate on his own terms until he feels comfortable with the new situation. If he reacts fearfully, stay calm and reassuring.
❍ See pages 154–155

Things to do

Buy a selection of new chews.

Make sure they're safe.

Look at your puppy's toys to see if any need updating or replacing.

Body shape

Are you happy with your puppy's body shape at the moment? If he appears too fat or too thin, take a careful look at his diet. He should be eating two or three small meals a day now - if you're confused, consult your vet, who will be able to give you advice and put your mind at rest or may recommend a special food or diet for your puppy.
▶ See pages 128-131

What you should do

Housebreaking: It is important to maintain your puppy's housebreaking schedule and not to slack off because he is older and should know what is expected of him – by now, you should be having some success, with fewer "accidents." If he does have one, never scold or punish him – this is counterproductive.
▶ See pages 122–125; 208–209

Fun and games: Make an effort to introduce more "fun" training in the form of stimulating games. Hide a treat somewhere in the house or outside in the yard and ask your puppy to find it. Playing hide-and-seek together can have very positive effects and will encourage him to come to you when you call him. Make it exciting and always praise and reward your puppy well when he gets it right.

Training: This should never be tedious or a chore – the more mutual enjoyment you both get out of it, the better behaved your puppy will be and the more motivated you will be to include this in your daily routine. ▶ See pages 182–189

Initiating a game of hide-and-seek with your dog's favorite toys will help with your dog's recall training.

Week 18
The individual

Anatomy

Muscle mass: At 18 weeks, puppies often require high amounts of protein to support the growth of their maturing muscle mass. Many owners are tempted to give their growing dogs a daily nutritional supplement, but this is not strictly necessary and a high-quality puppy food should be sufficient to supply most of your pet's nutritional needs.

Appetite: Your puppy may now be adjusting to a lower caloric need, which began at around 15 weeks, so you may notice that his appetite is diminishing slightly and he doesn't eat quite as much in a single meal. This is normal and nothing to worry about, although there is substantial variation among breeds.

Testosterone: An non-neutered male puppy's testosterone level increases, which may affect behavior, but he is not sexually mature yet.

Behavior

Sleeping alone: This is an important part of a puppy's security and maturity, and puppies that are not taught to sleep on their own can grow into adults that are anxious and fearful when they are separated from their owners, so don't take yours to bed with you.

Character: Similar to a young baby who grows into a toddler with individual likes and dislikes, your 18-week-old puppy has reached the stage at which his unique personality has begun to manifest itself.

Other dogs: He will be showing considerable interest in other dogs now as well as signs of independence. However, never let him off leash to play with other dogs until you are 100 percent sure that he is trained well enough to come back to you when called. ◗ See pages 148–151; 194–195

Check that your puppy's collar still fits.

If necessary, buy him a new one.

Make sure that it has an ID tag.

Get it engraved with your details.

Growing pains

Tummy upsets: Unless you have recently changed the type of food you're feeding your puppy, he should now be accustomed to his regular diet. Any sign of upset should be checked out with your vet.

Parasite and protozoa infections: These are among the leading causes of digestive upset in puppies and they need treating. ◗ See pages 270–271

What you should do

Recall practice: Decide how well your training regime is going. In particular, go through your recall routine and see if your puppy comes straight back to you. Practice doing this in a range of different situations and locations with a range of distractions, such as interesting toys, children and other dogs. Will he still come back to you as soon as you call him?
◗ See pages 194–195

Off-leash training: The time has come to practice some off-leash training in a controlled and secure environment, such as your yard. Always be sure to keep the sessions short, make them fun and reward your puppy well with treats or praise whenever he gets it right.
◗ See pages 184–189

Collar and leash: Check that your puppy's collar fits properly. You should be able to fit two fingers easily inside it, otherwise it is too tight and he needs a new one. Measure his neck or take him with you to buy a new one.

Practice recall training with your dog in a variety of locations; teach him to sit right in front of you when you call him to you.

Week 19
The junior

Anatomy

Maturing: Although your puppy continues to grow, major changes are now becoming less obvious. Even so, underneath his more adult exterior, his bones are getting progressively stronger, and his muscles and nervous system are maturing every week.

Weight gain: Your puppy's body mass and weight gain continue, albeit slowly, as he gradually fills out.

Coat: This is the time when he may start to lose his puppy coat, which is generally softer and fluffier than its adult replacement. Indeed, depending on his breed type, he may already have reached this stage in his physical development. Make sure that you groom him regularly not only to get rid of any excess dead hair but also to encourage healthy growth. ➤ See pages 228–231

Behavior

Hierarchy: Your puppy will still be going through his teenage stage as far as his behavior is concerned. As well as testing and challenging you, this is the time frame when he figures out where he stands in relation to other pets. Some degree of squabbling and play fighting is expected. It's a dog rule that older animals teach the puppy limits. ➤ See pages 148–151

Uncharacteristic behavior: Your puppy could have another "fear phase," lasting for up to a month, especially if he is a large-breed dog. This is normal and nothing to worry about – it tends to happen in conjunction with growth spurts. You may notice some "flaky" behavior or unwarranted aggression (becoming protective of toys, food or territory) but don't pay more attention to him – this would be counterproductive.

Review your puppy's diet.

Check that it is appropriate for his age and size.

Look at specially formulated foods made for junior dogs, not puppies.

Exuberance

Your puppy may become over-excited in certain situations. This is normal, but continue to use a firm "No" and ignore his behavior if he becomes too exuberant and boisterous. Making a fuss about it may be counterproductive as he may perceive it as a way of attracting your attention and this will only encourage him to behave in this way even more.

What you should do

Canine activities: Start researching activities in your area that involve other dog owners. Many rescue centers and dog homes organize fundraising dog walks, so why not join in? It will help to socialize and exercise your puppy. However, keep in mind that, at this stage, a 3-mile (5 km) walk will be too much for your puppy, however energetic he seems. Smaller, more frequent walks are preferable as they allow his bones and body to continue growing. ● See pages 242–243

Car travel: Start teaching your puppy some traveling manners. A good way to do this is to practice getting into and out of the car. Always make him sit and wait patiently until you tell him to get into the car – never let him barge in as soon as you open the door. Always reward him when he gets it right. By now, he should be turning into a well-rounded and pleasant member of your family, so keep building on his past successes and carry on with your gradual daily training routine. ● See pages 248 249

Your puppy needs to play with other dogs of different ages to learn how to behave appropriately within canine limits.

Week 20
The confident puppy

Anatomy

Weight: At 20 weeks, the average puppy will weigh 70 percent of his eventual adult weight and will be approximately 80 percent of his fully grown adult size.

Teeth: At this important stage in his physical development, his adult molars and canines are beginning to push through his gums, and therefore he may feel poorly at times. While he is still teething, do make sure that his food is not too hard as his gums may be sore.
❯ See pages 234–235

Sexual maturity: Male puppies will become sexually mature at around this time, so think about getting your dog neutered. Talk to your vet about the pros and cons of this simple procedure and what is involved. It is best to spay female dogs before they have their first season. ❯ See pages 226–227; 272–273

Behavior

Basic commands: Your puppy's learning capabilities are almost fully developed, so maintain your regular training routine. New experiences are all that he needs to continue learning. He should be able to play "Fetch" and follow basic commands, such as "Sit," "Stay," "Come," "Leave it" and "Go to bed."
❯ See pages 188–201; 244–245

Practice: He will not absorb new information as quickly as when he was younger, even though he is becoming mentally mature. For a 20-week-old puppy to remember what he has learned, you need to practice frequently.

Marking: Some male puppies of 20–24 weeks may start marking in the house and have selective hearing when they are running free outside. You must act quickly to stop this behavior from becoming ingrained.

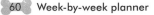

Things to do

Check if your puppy needs worming.

Buy some worming tablets if needed.

Purchase a toothbrush and toothpaste.

Clean his teeth.

Mood swings

These are normal for male and female puppies, and concentration problems may occur during hormonal changes. If your puppy is not well exercised and mentally stimulated, he may get bored and even develop behavior problems. Play games with him every day and always provide a range of interesting toys – be sure to offer new ones occasionally.
◐ See pages 158-159

What you should do

Encourage confident behavior: You should do this without allowing your puppy to become overconfident, which can lead to unwanted dominance issues later on.

Socialization: Continue to introduce him to different situations – perhaps a walk around a busy market, a visit to a café or a day out at the beach. If you have not already done so, take him on a bus or a train. Walk him along some busy roads past noisy traffic and trucks.
◐ See pages 142–143

How many meals? It's time to start thinking about cutting down your puppy's meals to just two a day: one in the morning and the other in the evening. Remember, as always, that routine is still the key to feeding him and avoiding unwanted dietary problems. If you have not already done so, check that his food is appropriate to his age and meets his nutritional requirements as he matures and grows. If you're unsure, talk to your vet.
◐ See pages 128–131; 236–239

You can have fun with your puppy and reinforce his obedience training by teaching him basic commands in the yard.

Week 21
The moody puppy

Anatomy

Physical maturity: Your puppy has nearly reached his full adult capability in terms of learning and mental capacity. He's also well on his way to being physically mature, and is beginning to resemble a smaller and younger version of what he'll look like as an adult.

Female dogs: It is possible that some females may come into season around now. If this is the case, keep your puppy well away from carpets and sofas, and contain her in a room with an easy-to-clean floor. If you have an non-neutered male dog as well, keep them separated.

Digestion and allergies: Puppies at this age do not generally experience digestion problems or develop new food allergies – they are accustomed to their diet and feeding schedule, and you will already have been alerted to any potential allergens.

Behavior

Teenage angst: This can be a difficult time for your puppy, and you may often find you are challenged or ignored. Stay patient, calm and consistent. Don't give in to him – be firm and motivate him to do what you want, rewarding him when you get the desired behavior.

Mounting behavior: Half of male dogs will display this behavior by now, and will also have the capacity to sire a litter at around this age. Indeed, some may even be able to do so before they reach 5 months. ❍ See pages 226–227; 272–273

Marking and scenting: These can become a problem around the house even if your puppy has been successfully housebroken. Keep an eye out for these behaviors and act quickly and decisively if you catch him in the act. ❍ See pages 208–209

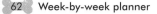

Things to do

Check your dog's boundaries again.

Remove or fence off harmful plants.

Provide a regular place to relieve himself.

Keep "chewable" items out of reach.

Sexual maturity

Is your male puppy becoming sexually mature? When this happens, the testicles start producing more testosterone, which can cause behavioral changes, such as roaming and domination. These actions can become personality traits if the dog is not neutered, or is neutered too late. Males have no season and there may be no signs. ◐ See pages 226–227; 272–273

What you should do

Lost dogs: What would you do if your adventurous puppy got lost? As long as he has an effective form of identification, such as a microchip, it is likely he will be found and returned safely. He should wear a collar with a tag engraved with your name and telephone number. If you do lose him, don't panic. Alert your family, friends and neighbors to keep a look out and also contact any special websites for lost dogs to report him missing. You might consider putting an advertisement in your local paper or putting up posters around the neighborhood. Remember that 95 percent of lost dogs return home safe and sound. ◐ See pages 246–247

Barking: Puppies can become quite vocal. If your puppy barks for no reason you must ignore him. Comments such as "What's that?" in a friendly or excited voice will tell him that he is pleasing you and will encourage him to do it even more. If he barks when left alone, leave a radio on for him. ◐ See pages 216–217; 224–225

When they are left at home alone, some puppies may be very vocal and bark incessantly until their owners return.

Week 22
The awkward puppy

Anatomy

Size matters: Small- to medium-breed puppies develop more quickly than large giant-breed ones. Whereas smaller breeds usually attain maturity by around 1 year of age, giant breeds can take up to 2 years.

At around week 22, a large breed, such as a German Shepherd, may weigh anywhere from 40 to 48 pounds (18 to 22 kg), while a Chihuahua or smaller dog may be between 4 pounds (2 kg) and 11 pounds (5 kg). ❍ See pages 260–261

Wet nose: Have you ever wondered why your puppy's nose is usually wet? The mucus on a dog's nose actually helps him smell by capturing scent particles. When a dog's nose is dry, he may lick it to help him smell things. ❍ See pages 174–175

Behavior

Independence: This is the age at which your puppy may become more independent and is likely to venture off on his own. Puppies that have always come when they are called or stayed close to their owner's side may now ignore them, often running off in the opposite direction. This period can last from several weeks to a few months. Take care and don't let your puppy off leash in public places until you are 100 percent confident that you have instant recall in all situations. ❍ See pages 194–195

Positive reinforcement: Don't worry about any reversal in your puppy's behavior. Use positive reinforcement (such as a tasty treat to reward good behavior) and ignore silly behavior. Never use physical punishment to stop him from doing something undesirable – a firm "No" will usually do the trick.

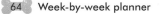

Things to do

Check your puppy's nails.

Make an appointment with your vet or local grooming parlor.

Ask your vet to show you how to trim his nails safely.

Trouble with recall

Most dogs go through a rebellious stage, which can include not coming back when called. Be consistent in your routine and praise and reward your puppy when he comes to you. The hard work you put in now will work eventually and he will soon get over his awkward stage. It will be a pleasure to own a well-behaved, polite and reliable dog. ◗ See pages 194-195

What you should do

Bonding time: If you have a puppy with a long coat, grooming should already be an important part of your regular routine. If not, now is the time to do so – it will be enjoyable for you both and is a good opportunity to bond. You can use your grooming sessions to check him over, looking for anything unusual – ticks and signs of fleas, cuts and scratches, matted hair in his ears or staining under his eyes. Talk to your vet about any concerns you may have. ◗ See pages 228–231; 256–259; 268–269

Bathing your puppy: Also, try introducing your puppy to an occasional bath – most dogs enjoy this when they grow accustomed to it. ◗ See page 232

Training: Continue with your training. If you are confident about your dog's recall, "Sit" and "Stay," progress to more advanced training and tricks, introducing them patiently and gradually as part of your routine. ◗ See pages 188 189; 244 245

When grooming your puppy, examine him physically and look for any cuts, unusual swellings and signs of parasites.

Week 23
The respectful puppy

Anatomy

Coat: You may notice further signs of your puppy's coat being replaced by an adult one, starting down the spine. An adult's coat is generally harsher, less fluffy and greasier. The natural oils will start to appear, and you must take care not to bathe your puppy too often or overbrush him, which may strip away these essential weather-resistant ingredients.

Color vision: Studies have shown that dogs see in various shades of blue and yellow. Purple and blue are both seen as shades of blue. Greenish blue is viewed as a shade of gray. Red is seen as black or dark gray. Orange, yellow and green are perceived as various shades of yellow, making bright orange toys the same yellowish shade as green grass. This is the vision your puppy will have as an adult, and other changes to his sight will be much more subtle.

Behavior

Learning: Your puppy is still energetic and eager to learn but he is also bigger and bolder. This is the point in his behavior and development at which you can combine all the different strands of your training to date and take stock of what you have both learned.

Earn respect: Continue to be the dominant pack member, so make sure you eat first and go through doors before him – don't get out of the way if he barges forward. All of this will assert your authority and earn his respect.

Eating feces: This is a natural behavior for dogs, especially puppies. Often it will just disappear when your puppy matures, but keep his waste area as clean as possible. Ask your vet to check for worms and other possible problems, such as a nutritional deficiency.
▶ See pages 218–219; 270–271

Body language

Take a daily look at your puppy's body language and familiarize yourself with some common signs. This will enable you to communicate better with him. Here are some postures to look out for:

· Ears pricked, relaxed and tail wagging are signs of happiness

· Ears back, eyes wide and tail clamped down signify nervousness.

▶ See pages 168-171

What you should do

Responsible behavior: It is important that you are aware of your legal responsibilities as a dog owner. For example, did you know that in some states, if your dog injures someone, he may be seized by the police and your penalty may include a fine or even a prison sentence?

Instant recall in public places: In a public place, always make sure that your puppy is under your control at all times — do not let him run freely off leash unless it is safe to do so and you have instant recall. ▶ See pages 194–195; 246–247

Identification: Your puppy must always wear a collar with your name and address engraved upon it, or on an attached tag. Your telephone number is optional (but advisable) in case your dog ever gets lost. You might also consider microchipping or even tattooing your dog. You must ensure your dog is safe at all times. ▶ See pages 246–247

To help you with your dog's energy levels make sure that he has plenty of toys, including chewable ones, activity toys and treat dispensers.

Week 24
Good communication

Anatomy

Adult nails: These may be appearing now. They will be harder and more durable than the baby nails, and some light roadwork is recommended to keep them at a reasonable length. If your puppy's nails are getting over-long (if they make a tapping noise on a hard surface), talk to your vet about clipping them. ❍ See page 233

Molting: Molting hair is a hassle, but it's natural for dogs to shed their coat, usually twice a year, although some shed all year round. There is no correlation to seasonal temperatures – it's due to fluctuations in the amount of melatonin secreted by the pineal gland in response to variations in sunlight. Allergies, indoor lighting, central heating and early warm spring weather can all have an effect on your puppy's shedding cycle. ❍ See pages 228–231

Behavior

Normal behavior: This will include barking, howling, digging, biting, chewing, mounting, marking territory with urine and feces, roaming, guarding, growling, trying to establish dominance and protecting food and sleeping areas. Most of the problems that arise from dog ownership are a result of an expression of normal behavior. If you find some of these behaviors unacceptable, take measures to stop them now before they become ingrained. ❍ See pages 176–179

Effective communication: This is the basis for building a good relationship with your puppy. He cannot talk and is unable to understand many words, but, by now, he will be extremely adept at picking up your body language. The key to communicating with him is to read his and to use your own to "talk" to him. ❍ See pages 168–171

Things to do

Find out about clicker training.

Buy a brightly colored clicker.

Carry it around in your pocket.

Use it to reward your dog.

Good behavior

If you groom your puppy regularly, are you happy with how he behaves? Most dogs love it, but some don't. If your puppy dislikes being brushed, start off by stroking him all over. Let him sniff the brush and then use it gently instead of your hand. Use tasty treats to reward good behavior and speak to him reassuringly all the time. Make it an enjoyable time for both of you.  See pages 228-231

What you should do

Consider clicker training: One of the most popular training tools in the world, this involves a small, hand-held "clicker," which you squeeze to make a noise each time your dog does something right during training. Used correctly and with patience, this method usually realizes a 100 percent success rate. ▶ See pages 184–185

Dog shows: Why not find out if there are any dog shows in your area? These are sometimes fundraising events for charities, and they're a great way to meet other owners and socialize your puppy. You might wish to enter him in a fun class, too. Many events cater to crossbreeds as well as pedigrees.

Sleep and rest: Remember that, in puppy terms, your dog is still like a human toddler. He needs plenty of sleep and some "down time" during the day, so ensure that he gets this. At this age, too much mental and physical stimulation can actually be counterproductive.

Providing your puppy with plenty of chews will help to keep his teeth healthy, and prevent boredom and unacceptable behavior.

Week 25
The bonded puppy

Anatomy

Growth: Your puppy's physical characteristics will be very much in place by now, but as he approaches the 6-month milestone, it's important to remember that he still has at least 6 more months of growing ahead of him. Moreover, some breeds don't reach their adult size until they are around 18 months of age. ◗ See pages 260–261

Whiskers: The touch-sensitive hairs found on the muzzle, above the eyes and below the jaws will be very evident now. You may hear them referred to as "vibrissa," and they can actually sense tiny changes in air flow.

Large paws: If your puppy is one of the larger breeds, he may have oversized paws, which look out of scale with the rest of his body, but he will eventually grow into his feet and appear more balanced and symmetrical.

Behavior

On the back: Puppies like to lie on their backs because they get instant "air conditioning" in this position. They even sleep on their backs sometimes, with their four legs sticking up in the air, which may look quite uncomfortable or even amusing to their owners.

Mastering commands: By now your puppy should be trained to walk at your side on leash without pulling as well as understand the basic commands. Well done if he has also mastered "Lie down" or "Paw." ◗ See pages 196–197; 212–213

Problem behaviors: Your puppy should be settled into a routine, and you shouldn't experience much inappropriate behavior. Address potential problems right away at this stage before they become ingrained. ◗ See pages 206–227

Things to do

Check your puppy's nails.

Trim them if they are too long.

Take him for more road walks to wear them down.

Refusing to let go of toys

This can be a common problem because puppies have no sense of fairness and sharing. They view all other members of their family as above or below them in rank order. Make your puppy sit while his food is being put down or offered and wait for permission to eat or take a treat. The same is true of toys and chews. ⬤ See pages 220-221

What you should do

Family day out: If you feel confident about your puppy's behavior, why not plan a family day out, such as a picnic or a trip to the beach, or even a holiday and include him, too? However, be aware that some beaches may have dog restriction zones or even ban dogs altogether during peak holiday periods, so check this out carefully beforehand to avoid possible disappointment. ⬤ See pages 248–253

Sports and activities: If your puppy is a very active and energetic breed that requires a lot of exercise and stimulation, you can keep fit together at agility or flyball classes. Find out if there are any in your area. A new fun activity is canicross in which owners run cross-country with their dogs attached to a harness.

Obedience: If your dog excels at obedience, attend more advanced classes. There are so many things you can enjoy participating in together. They will help to keep you healthy and will strengthen the bond between you.

Including your puppy in a family day out will not only help to socialize him but will also be a test of how well behaved he is.

Week 26
Changing behavior

Anatomy

Weight: Allowing your puppy to eat as much as he wants, whenever he wants, may well lay the foundations for adult obesity and even a shortened life span. Studies have shown that dogs that remain slim throughout their lives can live several years longer than their heavier counterparts that are allowed to eat freely. Watch your puppy's weight – he should have got rid of any puppy fat by now. If you're not sure, ask your vet to examine him. ◗ See pages 274–275

Teeth: By the time he is 5 to 7 months old, all 10 molars of a total 42 permanent teeth should be visible. They should look healthy, white and clean. If you haven't already done so, embark now on a strict dental routine to keep them like that – use a toothbrush and canine toothpaste and/or dental chews.
◗ See pages 234–235

Behavior

Stealing food? Many puppies go through a stage of being "scavengers," which usually takes the form of trying to steal food, often unintentionally provided by negligent owners, who unwittingly leave cakes, sandwiches, cookies and other delights on suitably low tables in their dog's territory. Dogs don't actually "steal" food – they eat what they find, so don't give your puppy the opportunity.
◗ See pages 210–211

Dominance and submission: As a puppy reaches sexual maturity, signs of dominant behavior may become apparent. Don't worry as this is relatively common, but nor should you encourage it. Also possible, however, at this stage is a tendency to more submissive behavior – rolling over on to his back and an obsessive desire to please – which means you may need to boost his confidence.

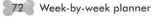

Things to do

Sign up for ringcraft classes if you want to show your puppy.

Check the canine press for local events.

Go to some shows to see what's involved and talk with other owners.

Stress

Is your puppy getting stressed in certain situations? The most common telltale signs include:

- Licking his lips
- Avoiding eye contact
- Shaking and hiding.

Find out what triggers the stressful reaction and then deal with it to desensitize him before the fear becomes ingrained and leads to behavior problems later in life.
▶ See pages 168-171

What you should do

Housebreaking: The time has come to review whether you are happy with your puppy's housebreaking. By now he shouldn't be having many accidents inside the house, if any. If he does, review your routine and make sure that you are letting him out often enough and reading the signs that he needs to relieve himself. If you see him waiting at the door or circling or he looks as though he is about to lift his leg on your table, put him outside immediately and praise him when he goes. Don't ignore him or you will set up potential problems for the future. ▶ See pages 208–209

Tricks: If your puppy needs mental stimulation and enjoys learning new commands, why not teach him some simple tricks, such as a high-five or offering a paw? Take this further by giving him little jobs, so he can help you around the house, such as fetching the mail, carrying shopping or bringing the remote. By learning basic commands, such as "Fetch," these training exercises are simpler to absorb.

Don't ever leave tempting food items lying around at your puppy's level within his reach – scavenging is particularly prevalent at this age.

6–9 months
Approaching maturity

Anatomy

Throughout the next 6 months, you will see your puppy growing into an adult dog. Many of the changes are not as noticeable as those that occurred when he was very young, as they are more gradual and subtle now.

Size: Most six-month-old puppies weigh approximately 75 percent of their adult body weight and will continue growing and gaining weight until they attain their full adult size, at between 9 and 16 months. There is a wide range of maturity between the various breeds, and smaller ones may have already reached their full-grown height and weight.

Senses: By 6 months, most dogs have a very keen sense of hearing, vision, taste and smell. At this age, they are learning to differentiate between different canine and human smells.
❯ See pages 174–175

Behavior

Sexual behaviors: Hormone surges at this age can cause challenging behavior, especially in males, which can act erratically to assert their dominance within their "pack" at home or by displaying aggression toward other dogs. This is usually a passing phase and you must be patient but very firm. Allow him to interact with other dogs, but if you have concerns, talk to your vet about neutering.
❯ See pages 180–181; 226–227

Fear aggression: Some young male dogs exhibit fearful behavior at around this age and become extremely possessive of their food, toys or even, in some cases, their owner. If this happens, always stay calm and reassure your dog without inadvertently rewarding the behavior, which can make it ingrained and even more problematic in the future.
❯ See pages 180–181; 220–221

Things to do

Talk to your vet about the pros and cons of neutering/spaying.

Ask him to check your puppy's weight.

Ask about heartworm disease (your dog may be at risk).

Chewing

Some puppies, when they get their full set of adult teeth, embark on a new phase of chewing. This phase is a form of territorial exploration and it will pass, but, while it lasts, be sure to keep all chewable items, such as shoes and children's toys, well out of your dog's reach and provide lots of edible chews and toys to keep him occupied. ◑ See pages 206–207

What you should do

Feeding: Feed your puppy twice daily at the same times. The manufacturer's guidelines for quantities are just recommendations. A puppy's weight needs to be just sufficient for you to feel – but not see – his ribs. He should have an hourglass figure when viewed from the side and above. ◑ See pages 236–239; 274–275

Housebreaking: A 6-month-old puppy can hold his urine for about 7 hours. This means you will need to take him out at least every 7 hours if you expect him to not have an accident. He should be able to sleep through the night without having to go out. ◑ See pages 208–209

Neutering: Six months is the most common age at which to have a female dog spayed, whereas most males are neutered between 6 months and 1 year. Neutering at this age means the dog's behavior should not change drastically. If you want to breed from your puppy, take precautions, especially if your dog is in heat and attracting the attention of amorous males. ◑ See pages 226–227; 272–273

This is the age at which some male dogs can engage in challenging or aggressive behavior to other dogs.

9–12 months
Problem behaviors

Anatomy

Immune system: Your puppy's immune system is maturing rapidly but he is still susceptible to infections, especially of the ears and skin. Check his ears for mites, a build-up of wax, and inflammation, especially if he scratches them. Skin infections may be associated with allergies or parasites, so treat at the recommended times with a flea preventative and take him to the vet if you have any concerns. Worms can also weaken his immune system, so worm him regularly.

Injury risk: This increases as your puppy gets stronger, more confident and exploratory and sometimes pushes his body to the extreme. Some energetic, playful puppies lack judgment and throw caution to the wind during exercise and boisterous games, and sprained joints and pulled muscles are relatively common.
❍ See pages 160–161; 278–281

Behavior

Being silly: Even at this age, your puppy will still have moments when he behaves more like a baby than a mature adult. Do not stifle his giddy, youthful behavior, but try to contain his natural exuberance or unruly episodes within safe areas, such as your home or yard.

Chasing: Some dogs have a built-in predatory instinct to chase other animals, joggers, cyclists or even cars, sometimes leading to dangerous and devastating outcomes. Although you may not be able to stop your dog trying to chase things, you can take steps to prevent potential disasters. Keep him on leash in public spaces and use a whistle or clicker to attract his attention. Channel his behavior into more acceptable outlets and encourage him to chase balls, toys and Frisbees instead. ❍ See pages 176–177

Things to do

Administer worming treatment, if required.

Buy flea preventative treatment.

Enroll in a canine first-aid course.

Check out local canine activities.

Tell-tale signs

Most puppies will sail through this period with no behavior problems whatsoever, but be aware of the following tell-tale signs:

- Barking excessively
- Submissive behavior
- Dominant tendencies
- Digging
- Biting excessively and not playfully
- Growling.

What you should do

Assess your puppy's progress and build his confidence by exposing him to new situations and finding new ways to interact with him, too.

Leash or no leash? The privilege of being off leash away from a confined area is reserved for puppies with good recall, who are trained to the point where they will not run away and fail to obey commands. It is irresponsible to release your dog in an open space if he has no recall, so don't do it. ◗ See pages 194–195; 212–213

Consistency: Everyone who has contact with your dog must praise the right behavior and use the same commands. This ensures that he always receives the same messages. Not doing so can be confusing and may even trigger problem behaviors in the future.

Ignore mistakes: All puppies make mistakes but it's not necessarily their fault – they haven't mastered the task at hand yet. Ignore mistakes and reward your dog when he gets it right.

Only allow your puppy to go off leash in an open space if he is well trained with good recall, returning to you on command.

1 year plus
The mature puppy

Anatomy

Muscle mass: To some extent, your dog's weight is determined by his diet and the amount and quality of exercise he does as well as his breed. Many large dogs, even at this age and beyond, continue to gain muscle mass and will do so until they are 18 months old.

Sexual maturity: The age at which this occurs varies between individuals and breeds, and the physical changes and sexual characteristics are different for males and females.

Males: Dogs will start lifting their rear legs to urinate and become more sexually aroused.

Females: Female dogs will experience their first season (estrus or heat) – their vulva will swell and they will have a bloody discharge for 5 to 7 days. ❯ See pages 180–181; 272–273

Behavior

Sexual maturity at around this age manifests itself in the development of a variety of different behaviors in male and female dogs.

Males: They often scent-mark around their neighborhood and sometimes in their homes, too. They may be very excitable, unruly and challenge their owners or pick fights with other dogs. They will be attracted to female dogs and may also try mounting stuffed toys, furniture or even people's legs.

Females: Many experience mood swings, alternating between affection and insecurity or even aggression. They may sometimes be subdued and withdraw from their family "pack." A few may even develop a condition called pica, characterized by eating strange substances, such as dirt or stones. ❯ See pages 180–181; 226–227

Things to do

Book annual checkup with vet.

Ask about neutering (if not done).

Administer worming treatment, if required.

Reassess nutritional requirements.

Begging

A lot of dogs experience an increase in appetite at this age or are naturally greedy, so don't be fooled into giving your puppy extra meals, treats or tidbits if he begs. If you never feed him from the table, he will soon learn to leave you in peace when you are eating meals, and begging will not become an issue. Make sure that all other family members do likewise.
❍ See pages 220-221

What you should do

Structure and routine: It is easy to be less rigorous, but any relaxation in your puppy's routine could have adverse effects, so continue with his usual training, feeding, play and bedtimes. Long-term success depends on reinforcement to create a well-rounded adult.

Feeding: Observe his eating patterns and check whether he's content with the amount of food he's offered. At this age, he should be happy to walk away from his bowl once it is empty. He should look "full," not like he is about to burst. If you think that he may be too thin or has a poor appetite, consult your vet.
❍ See pages 236–239; 274–275

Be aware of your demands: Don't assume that just because your puppy is older that he will be happy to be left, or able to hold his urine for hours at a time without accidents. Changes in his behavior are gradual, and any demands you make on him should be introduced gradually, too. ❍ See pages 208–209; 224–225

Your puppy may be quite big at this age and is maturing fast, but he still needs your guidance and an established routine.

PART 2
THE PUPPY ENCYCLOPEDIA

1 CHOOSING YOUR PUPPY

Lifestyle factors

HOW TO GET IT RIGHT

You've made the decision to get a puppy. However, before you do, there are many more choices to consider if the experience is going to be a successful one. A lot of puppies are returned or re-homed within months, with the owners citing cost, time commitment, unexpected behavior or obedience problems as the reason. By researching and preparing thoroughly, you can avoid the common pitfalls and have the opportunity to enjoy your puppy. Yes, they are hard work and time consuming, but there's a lot of fun involved, too.

Consider your lifestyle

There are many factors that will impact on the way you can care for a puppy and in the type of dog that will suit you. A busy family home will require a more robust, tolerant dog than a single professional would necessarily need. The spectrum of home situations is as wide as the range of puppy personalities and breed types, so some careful consideration is required before making a decision.

Available time

Adult dogs require social company, exercise and training, but a puppy needs so much more. One reason why dogs fit into our human lives so well is that they are a social species. While adults can learn to tolerate some "alone time," puppies require considerable social contact to keep them

Owning a dog can bring many benefits, including a less stressful, healthier life.

Assess your home

Inside	Outside
Is there space for a dog?	Is there a secure yard?
Are there steps into the property?	Is it shared?
Are you very fussy?	Is it suitable for play and can you create a waste area?
Can you puppy-proof a secure area?	Are you fussy about your lawn or plants?

happy. They need to be let out to relieve themselves regularly, so if you work, even part-time, think carefully about who will care for your puppy. Extended isolation will lead to otherwise avoidable behavioral problems. Before you take on a puppy, enquire about:

- Hiring a puppy-sitter or walker for the days when you are working away from home
- Whether neighbors or friends can help and, if so, doing what and how often.

Your fitness

Puppies bring their owners many health benefits, but never select an energetic breed to encourage you to exercise. While a treadmill can be ignored when you lose interest, your puppy cannot. If health issues prevent you from walking far, opt for a dog that requires the least exercise. If you have serious back or shoulder problems, choosing a strong dog may not be a sensible option.

Daily routine

- Can you adapt your day?
- Coming home during work breaks and lunches might be an option but is this always guaranteed?
- Will you have time to exercise a puppy? Initially, he needs short walks, but this soon increases, and play time, petting, grooming and training are a big commitment.
- What time commitments do you already have, e.g. children, other pets, courses, volunteering, gym?

Avoid some of the common pitfalls of dog ownership by thoroughly doing your research

Family event

It is important that your puppy is welcomed by your entire family. Everyone should be involved and play a role in your puppy's care. Anyone who dislikes dogs may find normal puppy antics (and mishaps) an irritation.

Owning a dog will change your life and you will be responsible for feeding, exercising and looking after him for many years to come.

What type of puppy?

WHICH DOG IS BEST FOR YOU?

Before you start selecting the specific breeds of dogs that you find especially appealing, you must make some sensible decisions about the type of dog that you can care for, depending on what you want from the relationship as well as your lifestyle, daily routine and commitments.

Factors influencing choice

Small, medium, large or giant?	It is easy to get carried away when looking at puppies, but you must think about what that little bundle of fur will ultimately grow into. Size impacts on the living costs, suitability for your home and car, suitability for children, how much and what type of exercise he will need and how much physical control you will have while walking and training him. Unfortunately, size also affects many aspects of a dog's health and its life span.
Coat type	A long coat requires more maintenance whereas shorter ones will shed, resulting in more frequent vacuuming. Regular grooming parlor visits will be costly and time consuming. People with allergies will have to think very carefully since a completely nonallergenic breed does not exist – individual differences will be important.
Other factors	Think about how tolerant you will be of a drooling dog, one that smells more "doggy" or requires daily cleaning between folds of skin.

Experience

You must take any previous experience with dogs into account when choosing your puppy, as some breeds are not ideal for beginners. If they were designed for fighting, guarding or protection work, then you need to be able to train them and know how to prevent problems from occurring.

Male or female

The correct choice is dependent on breed factors as well as your lifestyle and experience. Talk to your vet, breeders and trainers before deciding whether to go for a male or female dog. Remember that bitches have seasons and males can have mounting and roaming problems, so unless you are planning to breed or show your dog, get him or her neutered.

Suited to you

Your breeder should provide advice about which puppy may be best matched to your situation. However, the ultimate responsibility must be yours. It is important to seek out different opinions, so you are not influenced by any biased advice.

Different breed lines

Several breeds of dog, especially gundogs, have both showing and working breeding lines. The character and stamina differences (as well as their looks) can be remarkable, so make sure that you know what you are buying.

Pedigree or crossbreed

There are pros and cons to owning a dog from a single breed line, or one with mixed genetics. Experienced breeders are more likely to produce pedigree puppies, but don't assume that if a puppy is a pedigree it comes from a good breeder.

Type	Pros	Cons
Pedigree dogs	Know what puppy will look like.	More expensive to buy and insure.
	Know roughly what size he'll be.	May have to travel to buy.
	Can research family lineage.	May have to wait for a puppy.
	Know of potential health risks.	Increased risk of theft.
	Good breeders give support.	May have increased risk of certain conditions.
Mixed-breeds and crossbreeds	Cost less to buy and insure.	Not sure what he will look like.
	Can be healthier.	Not sure of his adult size.
	Usually shorter waiting time.	Not entirely sure of his inherited characteristics.
	Rescue shelter puppies usually come already partly vaccinated.	"Fashionable" cross-breeds often cost a disproportionate amount.

What do you want from a dog?

- Companionship only
- Exercise and fitness
- Showing
- Obedience competitions
- Working trials
- Agility or flyball
- Assistance dog work
- Security work
- Volunteer work, e.g., pet therapy dogs

Both your lifestyle and commitments will influence your choice of dog

Think hard about what sort of dog will be right for you, especially if you are a very active person who likes to keep fit.

Selecting a breed type
WHICH WILL SUIT YOU?

If you have decided that a pedigree puppy will suit you, or you know of a crossbreed puppy and want to understand his potential characteristics, then you should look closely at the breeds and what they were originally bred to do. Knowing what his instinctive behavior is likely to be will improve your ability to assess whether a particular type of puppy will suit you.

Canine events

These are very interesting and useful places to go in order to meet breeders and owners and learn about the different breeds and their individual requirements. At events, like pet and dog expos, you can find out more about your favorite breeds and which is the best choice for your own personal circumstances. You should also consider attending some dog shows, gundog trials, agility and flyball events and obedience competitions, depending on the sort of dog you are interested in buying.

Puppies from some breed groups, including herding and gundogs, will be more energetic and active than others, such as toy breeds.

Dogs of different breeds, sizes and temperaments can get along well together.

Breed groups

Dog breeds are categorized according to their original purpose and common behavioral traits. The recognized breed groups are: hounds (hunting dogs that hunt either by sight or following trails); sporting group (dogs bred to help hunters find and retrieve game); herding dogs (dogs that helped shepherds by herding or guarding flocks); working dogs (dogs bred for other work, such as guarding, fighting and pulling sleds); terriers (dogs bred to catch and kill vermin); toy dogs (small companion dogs); and non-sporting or utility dogs (breeds that do not fall easily into the other groups).

Look at the instinctive behavior of your chosen breed and what it was originally bred to do

Breed group characteristics

Hounds Including: Basset Hound, Beagle, Bloodhound, Dachshund, Foxhound, Greyhound, Irish Wolfhound and Rhodesian Ridgeback	Bred for their ability to locate and chase prey by sight or scent. Active dogs requiring early and consistent training although often relaxed and lazy at home. Can be easily distracted. Loud bark and some will "bay" while exercising.
Working dogs Including: Alaskan Malamute, Bernese Mountain Dog, Boxer, Bull Mastiff, Doberman Pinscher, Great Dane, Newfoundland, Rottweiler and Siberian Husky	A large group of dogs used for many purposes, including guarding, fighting, hunting and tracking. These dogs are typically large and strong, making them less suitable for inexperienced owners. Intelligent dogs requiring socialization and regular training.
Sporting dogs (sometimes known as gundogs) Including: English Pointer, German Shorthaired Pointer, Golden Retriever, Labrador, Irish Setter, Cocker Spaniel, Springer Spaniel, Hungarian Vizsla and Weimaraner	Selected for their ability to find and retrieve game. Some breeds have particular skills in and around water. Highly active group that require a lot of exercise, mental stimulation and obedience training to keep them satisfied. Not suitable for sedentary lifestyles.
Terriers Including: Airedale Terrier, Staffordshire Bull Terrier, Fox Terrier, Parson Jack Russell Terrier, Border Terrier, Welsh Terrier, and West Highland White Terrier	Originally used for hunting vermin and still retain a brave and tenacious temperament. Independent dogs requiring lots of training and socialization to remain friendly and tolerant of other dogs and pets. Require an active lifestyle.
Non-sporting dogs Including; Akita, Boston Terrier, Shar Pei, Chow Chow, Dalmatian, English Bulldog, Lhasa Apso, Poodle, Shih Tzu and Tibetan Spaniel	A very diverse group of dogs with variable purposes, including hunting, fighting and even companion breeds. Research the characteristics of the breed you like since this group includes a range of personalities and physical abilities.
Herding dogs Including: Australian Shepherd, Border Collie, German Shepherd, Old English Sheepdog, Shetland Sheepdog, Smooth Collie, Norwegian Buhund and Welsh Corgi	Highly intelligent breeds with a fantastic training potential. However, they require a lot of exercise and early socialization. Not well suited for a lifestyle with minimal stimulation.
Toys Including: Bolognese, Chihuahua, Chinese Crested, Cavalier King Charles Spaniel, Maltese, Miniature Pinscher, Papillon, Pomeranian, Pug and Yorkshire Terrier	With many different origins, these smaller breeds are now companion pets. Small stature makes them more suitable for smaller homes. Often require particular grooming care and must be trained and socialized thoroughly as often have strong personalities.
Miscellaneous	Some breeds are recognized by particular countries or are so new that they are not yet categorized by group. Research your breed of interest to determine its likely characteristics.

Terriers

INDEPENDENT AND ACTIVE DOGS

Terriers are typically active and fearless dogs. The breeds vary greatly in weight from just 4 pounds (2 kg) to over 70 pounds (32 kg), and they are usually categorized by their size or function. The word "terrier" comes from the French word "terrain," which means ground. This is because many breeds were originally bred to "go to ground" to dig out rabbits and foxes, while others were used for ratting and even bull-baiting.

Temperament

Most terriers are intelligent, friendly, stable and loyal pets. Indeed, the Staffordshire Bull Terrier is often referred to as the Nanny Dog, due to his built-in love of children. Although small in stature, terriers often behave as though they were giants – they have a reputation for being fiery and feisty. Even the smallest ones are ready to take on any opponent – a necessary attribute when hunting and killing vermin for which they were bred originally. Terriers are often protective of their family and home and they can also be very vocal and make good watchdogs. They are independent by nature, which can make some individuals notoriously difficult to train. In addition, the puppies need very careful socialization as some terriers can be aggressive toward other dogs or may be excitable and nip small children, especially during games.

Size

The breeds in this group come in a wide range of sizes, from the diminutive Cairn Terrier to the tall and majestic Airedale Terrier. Terriers are not lap dogs and you should not assume that the smaller breeds require minimal exercise and play time. They are active, fun dogs and they will make demands on your attention and time.

Small: Cairn Terrier, Norfolk Terrier, Norwich Terrier, Scottish Terrier, West Highland White Terrier.
Medium: Bedlington Terrier, Border Terrier, Jack Russell Terrier, Fox Terrier, Manchester Terrier, Staffordshire Bull Terrier.
Large: Soft Coated Wheaten Terrier, Airedale Terrier, Irish Terrier.

The strong-willed Staffordshire Bull Terrier is affectionate and loyal to his family but needs careful socialization as a puppy.

Your duties as an owner

Exercise: An adult terrier will need at least an hour of exercise daily (leash walking and free running) – many sturdy terriers from working lines never seem to tire and can literally keep going all day. They also require plenty of mental stimulation to prevent boredom and problem behaviors, and keep their clever minds busy and occupied.

Grooming: Many terriers are short-coated, so a quick brush once a week might be sufficient for some breeds. However, others, such as the Soft Coated Wheaten Terrier and the Bedlington, have longer coats that need more attention. Some, like the Border Terrier, have to be hand-stripped occasionally to get rid of dead hair, while the Airedale, Kerry Blue and West Highland White Terrier need regular trimming and clipping to keep their coat in shape and good condition.

Health

Terriers tend to be very healthy dogs and usually have a good life span and can live well into their late teens. These dogs are very robust and active, with lots of stamina, and they don't get injured easily – in fact, it may sometimes appear that a terrier is almost incapable of experiencing pain. Hereditary diseases are few, and modern testing has eradicated many of the more common ones.

Working dogs

Terriers were bred originally as working dogs: to catch vermin (mice and rats), to dig and go underground after rabbits and foxes, or as fighting dogs (as in the case of the Staffordshire Bull Terrier). Our pet dogs retain some of their inbred working traits and they need to be kept busy, physically and mentally, or they can experience behavior problems as adults.

Originally bred to kill vermin, the little West Highland White Terrier is an extremely feisty, energetic and spirited dog.

Is a Terrier for you?

Terriers are undoubtedly the clowns of the canine world. If you have the patience to socialize and train a terrier, and also the time and ability to play lots of games and take him for plenty of walks, one of these affectionate, loyal and energetic dogs will make a great family pet.

The Jack Russell Terrier is an ideal country dog that loves to scent and hunt and retains all his natural instincts for killing vermin.

Hounds

BRED TO HUNT BY SIGHT OR SCENT

Hounds are very sociable, gentle and friendly dogs, which were originally bred to assist hunters. They were used for tracking, chasing and/or killing wolves, deer, hares and rabbits, making them different from the sporting group, which were bred to locate prey and recover shot quarry.

Temperament

Three words can probably sum up the Hound Group: active, intelligent and friendly. Of course, all dogs have their different quirks, but most hounds are eager to please and are extremely responsive to members of their family. The Basset Hound can be quite independent and may need a very patient owner, whereas the affectionate Greyhound is possibly the most laid-back of any breed in all the dog groups. Hounds are generally gentle and good with young children as well as amicable toward other dogs.

Your duties as an owner

Exercise: It can be a misconception that hounds need more exercise than other dog breeds. The

With its excellent vision, great speed and remarkable endurance, the even-tempered Greyhound makes a gentle and affectionate pet.

Size

The Hound Group is one of the most diverse when it comes to size. They range from the short-legged, low-to-the-ground Basset Hound to the king of dogs, the huge and majestic Irish Wolfhound, which can stand over 6 feet (1.8 m) tall on its hind legs. In between these two extremes are the tall and willowy Afghan Hound, the compact, small and sinewy Whippet, and the large and very fast Greyhound.

Small: Dachshund, Whippet, Basset Hound.
Medium: Basenji, Beagle, Elkhound.
Large: Afghan Hound, Irish Wolfhound, Borzoi, Greyhound, Bloodhound, Deerhound, Saluki.

Greyhound, which is known for its size and speed, is actually very relaxed at home. The sight hounds need short bursts of exercise rather than hours of free running. As with all puppies, don't over-exercise a young hound, as he can withstand only the same amount as a much smaller, slower breed.

Grooming: The Afghan Hound and some of the longer coated Dachshunds need daily attention when it comes to maintaining their coat. These dogs have fine, silky hair, which can soon become dirty and matted after a run in a muddy field. They also require frequent bathing. However, the short-coated Basset Hound, Smooth-haired Dachshund or Beagle requires minimal fuss, and a good brush once a week will usually be sufficient.

Health

Some hound breeds are affected by specific eye diseases, and responsible breeders test and only breed from those individuals that they know to have certified normal eyes. Basset Hounds have been in the spotlight recently for being too low and long in the back, with too many skin folds. However, Bassets from working lines and those bred by careful breeders should not experience these health problems. Dachshunds, too, can suffer spinal problems, especially if they are allowed to become overweight, as this puts more strain on their elongated backs. If you intend to buy a hound puppy, do your research carefully and check with the breeder whether the puppies and their parents have been tested for any genetic diseases. Ask to see the test results before you buy.

Is a hound for you?

One of the most important things to consider with a hound puppy is his eventual size. Make sure that the house you welcome your Irish Wolfhound or Deerhound puppy into will be big enough when he grows to his full adult size. Hounds make excellent family pets, and although they are sometimes more aloof than other breeds, they are fiercely loyal and great companions. If you are a very active person, a Beagle could be a good choice as it needs a lot of exercise. However, if you are more sedentary by nature, it might be better to consider getting a Greyhound, which will not require much walking – just bursts of speed and free running in the park.

The gentle, dignified and friendly Deerhound is usually eager to please his owner, making him easier than some of the other hounds to train.

Working and Herding

BUSY AND ENERGETIC WORKING DOGS

These two groups include lots of different breeds in many shapes and sizes. As their name suggests, most were initially used for some type of work, such as herding sheep, pulling carts or rescuing people lost in the mountains. Some breeds are ancient, like the tiny Swedish Vallhund, which was believed to have herded cattle as far back as Roman times.

Temperament

It is not a coincidence that many dogs from these groups are used as guard dogs and police dogs. They are extremely loyal and protective toward their family and they will unconditionally devote themselves to you. Often supremely intelligent, working and herding breeds are quick and eager to learn, easy to train and very obedient. However, they need to be kept busy, physically and mentally, with games and activities, such as obedience and agility at which they excel. Remember that due to their guarding instincts, some of the larger breeds can display challenging behavior during training and they are more suited to experienced owners, but these problems are easily overcome in most cases by firm handling and good socialization.

Your duties as an owner

Exercise: Larger dog puppies, such as Great Danes and German Shepherds, need to be exercised carefully to allow their bones to grow adequately in the formative months. Larger breeds benefit from some leash walking on pavement (as well as free running), which helps not only to build muscle tone but also keeps feet and nails in good condition. Collies and German Shepherds, in particular, require a lot of exercise, whereas the protective, guarding breeds are less energetic. Owing to their intelligent nature, many dogs in this group also

Size

As diverse as the Hound Group, the Working and Herding Groups include the huge Great Dane and all the varieties of medium-sized collies as well as the smaller Hungarian Puli and Welsh Corgis. It's important to consider the adult size of the puppy you are thinking of getting, and to be confident that he will be comfortable in your home and the surrounding area.

Small: Swedish Vallhund, Hungarian Puli, Shetland Sheepdog, Welsh Corgis.
Medium: Border, Rough, Smooth and Bearded Collies, Siberian Husky, Samoyed.
Large: Great Dane, Bernese Mountain Dog, Boxer, Doberman, German Shepherd, Giant Schnauzer, Newfoundland, Pyrenean Mountain Dog, Rottweiler, St. Bernard, Komondor.

Working instincts

The dogs in these groups were bred originally to round up and herd sheep, cattle or reindeer, or to protect them from predators, or to be guard dogs. These instincts are still inbred, and the herding dogs (Collies, German Shepherds and Corgis), although reliable and obedient, need a lot of stimulation and exercise. Many of them excel at ability and obedience training. The protective dogs (Samoyeds, Komondors, Pyrenean Mountain Dogs) are powerful, strongwilled and can be stubborn; they need good socialization, especially with other dogs.

The inquisitive Border Collie requires a huge amount of exercise as well as mental stimulation, making it a big commitment for any owner.

The intelligent German Shepherd excels at obedience and needs a lot of stimulation and exercise.

need plenty of mental stimulation, often in the form of additional training, games and agility.

Grooming: Many working and herding breeds are heavily coated. This is due to the prevailing weather conditions in which they were bred to work, making a warm and weatherproof coat essential to their survival. The longer coated dogs require frequent grooming and bathing as their coats get muddy and become matted easily, so you must take this into account when choosing a puppy as it can be time consuming. Some working dogs, such as the St. Bernard, also have a tendency to drool down their fronts and will need regular cleaning.

Health

Larger dogs tend to have a shorter life span than their smaller cousins, although this is not related to any prevalence toward disease, more the case of a heart working harder to maintain a larger body. This does not mean that all large dogs die early, however, and many live to a ripe old age. Despite their size, working dogs require the same routine health and preventative care as any other dog. Some breeds, including the Collies and German Shepherd, are affected by inherited diseases and genetic conditions in their bloodlines, and you must check these out carefully before buying one.

Is a working or herding breed for you?

As with any other breed, an area of consideration has got to be size. If you choose a large dog, it will eat more, take up more room and require more exercise than, say, a small Toy dog. The working and herding breeds can make wonderful pets as they are extremely loyal and protective of their family. However, due to their working intelligence, they can be challenging dogs to own.

Toy dogs
ENTERTAINING COMPANIONS

Toy dogs are still sometimes referred to as lap dogs because their original function was to sit in the lap of their owners (usually rich ladies) and to provide nothing more than amusement and companionship. These small dogs have a lot to offer and they can make adorable and fascinating pets. A toy dog is an entertaining addition to any family as well as a great pet for retired people, as they tend to need less exercise, are easier to care for and keep clean and are cheaper to feed than bigger dogs.

Temperament

Toy dogs are very loving and more than make up for their diminutive stature with their strong-willed, big personalities. Some breeds can be hyperactive at times, and they all demand attention and crave mental stimulation, enjoying playing games and entertaining their owners. Some breeds, such as the Chinese Crested, are prone to "yappiness," which can sometimes be a problem for people who live in apartments. Some of the smaller breeds may appear timid with other dogs and children, but they are happy and confident with people they know.

Your duties as an owner

Exercise: Toy dogs and small breeds cannot get enough exercise inside their house and yard (contrary to popular belief). Pugs, for example, have

Size

As their name suggests, toy dogs don't come in large sizes. The smallest is the Chihuahua, which may measure about 6–9 inches (16–22 cm) in height and weigh around 2–6 pounds (1–3 kg). The fun-loving and companionable Pug is one of the bigger, stockier and heavier examples of a toy breed. In between these extremes you will find the feisty, silky-haired Yorkshire Terrier as well as the graceful Chinese Crested Dog, which comes in coated and non-coated varieties.

Small: Chihuahua, Yorkshire Terrier, Papillon, Pomeranian, Toy Poodle, Maltese, Miniature Pinscher.
Medium: Chinese Crested Dog, Pekingese, Affenpinscher.
Large: Pug, Cavalier King Charles Spaniel.

The graceful Chinese Crested Dog is happy and alert, loves to play and craves the attention and companionship of his family.

Dealing with large dogs

Many small dogs, when they are well socialized, have developed effective strategies for coping with bigger dogs and can hold their own with confidence, even though their owners are sometimes overprotective toward them. Toy dogs need to engage with other larger dogs in normal canine behaviors, and you should not try to shield your dog from meeting others as long as they do not pose a threat to him.

a tendency to obesity and need much more exercise than their owners usually give them. Remember that a dog that has not exercised enough is more likely to be destructive at home – as a way of burning off excess energy and combating boredom. Common sense will tell you how much exercise is enough for your dog, but a toy puppy will need at least 1 hour of exercise a day when he reaches 6 months.

Grooming: Toy dogs have a variety of coat types. The silky-haired Yorkshire Terrier and Powderpuff Chinese Crested Dog require a lot more attention and grooming than the short-coated Pug. The Affenpinscher has a wiry coat, which is supposed to look slightly "shaggy," whereas the Long-coated Chihuahua is meant to have a pristine coat, which needs regular grooming. Before you buy a puppy, be aware of the type of coat care that your favorite breeds will require, and decide how much time you will have to dedicate to grooming.

Health

Most toy dogs live long and very healthy lives, although there are exceptions. Pugs that have not been bred properly may suffer from breathing problems, and some strains of Cavalier King Charles Spaniels are prone to several hereditary diseases, including degenerative mitral valve disease (MVD), which can be fatal, but a good breeder will always breed away from these genetic problems and you need to check that the proper tests have been done before buying a puppy. Care needs to be taken with the hairless Chinese Crested, as sunburn can be a problem. In general, a toy dog's life span can be well into its late teens.

Is a toy dog for you?

Larger than life, full of energy, always entertaining and often demanding your full attention, a toy dog is perfect for people who have time on their hands. A well-trained one will fit into almost any environment, and is well suited to families or older people who live in urban areas with minimal space or small yards. Although most toys are good with children, if you have a very busy family life, make sure that you can dedicate enough time to your dog's development, both socially and mentally, as he will demand your attention and requires a lot of stimulation and human companionship.

The characterful Pug is a small dog with a big attitude and likes nothing better than to keep his owners amused and entertained.

Sporting dogs

BRED TO FIND AND RETRIEVE GAME

Sporting dogs (also known as gundogs) were developed specifically to help hunters find and retrieve game, usually birds. They are divided into three main types: retrievers, flushing dogs and pointing breeds. Pointers assist the hunters by telling them where the game is; flushing dogs literally "flush out" the game; and retrievers collect the game from the ground. Obviously, not all sporting dogs are working dogs, and they also make excellent pets.

Temperament

A well-bred sporting dog makes a great companion and will almost certainly have a friendly and steady temperament and is very easygoing and willing to please. Sporting dog puppies tend to be fearless and soft in equal quantities and can change their mood depending on whether they are working in the field or relaxing at home.

Assuming that you will not be hunting game, you will find that most sporting dogs are loyal, robust and ready to have some fun. They are particularly

Size

There is less variation in size among the breeds in the Sporting Group than any other. All the spaniels are included in this group, as well as all the retrievers and setters. Among the largest breeds is the exuberant Irish Setter at 25–27 inches (64–69 cm) in height, while the smaller Brittany, at 18–21 inches (46–52 cm), is fast becoming a favorite pet. The Labrador makes a great family dog and is always one of the top three most popular breeds.

Small: Cocker Spaniel, Brittany.
Medium: Springer Spaniel, Clumber Spaniel.
Large: Irish Setter, German Shorthaired Pointer, English Pointer, Spinone, Labrador Retriever, Golden Retriever, Hungarian Vizsla, Weimaraner.

receptive to obedience training and willingly obey commands, although they can sometimes show more enthusiasm for playtime than training time.

Your duties as an owner

Exercise: Most well-bred sporting dog puppies have high energy levels and are structurally sound, so a 4- to 6-month-old puppy should be capable of 30 minutes' exercise per day, consisting of road walking and some free running. The puppies love to run, so allow yours free time in the yard or a safely enclosed area. Be guided by your dog – a Labrador puppy will let you know when he is tired. Adult dogs require a great deal of exercise to stay fit and slim, so don't buy a sporting dog unless you are a very active person and are prepared to invest a lot of time in walking your dog.

Grooming: Sporting dogs have very tough, weather-resistant coats and it is usually best to leave them as natural as possible. The grease on their coat is an effective form of protection, and too much grooming and bathing can strip away the essential oils. A good brush on a regular basis is usually all that is required. A very dirty coat may need a more thorough clean, but check with your vet as to which shampoo is best to use.

Health

The keys to good sporting dog health are a sensible, well-balanced and nutritious diet and plenty of aerobic exercise. Labradors and Golden Retrievers,

Chewing

Some non-working sporting dogs tend to have an insatiable desire to chew, which can lead to problems if you do not provide enough interesting edible chews and toys to satisfy this craving. It is probably due to the oral dexterity that was needed in working strains to retrieve small birds and animals. Do not leave shoes or any chewable items lying around at ground level or within your dog's reach if he enjoys chewing. Keep him occupied instead with a variety of toys.

in particular, can be predisposed to obesity, and it is very important to get them accustomed to exercise from puppyhood. As with any young dog, exercise should be gradually built up over a period of about 12 months to avoid bone and muscle damage.

Canine hip dysplasia (CHD) is a congenital disease that causes the hip joints in affected dogs to grow abnormally, thereby causing the joint to become loose and wobbly. It eventually leads to a form of arthritis that is commonly referred to as degenerative joint disease (DJD). This can occur in sporting dogs, mainly Labradors and Golden Retrievers, but screening for it is now readily available. Always check the hip scores before buying a puppy.

Is a sporting dog for you?

Great with children, loyal, dependable, laid back and often silly, a sporting dog puppy makes an adorable family member. He will eventually need lots of space and exercise as well as a close eye on his diet. Faithful and loving, a sporting dog will thrive if he has plenty of space to run and to grow into his full potential as well as physical and mental exercise and activities to keep him occupied.

The affectionate Springer Spaniel has boundless energy and requires a lot of exercise, free running, retrieving games and companionship.

Non-sporting dogs

A DIVERSE RANGE OF BREEDS

Sometimes referred to as utility dogs, the Non-sporting Group is rather mixed, consisting of breeds that are hard to put into any of the other categories as they have been bred to fulfill such a diverse range of tasks. Here you will find the small, heavily coated Shih Tzu alongside the tall and imposing Dalmatian, the Bulldog with his distinctive short face and the regal, large Akita. Utility dogs come in all shapes and sizes and with so many hugely differing characteristics and temperaments, it is no wonder that many owners choose a breed solely for its appearance.

Your duties as an owner

Exercise: Because of the huge differences in shape and size of the dogs in the Non-sporting Group, exercise needs can vary immensely between breeds. A larger puppy, such as a Dalmatian or Akita, needs more exercise than a stockier Bulldog or a shorter legged Lhasa Apso or Shih Tzu. It is, however, essential that the smaller breeds get sufficient exercise, including some road walking and free running as well as playing games in the yard.

Size

In this group there's a dog for almost anyone. Whereas the Bulldog is a fearless, stocky dog, short in stature – only 12–14 inches (30–35 cm) – but big in personality, you may prefer an imposing Akita with a height of 24–28 inches (60–70 cm), an elegant Dalmatian with its sleek, athletic body, or even a small, sweet-looking Shih Tzu. The Non-sporting Group is always worth a look, but brush up on your chosen breeds as they are a diverse bunch.

Small: Shih Tzu, Lhasa Apso, Miniature Poodle.
Medium: Bulldog, French Bulldog, Schnauzer, Boston Terrier, Tibetan Terrier.
Large: Akita, Dalmatian, Chow Chow, Standard Poodle, Shar-Pei.

Grooming: The longer coated breeds, such as the Lhasa Apso or Shih Tzu, require regular daily grooming to keep their coats healthy. Some busy owners prefer to keep their dogs' coats short and trimmed. Shorter coated breeds, like the Dalmatian or Bulldog, need brushing but are less likely to pick up mud and grass on their daily walk. As with all the other breed groups, diet plays an important role in coat health, so make sure that you feed your dog a healthy, nutritionally balanced regime.

Health

Recently, there has been considerable controversy concerning the health of the Bulldog and Shar-Pei, due to the actions of disreputable breeders who put

Inquisitive, alert and very vocal, the Tibetan Terrier is not a true terrier and was originally bred by Buddhist monks as a watchdog.

Temperament

Again, the range of temperaments in this group is very varied, from the aloof Akita, which was bred originally as a fighting dog, to the gentle Lhasa Apso and good-tempered, intelligent and playful poodles. Some of these breeds, however, are not suitable for first-time novice owners: the independent Chow Chow and Shar-Pei can be challenging, although they are loyal and devoted to their owners and make affectionate pets with the correct socialization and training. The French Bulldog is fun-loving and affectionate, while the Shih Tzu is a friendly, intelligent little dog.

profit before health and have bred unhealthy dogs. However, the Bulldog's short face and Shar-Pei's wrinkled skin are unlikely to cause problems if you do your research and only purchase a puppy from a reputable breeder who has bred responsibly and focused on their dogs' health rather than appearance. Most other Non-sporting breeds enjoy good health and a long life span.

Is a non-sporting breed for you?

The wide range of sizes, coats and temperaments make this an interesting group to choose from. These dogs are almost always loyal, affectionate and intelligent and make good companions, but you must take special care to select one that suits both your lifestyle and family. Thus a big Akita or Chow Chow may not be suitable if you have young children or live in a small apartment, whereas even a little Lhasa Apso or Shih Tzu will require lots of mental stimulation to keep its mind active as well as regular grooming and exercise. It is really important to do your research and to find out everything you can about the breeds you like. Never select a puppy on the basis of appearance alone – lots of people do this and their dogs subsequently may end up in shelters looking for new homes.

The graceful Dalmatian with its distinctive spotted coat was originally bred as a carriage dog and it has great endurance as well as speed.

Challenging dogs

Some of the breeds in the Non-sporting Group have particularly strong-willed natures and need careful socialization, especially with other dogs. Breeds such as the Akita and Chow Chow are best suited to experienced owners, who can handle them calmly and earn their respect and loyalty. Because they are so independent, aloof and occasionally stubborn, they can be more difficult to train than more easy-going breeds, like many sporting dogs, which are eager to please.

Crossbreeds and mixed-breeds

UNIQUE DOGS WITH PERSONALITY

A crossbreed is a dog with two pedigree parents of different breeds, whereas a mixed-breed is a dog with a hybrid background with several or no obvious pedigree breeds in its makeup. Crossbred so-called "designer breed" dogs, such as the Labradoodle (Labrador x Poodle), Jug (Jack Russell x Pug), Cockapoo (Cocker Spaniel x Poodle) and Puggle (Pug x Beagle), are a new and fashionable phenomenon in dog breeding.

Pros and cons

Many crossbred dogs are popular nowadays, with some new "designer" breeds being highly sought after. There is a tendency with these new breeds, however, for some less responsible breeders to cash in, and that means that health checks are sometimes overlooked in the quest for the perfect mix and attractive appearance. If you acquire a crossbreed or mixed-breed puppy, check whether it has been wormed and vaccinated and get it checked by your vet as soon as possible.

Crossbreeds and mixed-breeds come in all shapes, sizes, coat types and colors, and it can be quite difficult to predict their eventual appearance.

Crossbreeds

These puppies usually result from an accidental mating between pedigree dogs of different breeds. If you are interested in getting a crossbreed, take a careful look at the breeds of both the parents, work out their singular traits and build, and then decide whether this is a mix that you can cope with.

Mixed-breeds

These are more common when irresponsible owners give their dogs the freedom to roam. Mixed-breeds usually have many breeds in their makeup, which often gives them a larger gene pool, hybrid vigor and better health than many pedigree dogs. However, buying a mixed-breed puppy is a gamble and will almost always leave you guessing as to its eventual adult appearance, size, weight and temperament. What is certain is that each mixed-breed is unique with his own individual character

Labradoodles

This crossbreed was developed specifically for owners who are allergic to fur and dander or who wanted a dog with a nonshedding coat. A cross between a Labrador Retriever and a Standard Poodle, the intelligent Labradoodle is often trained and used as an assistance or guide dog as well as making a great family pet. It has a friendly, affectionate temperament and is very receptive to obedience training.

The Cockapoo, with its distinctive curly coat, is one of the new so-called "designer" breeds, which are now becoming increasingly popular.

and appearance, which makes owning one very appealing for some people. In addition, a mixed-breed will be cheaper to insure than a pedigree dog and is less likely to be stolen.

New "designer" breeds

Many of the new crossbreeds are attractive and desirable pets with good temperaments. Because they are fashionable, the puppies are often sought after and relatively expensive. They include:

Chipoo: Chihuaha x Poodle
Newfypoo: Newfoundland x Poodle
Maltipoo: Maltese x Poodle
Cockapoo: Cocker Spaniel x Poodle
Labradoodle: Labrador x Poodle
Puggle: Pug x Beagle
Chug: Chihuahua x Pug
Jug: Jack Russell Terrier x Pug
Snorkie: Miniature Schnauzer x Yorkshire Terrier.

These puppies will not come with any Kennel Club registration papers, and it is unlikely that they will have had veterinary checks and tests for hereditary

Rescue dogs

Welcoming a rescue dog into your home can be very rewarding. There are thousands of these dogs looking for kind and loving owners and the benefits can be huge. If you have lots of patience and time, why not consider rehoming a puppy?

Most of the puppies in rescues are crossbreeds and mixed-breeds that end up there through no fault of their own. They can make wonderful companions and loyal family pets, and their requirements in terms of socialization, training, diet, exercise and daily care are similar to that of a pedigree puppy from a recognized breeder.

Acquiring a rescue dog: If you are interested in getting a rescue puppy, contact the humane societies and your local rescue shelters. Visit them, look at the available dogs and talk to the staff. They will ask you some questions about your home, lifestyle and working hours to find out what you can offer a rescue dog and to match you to one in their care.

They may arrange a home visit to check that you are a suitable owner and can offer a dog a loving home in a safe environment. They will also offer advice on which is the best puppy for you and will recommend a suitable match.

diseases, so you must take special care if you are thinking of purchasing one. That is not to say, of course, that they are not healthy or have good temperaments, but do exercise caution with the breeders. Although many of these crossbreeds are healthy, they are not necessarily healthier than pure-bred pedigree dogs; indeed, they can inherit the worst health problems of both parents' breeds, so you can end up with double trouble.

Sourcing your puppy

HOW TO DO IT

You need to have your wits about you when finding the perfect puppy. Unfortunately, there are many unscrupulous people with poor breeding practices who will try to part you from your money, so here are some sensible guidelines to help you find a healthy puppy that will be right for you and your family as well as your lifestyle and circumstances.

Finding a breeder

The Kennel Club and breed clubs can recommend breeders. Avoid newspaper or online advertising offering several breeds or "bargain" prices. Ask:

- Will they let you visit the mother and puppies?
- Can you handle the puppy before buying it?
- Is the breeder a member of the Kennel Club?
- Are the puppies registered with the Kennel Club (if being sold as pedigree)?
- Are the parents kept as pets or working dogs (if relevant to the breed)?
- Are the puppies living inside the home?
- What health checks have the puppies had?
- Are the puppies suitable for your intended purpose, e.g., companionship, working dog?

Adopting a rescue puppy

Animal shelters often have pregnant dogs and unwanted litters. You will have to go through their adoption process to ensure that you can provide a good home for a puppy. Usually you will need to:

- Visit your local rescue shelters. Do not expect to take a puppy home that day.
- Complete a home-finder questionnaire and talk to the rescue staff. They will want to know about your lifestyle and personal circumstances. Do not be offended if they ask you a lot of questions.
- A home visit may be arranged and you will be notified when the puppy can be homed.
- There will be a homing fee, which covers the cost of the puppy's care while in the shelter.
- A puppy should be vaccinated and microchipped.

Pedigree rescues

Sometimes, pedigree dogs need new homes. You may need to wait for a rescue puppy to come up for homing, but you can search through the Kennel Club or through specific breed clubs. A dog acquired in this way is likely to be slightly older since young puppies are usually returned to their breeder if and when problems arise. However, if he has been socialized, you should not experience any additional problems.

Your puppy will live an average of 12 years, so it is worth taking the time to find the right one for you

Puppies are very appealing but never buy one on impulse – consider your lifestyle and how much time you can devote to caring for a puppy.

Never buy a puppy from...

Pet stores: You should always see the puppy with his mother and siblings. Puppies in pet shops often come from puppy farms and are removed from their mother too early. The trauma of being transported, or from living in a cage (often during the fear-imprint stage), in addition to poor health care often results in long-term problems. A good breeder would not send their puppies to a store for sale, no matter what you are told.

"Puppy dealers": These are the "middlemen" for puppy farms. These people often pretend to be the breeder, making excuses as to why the mother and siblings cannot be viewed. They may even offer to bring the puppy to your home or to meet you at a gas station, supermarket or parking lot. A reputable breeder is very unlikely to ever agree to this arrangement.

Why are puppy farms so bad?

Mass production of puppies with the aim of making a profit will never be in the interest of the animals. The conditions in puppy farms are unacceptable and cause undue suffering.

- The puppies are often in poor health and many do not survive.
- They are bred without regard to responsible practices or consideration for inherited diseases and genetic health conditions in certain breeds.
- They do not receive adequate socialization or the right environment to begin housebreaking.
- The breeding dogs spend their lives in appalling conditions. They are bred too often, without the right nutrition or health care.

Selecting your puppy

CHOOSING THE RIGHT ONE

Although you are presumably excited about acquiring a new addition to your family, you must carry out the puppy selection process with due consideration. After all, when you bring your new puppy home, it would be heartbreaking to realize that you had made the wrong decision.

Who's available?

You might not have the pick of the litter. The breeder might keep a puppy they see as having good showing, breeding or working potential, and others may already be reserved. You will be told which puppies are available, but if they do not fit your criteria, do not be tempted to buy one.

Signs of good health

While observing the litter, you can assess whether they appear healthy and are responsive to their surroundings. When you get a chance to handle them, look more closely to make sure there are no signs of discharge from the nose, eyes or ears and that the coat is clean. The tummy should not be

What to look for in a puppy

Desirable characteristics	Undesirable characteristics
Active, playful character	Bullish and overbearing with littermates
Willing to approach you with confidence	Shy or fearful, unwilling to approach
Relaxed when held and examined	Excessive struggling or avoidance when handled

You may see the mother with her puppies at a very young age indeed but you will have to wait until they are 6 or 7 weeks old before choosing one.

disproportionately rounded; if it appears so, ask the breeder when the puppies were last wormed.

A good match?

Once a particular puppy has caught your eye, ask the breeder about his or her character. You need to know that this puppy is suited to the home you have to offer. Mixed personalities can exist within a single litter even though they are bred from the same parents. If you are unsure why the breeder has selected a specific puppy for you, ask them to explain their reasons for this decision.

Can you hear me?

Owning a deaf dog is always a challenge. With the breeder's permission, satisfy yourself by conducting a little hearing test. While the puppy is looking away from you, clap your hands or jangle your keys. He should respond immediately – hopefully coming up to you to investigate the source of the noise.

Do not buy a puppy if...

- **You feel sorry for him**: Being timid or the last one available will not make him a great pet.

Handle the puppies and look at them carefully, checking for any signs of nervousness or poor health – they should be bright and alert.

- **You have not seen the mother**: You have no reference for how he may turn out and need proof that this breeder is genuine and not a dealer.
- **The litter does not appear to have been handled**: Early experience is essential.
- **You're feeling pressured**: A good breeder will talk you through all the options without rushing you as they want you to make the right decision, too.
- **Your gut instinct tells you something isn't right**: You are probably correct. Walk away and find another litter. Living with a mistake can be emotionally and financially draining.

How many?

Two is not better than one. Many owners buy two puppies on impulse rather than picking between them. This is a terrible idea and, more often than not, causes difficulties. Two littermates can cause:

- A reduced bond with you, the owner
- A dramatic increase in the time needed to care for them since it's vital that they are separated and not left to play and romp together all day
- Less socialization since two puppies are harder to carry around and take to puppy parties (two people will be required for these tasks)
- Increased cost of food, insurance, vet bills, grooming, equipment and kennels.

Always take your time and choose a healthy, active puppy, not one you feel sorry for

Puppy-proof your home

MINIMIZE POTENTIAL HAZARDS

You're about to welcome your puppy into his new home, so the time has come to minimize potential hazards. This may be time consuming but prevention is easier than resolving undesirable habits, replacing damaged items and emergency veterinary treatments later on.

From your puppy's point of view

Before your puppy arrives ensure that all safety measures have been taken. Crouch down to puppy height, so that you can see anything that might catch his attention. Think "puppy": he will sniff, taste, paw and jump, and therefore furniture and fixtures must be stable and nontoxic. Houseplants should be moved out of reach as many are toxic and all are vulnerable when a puppy is around.

Compelled to chew

While exploring, cables, wood and carpet edging are commonly targeted for chewing, so protect these with plastic covers or remove them completely for now. Once your puppy has matured and learned to play with his toys he will be less inclined to start the habit. Taste-deterrent sprays may be useful if he is determined to chew furniture or fixtures (see Chapter 8 – Avoiding problems).

Coping with mistakes

Puppies cannot place monetary value on mobile phones, glasses or shoes, and most will happily spend time playing with and gnawing on them. Unfortunately, the best solution is to reprimand yourself for leaving them within your puppy's

Puppies love to sniff and explore their surroundings, so make sure that everything at your dog's level, including all the woodwork and furnishings, is dog-friendly, nontoxic and safe.

reach and then take the time to move other items to prevent a repeat occurrence. If your puppy has something of yours in his possession you should stay calm. If you have already taught him to "Leave it" (see pages 200–201), then use this command as practiced. If not, find something else to exchange it with. Pick a favorite toy and get his attention by jiggling it, then gently make the switch.

Reacting angrily may be instinctive, but your puppy won't understand why and further problems could develop

Make your home safe

Kitchen	• Purchase a tall, top-opening container for garbage and recycling.
	• Install child locks on cupboard doors and on the fridge.
	• Clear any low corner shelves and move dish towels out of reach.
	• Move or cover wine racks; corks are a chewing risk.
Living room	• Knicknacks should be moved to higher levels and the coffee table cleared.
	• Place bowls of potpourri and candles out of reach.
	• Place screens in front of fireplaces and prevent access to logs or coal.
	Caution! Blind cords should be tied high up to prevent strangling.
Hallway	• Keep the front door closed – fix loose latches and start good habits.
	• Position a safety gate at the base of the stairs.
	• Move shoes, umbrellas, cycling helmets, sports rackets to a closet or storage box.
	Caution! Inquisitive noses love to investigate handbags but painkillers, candy, chocolate, cosmetics, coins or key rings can be potential risks. Keep your purse out of reach!
Laundry room	• Ensure electric cables and pipes are adequately protected.
	• Move laundry baskets and clothespin bags onto high surfaces.
	Caution! Move all cleaning supplies into a secured cabinet.
Bedrooms	• Use cable protectors, including under the bed, where a puppy may chew undiscovered.
	• Move all medicines from bedside tables into a secured drawer or cabinet.
	• Fit a child safety gate on children's rooms where puppy-proofing is difficult.
	Caution! Never leave hot hair appliances switched on while a puppy is present – he could pull them down, burning himself or causing a fire.

Child safety gates

These are useful for preparing puppy zones to keep him safe: within the confines of a room or to block off stairs and doorways. A tumble down a flight of stairs could severely injure a puppy and make him nervous about climbing steps later in life. Open-tread staircases pose a particular problem for many dogs, even those who happily use traditional stairs.

A puppy pen or crate can keep your puppy safe while you are busy doing other things as well as providing a quiet haven for him.

What your puppy needs

CHOOSING THE RIGHT EQUIPMENT

A new puppy owner can sometimes feel overwhelmed by the wide range of pet products and the potential expense involved. While all puppies will differ in their needs, there are a few key items of equipment that you should have ready and waiting for your new puppy's arrival.

Immediate need

Food bowl: Your puppy will need his own dish for meals. However, while training him, you may prefer to offer at least some of his food by hand to reward good responses, or you can place it inside an activity toy to occupy him for longer.

Water bowl: A heavy, ceramic dish is probably best as it is difficult to tip over and easy to clean. You will require at least one as fresh water should be available to your puppy at all times.

Bed: Positioned in a quiet but inclusive place, this will become your puppy's safe space.

Required after a few days

Puppy collar: A flat, soft collar with a buckle is perfect for a puppy. There is no need for anything fancy and you should avoid chain versions. Your puppy will grow quickly, so the collar should be comfortable and easy to adjust.

Leash: Your puppy will need a regular leash that you can use for walks and training. His size will influence its width and length, but, in general, it should allow some freedom of movement without trailing on the floor. Always avoid chain leashes as these are too heavy for puppies and the noise they make can cause a fear reaction.

House line: This is the name given to a long, light leash that is typically used within the home for extra control. It has a small clip at one end to attach to the collar. The long end can be held or can trail behind the puppy as he moves around. Use it to gently guide him away from things he should not

be doing, such as raiding the garbage can or trying to chase your cat. Having distance control without the need to chase or grab at your puppy is of great benefit in many areas of his training. Supervision is necessary while the house line is being used.

A responsible dog owner will ensure that their dog has an ID tag on his collar in case he gets lost.

A long training leash is invaluable in training your puppy, especially teaching him recall. It enables you to stay in control at all times.

Long training leashes: A long training leash, which is usually between 10 and 30 feet (1 and 2.8 m) long, is an extremely useful piece of equipment, which will help you to safely build up your puppy's recall training skills. It not only enables him to run around and play with a feeling of freedom but, while he does so, you have the ability to prevent him running away or getting into trouble with other dogs.

The length and weight of the training leash will depend upon your puppy's size, and he may need to be familiarized gradually to its feel and the noise it makes over the course of several walks.

Harnesses: Ideally, a long training leash should be attached to a body harness rather than a collar to prevent any potential jerks to a puppy's neck, although this is more likely with slightly older and heavier dogs or those that can run at great speed right to the end of the line. A harness is also a good option for short-necked breeds, like Pugs.

Name tag

Your puppy should always wear a name tag (ID) that clearly states your contact details. Make sure that this is securely attached to the D-ring on his collar. You may receive an additional tag from your microchip company that can be attached alongside the name tag.

Buy a few essential items of equipment in readiness for your puppy's arrival

Puppy-proof your yard

KEEP YOUR PUPPY SAFE OUTSIDE

Securing the boundary of your yard is essential unless you intend to supervise your puppy on a leash during every single outside break or play time. If this is impossible, perhaps due to hedging (rather than fencing or walls) or the yard's sheer size, you can still create a secure puppy enclosure. Your puppy will enjoy the freedom to run off leash, burn off excess energy and to find a suitable place in which to relieve himself.

Careful selection and storage

Your yard will be an extension of your puppy's territory, and to enable him to play safely and explore, you must make sure that not only is it escape-proof but also that you keep all yard products and tools safely locked away in a shed. Place any cans of paint, weatherproofing products, weedkillers and insecticides as well as all sharp tools high up out of your dog's reach. Avoid using rodent poisons and opt for safely positioned traps instead. Beware of using cocoa mulch; it has a similar toxicity to chocolate and therefore is not suitable for use around puppies.

Slug and snail pellets, granules or liquids: These can contain metaldehyde, a chemical that can be fatal to dogs if ingested. Always check the label as "pet safe" versions are available.

Antifreeze: This is fatal even in tiny doses, so containers should be sealed and kept away from your puppy. Check for leakages from your car as he may be tempted to lick up the sweet liquid.

Weedkillers: These can be toxic and carcinogenic. Select "pet safe" brands and don't allow your puppy to approach or lie on treated areas for 24 hours.

Other backyard hazards

- Fence off swimming pools and ponds to prevent drowning. An excited puppy may easily run off the edge, onto a pool-cover or frozen surface.
- Many gardens include decorative stones, which puppies often love to chew or carry in their mouths. These pose a danger but removing them can be difficult. Instead, make sure that your puppy has plenty of toys and safe items to play with and encourage him to spend time in safe areas. Praise him for performing desirable activities every time.

Puppies like to chew, so you must ensure that there are no poisonous plants (see Poisonous Plants opposite) at a low level within your dog's reach.

If you think your puppy has eaten a poisonous plant or substance, contact your vet immediately

Poisonous plants

During his investigations, your puppy will taste many of the plants in your yard. Although the most toxic plants should be removed completely, where this is impossible plants should be moved or safely fenced off. Most puppies love to dig and the discovery of bulbs beneath the soil can encourage this destructive and potentially dangerous habit. Laying protective wire mesh over the soil will limit the chances of a poisonous bulb or tuber being consumed.

May prove fatal

- Aloe vera
- Holly (berries)
- Azalea (all parts)
- African violet (leaves)
- *Clematis arnandii*
- Privet
- Wild cherry tree (twigs and foliage)
- Amaryllis (bulbs)
- Bracken
- English ivy (berries and leaves)
- Wisteria (pods and seeds)
- Cyclamen
- Elephant ears
- Oleander
- Autumn crocus (bulbs)
- Daffodil and narcissus (bulbs)
- Yew (berries, bark and foliage)
- Dumb cane
- Virginia creeper
- Jasmine
- Lupin

Minute doses fatal

- Ragwort

Fatal

- Mistletoe (berries)

It is important to make sure that your yard is secure and that your puppy cannot escape – check the fencing and hedges for any gaps.

Getting ready
AGREE ON THE GUIDELINES TOGETHER

Each member of your family will have their own thoughts about what owning a puppy will entail. You are all likely to have different ideas and varied tolerances, but to help your puppy to understand what is expected of him you must all sit down together and discuss these issues. If each person has different rules, your puppy will feel understandably confused and behavior problems could soon develop.

Which areas of the home will your puppy have access to?
Agree as a family on the house rules for your new puppy. Start by deciding which gates or doors will be kept closed and which rooms are out of bounds. Decide upon whether or not he can get up on sofas and beds and agree to abide by this rule.

Who will be responsible for his daily care?
Everyone should have a role in your puppy's care, although adults will need to have overall responsibility. Agree on a schedule for meals, taking him out to relieve himself, cleaning up afterward, grooming, playing, walking and attending training classes.

How will you correct your puppy?
Agree on how to respond to any mistakes that your puppy makes and where best to put him for some "time out" when necessary.

Decide whether your puppy will be allowed to get up on the sofa and stick to this rule.

Example of training plan

What your puppy does	How to respond
Jumps up to say hello	Turn away and ignore him until all four paws are on the floor, or he is sitting. Try to remember this every time you come home.
Steals a sock	Don't chase him or shout at him. Try to swap the sock for a tasty treat or toy and then praise him.
Relieves himself on the floor	Take him into the yard in case he needs to go again. Clean up and try to remember to take him out more often.
Climbs on the sofa	Encourage him "Off" and reward him for responding. Ask him to settle on his own bed and praise and reward him for that.

Shared responsibility

One person in the family often takes responsibility for all training and walking. This may suit you but could mean that your puppy won't be as obedient for, or bonded to, other members who are less involved. It is also unlikely that there will be consistency in the methods used if only one person attends training classes and hears the instruction.

What's his name?

Your choice of potential names is limitless but it helps if everyone uses the same name and if it can be called out clearly in the park. It's common to use nicknames for pets, but, while he is young and learning to respond, it will help your puppy to hear the same word used in reference to him. Short names are fine but it is an advantage to have two syllables for emphasis, e.g., "La-ra" or "Ri-cky."

It's also worth considering that your puppy's name will influence how people perceive him. While "Snoopy" might get away with being a little disobedient, "Tyson's" similar behavior may be interpreted as unruly and dangerous. It may not be fair but perception is important when it comes to the way other people interact with your puppy.

Get together and decide as a family how to look after and train your new puppy

Decide who will walk the new puppy and make sure that he walks nicely on a loose leash without pulling for everyone.

Training preferences

As a family, you must agree upon what you want to train and how to do it. Mixed messages will compromise any training attempts. Everyone should know where to find treats and what your puppy can do to earn them.

Your puppy's space
PROVIDING A SECURE ENVIRONMENT

Wherever your puppy will spend his time, he must feel safe and secure. Whether you have chosen to use a puppy crate or a dog bed, you must ensure that the environment you provide is welcoming for him. He will then settle in to his new life with you much more quickly and will also be less likely to exhibit distress when he finds himself alone.

A place to sleep

It is tempting to purchase a fancy dog bed for your new arrival, but the reality is that your puppy won't mind what his bed looks like as long as he is comfortable. His rapid growth over the coming months will mean that a replacement will be needed at some stage. A bed with sides reduces drafts and creates a sense of security.

However, some of the larger breeds, those with thicker coats or dogs that are susceptible to overheating (such as Bulldogs) are better with a bed they can stretch out on. A teething or under-stimulated puppy can destroy a cloth or wicker bed in a few short hours, and while there are solutions for both of these situations, it may mean that you would prefer to wait until he has matured before making any significant purchase.

Blankets

While these provide warmth and extra security, particularly for breeds that like to burrow, a blanket will typically become a play item. It's likely to be dragged from the bed and possibly chewed or soiled. Therefore an easily replaceable, washable blanket is required. Vet bedding is a type of fleece bedding that is absorbent and nontoxic and easily cut to size. This makes a good option for inserting into a dog bed, or as a standalone bed option.

- **Traditional cushion or duvet-style beds**: These beds often have washable covers, making them particularly suitable for young puppies, as well as allowing the dog to stretch out.
- **Donut-style beds**: These beds are cushioned all around and are extremely comfortable, although they may be tricky to climb into.
- **Nest-style beds**: These beds have raised sides to reduce the likelihood of drafts and an opening to make entry and exit easy.
- **Igloo-style beds**: The puppy is enclosed and secure; they are usually made from soft material.
- **Other styles**: These include memory foam or orthopedic mattresses, or specialized beds that can warm or cool the dog.

Some puppies enjoy the security of their own crate, in which you can place some comfortable bedding as well as interesting toys and chews.

It is not advisable to let your puppy sleep on your bed, especially if he is damp or muddy or is a particularly large breed of dog.

Heat and heartbeat: Some puppies may become distressed when they leave the security of their mother and siblings. It is possible to purchase a heated pad that is safe to use with puppies (hot water bottles are easily chewed and therefore should be avoided). Often these pads come with a heartbeat simulator, so that your puppy feels as though he is cuddled up beside his mother. Once he has settled in and familiarized with his environment he will have less need for these.

Help your puppy relax and feel safe

There are many products that are available now from pet stores that can help your new puppy to settle into his new home environment and relax.

Pheromone diffuser: Pheromones are produced by one member of a species to influence the emotional state of another member of the same species. Pregnant and lactating dogs secrete an appeasing pheromone that has been shown to calm their puppies. Scientific studies have shown that puppies that are exposed to a synthetic copy of this pheromone find it easier to settle down after environmental changes. A diffuser can be plugged in near to where your puppy will sleep or spend the majority of his time. Diffusers have no impact on the humans or other animals who inhabit the house as they are species-specific.

Bedtime

When your puppy arrives, get him accustomed to a bedtime routine at a similar time each night. Before settling him down, take him outside to relieve himself and praise and reward him when he does so. Put some sheets of newspaper or a training pad down on the floor near his bed in case he has an accident during the night. Puppies usually adapt quite quickly to the rhythms of their new home and take themselves off to bed

You can help your new puppy feel safe by providing a comfortable bed in a secure environment

3 SETTLING YOUR PUPPY IN

Collecting your puppy

HOW TO MAKE IT TROUBLE-FREE

The big day has finally arrived! Getting organized before you go to collect your puppy will make his transition into your home as smooth and as stress-free as possible. Prepare for your journey by checking the directions and planning stops in advance. It's extremely helpful to have another person accompany you, either to drive or to hold your puppy.

Collection

Before accepting him, check that your chosen puppy is interactive and bright-eyed, without runny eyes or nose, or signs of an upset stomach. Ask the breeder not to feed him just prior to your arrival, so that he will not be traveling on a full stomach. If possible, try to ensure that he has recently relieved himself before you begin your journey. Complete all the paperwork and pack the car before you take your puppy away from the breeder's house.

Collection checklist

- The correct documentation relating to your puppy's purchase and pedigree (if applicable).
- A receipt for the purchase price.
- Your copy of the contract (if applicable).
- Your puppy's veterinary records complete with dates of worming and any flea treatments.
- Paperwork relating to any free insurance offered by the breeder.
- Instructions on what to do if there is a problem with your puppy (often within the contract but worth discussing).
- Familiar blanket and/or toys.
- A sample of his current food.

Get everything ready well in advance for when you bring your new puppy home.

Safe journey

Normally your puppy should travel within a car kennel, puppy crate or secured by a car harness but he may find these choices upsetting, especially on his first journey away from his siblings. Puppies should never travel on the driver's lap or be free to move around inside the vehicle. Ideally, your puppy should sit on your helper's lap or beside them in the rear of the car. Talk calmly and quietly to your puppy during the journey. Try not to become agitated if he's upset, as this could exacerbate his anxiety and distract you from driving.

Motion sickness

Young puppies often experience "travel sickness." This is typically due to the type of motion being unfamiliar and therefore their movement-detection receptors become overstimulated. However, anxiety plays a significant role in triggering sickness, too. Protect your car seats with layers of old towels. A waterproof sheet is useful but you must ensure that this does not cause the top blankets or towels to slide around. There's the least movement in the passenger footwell, so this can be a good place to transport your puppy if his size allows and if your helper can prevent him from moving around.

Caution! Your puppy's first journey in the car should be as relaxing as possible, so stay calm and don't play loud music. Drive carefully without any sudden braking. He will feel unwell if you drive too fast around corners or over bumps. Slow down.

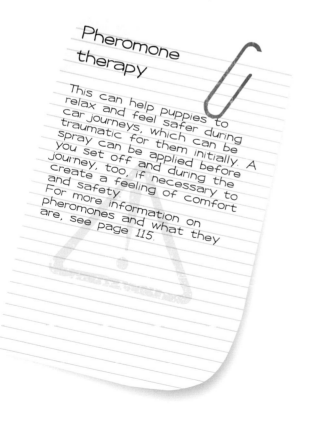

Pheromone therapy

This can help puppies to relax and feel safer during car journeys, which can be traumatic for them initially. A spray can be applied before you set off and during the journey, too, if necessary to create a feeling of comfort and safety. For more information on pheromones and what they are, see page 115.

This is a very important day for you and your puppy as you embark on a new life together.

Refreshments

For you: Make sure that you carry some water or a vacuum flask of tea or coffee and some snacks to minimize non-essential stops on the way home.

For your puppy: Travel bowls allow easy carriage of water. Get into the habit of always taking a large bottle of water on journeys and for the end of walks. A few tasty treats might be appreciated, although a tummy full of new treats is likely to cause an upset when combined with travel.

Plan your journey and pack the car in advance, so that everything goes smoothly

Coming home
MAKING THE TRANSITION GO SMOOTHLY

Arriving home with your new puppy is usually fraught with excitement. If you have done your homework properly and prepared your family and children in advance, everyone should know just how important it is to stay calm and quiet, so as not to frighten the puppy, who may well be feeling anxious or even distressed at being separated from his mother.

Are we ready?

Leave your puppy with your helper in the car or call ahead to make sure that the house is ready. Other existing pets should be shut away in another room. It may be easier for everyone concerned if resident dogs have just been walked and are resting.

Make a fuss of your puppy and set some time aside to play games together and start the mutual bonding process.

Comfort break first

After his journey your puppy will probably need to go outside to relieve himself. Ideally, you should carry him to the place that you want him to use, usually into the yard, and give him the opportunity to "go." However, if your puppy has never been outside, if the weather is adverse, it is dark or there is no safe area, you may want to put him on a puppy training pad.

These are typically placed near to the door where he will eventually exit to relieve himself, but they need to be accessible at all times, so you may need to start off within his secured area. These absorbent pads are also useful for those times when he can't be taken out, although it's usually easier in the long run to teach your puppy to go outside early on. Puppies make associations with the types of substrate, and the sort of area where they "go." Ideally, all these associations will be with outdoor places to minimize confusion and the probability of any future accidents inside the home.

Sleepy puppy

Your puppy will tire easily. Little baby brains can take in only so much new information before a rest is necessary, and the excitement of meeting everyone and exploring will physically tire him, too. Let him rest without disturbing him; he'll soon be awake and ready to restart the fun.

Pick a place and a surface where you would like your puppy to relieve himself and encourage him to go there – always accompany him.

When you arrive home, begin good habits immediately by letting your puppy "go" outside in the yard before you take him indoors.

Hello!

Everyone should sit on the floor while your puppy explores the room and says "hello." He needs to learn that everyone is friendly and fun to be around. Pet him gently when he approaches you. It's important to prevent children becoming overexcited and crowding him or squabbling for their turn. Take care when lifting him up – suddenly swooping down to pick him up could startle him and make him nervous about being carried again.

This place is fun

Place several of your puppy's toys on the floor for him to discover. There may be too much going on for him to focus for long on any one toy, but you can try to entice him to play by wiggling a toy on the floor at his level. Praise him for joining in.

Be prepared and calm to make your puppy's homecoming welcoming and less frightening

Busy children

If your children are home, give them helpful jobs related to the puppy.

· Water bowls need to be filled.

· Your puppy's first meal must be measured and placed in his bowl.

· His blanket and toys should be placed in his bed.

· If you are using one, the heating pad can be turned on.

· Offer existing pets, shut in other rooms, some treats, too.

Introducing equipment
SELECTING THE RIGHT ITEMS

Once your puppy has settled in to his new home and is feeling much more relaxed, you can gradually introduce essential items of equipment, including his collar, leash, a harness (if you use one) and a crate or cage.

Collar

Adjust the collar to roughly the correct size first. Sit with your puppy on your knee or in front of you, stroking him, so he is relaxed before putting the collar on. Slip two fingers between his collar and his skin to check that it's fitting correctly. The collar will feel unusual, so your puppy might scratch at it initially. Distract him with a favorite game or meal time and he will soon get used to wearing it.

Leash

Introduce a leash well before your puppy goes on his first walk in order to reduce the number of new experiences at one time. Practice clipping the leash on to and off his collar, offering him a treat each time. Avoid dangling the leash in his face while you do this. Try spinning his collar around so that the strong D-ring is at the back of the neck, allowing easy attachment of the leash. After a minute or so, remove the leash and practice again later.

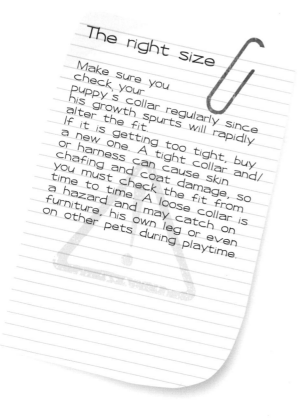

The right size

Make sure you check your puppy's collar regularly since his growth spurts will rapidly alter the fit. If it is getting too tight, buy a new one. A tight collar and/or harness can cause skin chafing and coat damage, so you must check the fit from time to time. A loose collar is a hazard and may catch on furniture, his own leg or even on other pets during playtime.

Regular collar checks will keep your puppy comfortable and safe. You should be able to insert two fingers between the collar and his skin.

Gradually leave the leash on for longer periods while your puppy walks with you around the house, and then in the yard. Always make sure that you praise and reward him for walking nicely. Some puppies are not fazed by their leash whereas others panic and won't walk at first. Take the necessary time to practice until your puppy is relaxed and confident, ready to face the outside world on his walks, which can start as soon as he finishes his set of vaccinations.

Harness

A harness may suit a tiny or short-nosed breed, such as a Pug, or can be used for car travel. Either way, it pays to introduce this item of equipment slowly and patiently and to link it with a rewarding experience. Familiarize yourself with the harness and how it fits and fastens before you begin, since they can be tricky to master. Take your time and reward your puppy for each step of the process.

Playing games with your puppy serves as a distraction from the unfamiliar sensation of wearing a new harness.

Indoor kennel

An indoor kennel (sometimes also called a crate or cage) should be a place of safety for your puppy. Set it up with some familiar bedding, a few safe toys and a secured bowl of water.

- Leave the crate open and let your puppy sniff it and enter.
- Hide tidbits and fun toys inside the crate to encourage him to explore.
- Include some familiar scents via an old T-shirt or pillowcase.
- Place your drowsy puppy inside the crate to sleep, leaving the door open at first.
- Gradually accustom him to the door closing but remain nearby until he relaxes.
- Slowly build up the time he spends inside.

Avoid...

- Forcing your puppy into the crate.
- Shutting him in the crate right away.
- Leaving him for prolonged periods on his own shut inside the crate.
- Using the crate as a place of punishment.

Choosing the right size

This depends upon the breed of puppy, his temperament and what the space is intended for. Some puppies like a large crate while others prefer the security of a smaller space. Your puppy should be able to stand up, turn around and lie down comfortably. As he grows, you must ensure that these essentials are still possible.

Housebreaking

CONSISTENCY AND WATCHFULNESS ARE IMPORTANT

Housebreaking can start as soon as your new puppy comes home. If it is approached consistently and with dedication, good habits can form within weeks, although you must expect the occasional mishap because he won't have full bladder control until he is at least 5 months old. Never punish him for any "accidents" – just take him outside immediately.

Early experience matters

It's much harder to successfully housebreak a puppy that has been confined to a tiny area where the puppies had little choice but to relieve themselves, play, sleep and eat within the same space. Thankfully, puppies naturally want to move away from their sleeping areas to "go," so you can use this instinct to encourage your puppy to go to the area you would like him to use. Your puppy will begin to learn about the rules of his new environment as soon as he arrives in your home.

Your puppy will give out clues to indicate that he needs to relieve himself.

When?

Your puppy needs to relieve himself regularly. Until you know his habits, take him to his area at the following times and establish a routine:

- When he wakes in the morning
- After meals
- After playtime or other exercise
- After big excitements
- When he wakes up after a nap
- At least once every hour
- Last thing at night.

Looking for the signs

Every accident within the home is an opportunity for your puppy to make the wrong associations, and the emphasis is on you to make sure that this does not happen. If you are vigilant and observe him closely, you will soon learn to spot the telltale signs of when your puppy is thinking about "going." These are listed below.

Puppies will often...

- Stop playing or chewing
- Begin to sniff the floor
- Circle while sniffing
- Appear to have a vacant or distracted moment
- Wander off toward the door or to an area previously used to relieve themselves.

Going out

Take your puppy into the yard and be prepared to wait for him. The world is very exciting for a young puppy, so he may be distracted at first and

Pads or paper?

You may wish to use pads or newspaper to protect your floor against accidents, but, unless you have good reason for using them, such as a high disease risk, illness or adverse weather, try not to rely on them solely. A puppy may learn to target the pad or paper but you will then have to go through the transition process of teaching him to go outside, usually by inching the paper gradually toward the door and then out into the yard, finally reducing the size of the paper until he is going on the ground. It is simpler to teach him to go outside right from the start.

If you see your puppy sniffing and circling, a swift exit into the yard increases the likelihood that he will relieve himself in the right place.

you must be ready with shoes and a coat by the door. Trying to hurry him will only slow things down whereas waiting in the warmth while you send him outside will only encourage him to rush to get back to you, meaning that he doesn't empty his bladder properly, increasing the chance of a mistake.

Reinforcing the right action

• When your puppy does "go," always say the phrase that you've chosen as your signal, such as "Hurry up" or "Be clean."
• When he's finished, praise him and offer him a tasty tidbit as a reward.
• While he is distracted with his treat, you can pick up the feces, or go back later to clean up.

If you spot these signs you should do the following.
1 Quickly call your puppy to you in the most excited voice you can muster.
2 Rush to the outside door, encouraging your puppy to come with you.
3 Pick him up if you think there is no time, or if the distance outside is too far.

Hopefully, your reaction will cause him to pause for long enough to get him to the appropriate place.

Where?

No matter whether you want your puppy to "go" in a specific area or are happy for him to use the whole yard, establishing these rules as early as possible is helpful. Before you decide to teach him to "go" on one surface only (grass, concrete or bark chips), consider whether you will always have this surface available in the future. Repeatedly take him to the area where you want him to go and the habit will soon start to form.

Accompanying your puppy

It is very important that you go outside with your puppy, whatever the weather or the time of day. It is not enough to put him outside and close the door behind him. Stay with him at all times, no matter how cold or wet, and encourage him. Praise and treat him when he performs the required action. He will soon learn what is expected and where to go.

When accidents occur

They might feel frustrating but remember that your puppy is just starting to learn. He does not relieve himself inside deliberately through spite or as an act of dominance. In reality, perhaps it was just too long since he was last taken out or you missed the signs while you were distracted.

Punishing your puppy after he "goes" is always counterproductive. He will not be able to associate your response with the act of going but he may become anxious when you arrive home or walk into the room. It is not uncommon for a punished puppy to avoid relieving himself when their owner is present, which not only makes walks very tricky but may also make him more likely to sneak away to find a quiet place inside the house to go in private.

Cleaning up thoroughly after he has urinated or defecated on the floor is important for hygiene purposes and for the prevention of further accidents, as you need to remove the scent.

- Soak up urine or lift feces with paper towels.
- Use a quality pet mess cleaner or a hot biological washing powder solution to clean the area.
- Rinse the area afterward with clean water. Soak up any excess water with clean paper towels.

Choose your phrase carefully

"Be quick" or "Hurry up" are common phrases, but these are less ideal, of course, if you usually shout them out to your children every morning as they get ready to leave for school. Make sure you choose your phrase carefully.

Accompany your puppy outside and quietly supervise and encourage him while he sniffs the ground and prepares to "go."

Picking up

All dog owners must pick up after their pets. Even a tiny piece of feces contains millions of bacteria that can contaminate the ground, water, and shoes and toys of adults and children. Puppies may also want to explore the feces, playing with or eating it (see pages 218–219 for how to cope with this problem). This undesirable habit, known as coprophagia, can continue into adulthood if it is not dealt with effectively early on or prevented.

- Keep a supply of plastic or paper bags by the door and in your coat pocket.
- Pooper-scooper tools are available for those who prefer them.

Caution! Don't leave pickup bags on the ground, even if you intend to retrace your steps later. Many owners forget or cannot find the bag again, causing litter problems in dog-walking areas.

Reward your puppy and make a fuss over him when he relieves himself appropriately in the correct place.

No yard?

If you live in an apartment and have no yard, housebreaking your puppy will be more problematic and may take longer, and you must be consistent, patient and proactive.

· Take him out for regular walks to the same patch of grass.

· Go outside with him first thing in the morning, after meals and naps, and last thing at night.

· Supplement this with a puppy training pad in your home.

Successful housebreaking guidelines

Housebreaking isn't very difficult if you are consistent in your approach and apply these rules.

- Be vigilant and proactive about taking your puppy outside to relieve himself.
- Take him out immediately you spot any of the warning signs (see page 123).
- Use the same command each time.
- Praise and reward his behavior – he will soon associate "going" with pleasing you.
- If he has an accident indoors and you catch him in the act, say "No" firmly and take him outside.

Don't take risks

If you are immune-suppressed due to illness, or you are pregnant, it is essential that you take extra care whenever you are picking up your puppy's mess – latex gloves or double bagging will provide you with additional protection. Make sure that you always wash your hands thoroughly or use some antibacterial gel immediately afterward. Don't take risks.

Strongly scented household cleaners may mask the smell to you, but your puppy's sensitive nose may detect traces, so clean up thoroughly indoors

Housebreaking checklist

WATCH YOUR PUPPY CAREFULLY

When you collect your new puppy and bring him home he will probably have had very little housebreaking training. Most breeders keep very young puppies in an enclosed environment and simply put newspaper down on the floor in case of accidents. It will be your responsibility to teach him the ground rules, and, with a little time and patience, it will not be long before you have a clean and well-trained puppy.

Housebreaking rules

- Take your puppy outside to "go" every hour.
- Take him out after games or exercise.
- Always take him outside last thing at night immediately before you go to bed.
- Do not leave water down for him after the final elimination just before bed.
- Take him outside as soon as he awakens from a sleep, even if it's a nap during the day.
- Take him out after every meal.
- Never offer him food after 7 pm.
- Take him out immediately if you see him circling, sniffing or squatting inside the house.

You must stay outside and wait for your puppy to relieve himself – if you stay indoors he may not go and will scratch the door to get back inside.

Patience is key

Housebreaking a puppy takes time, observation and patience. Its success depends, to a great extent, on watching your puppy for telltale signs of needing to go, such as sniffing and circling indoors, and then taking him out immediately. Some breeds are quicker to learn than others, and the smaller toy breeds can be notoriously slow. However, most puppies are housebroken by the time they are 7 months old – some much earlier than this.

Top housebreaking tips

- Learn to recognize the signs your puppy makes when he needs to go, such as restlessness, circling, sniffing the floor and, finally, squatting.
- When he relieves himself outside, encourage him and praise him immediately – give him a treat to reinforce the behavior.
- Use a standard command every time he goes, and make sure everyone else uses the same one – he will soon associate this with the act.
- Don't have just "one place" where he can go. If he is only used to relieving himself on grass, eventually he may not like using gravel or soil.
- Every member of the family must be prepared to take turns at going outside with him.
- Don't panic if your puppy has an accident inside the house, and do not punish him – clean it up and continue your training.

Housebreaking methods

Going outside	This is the best and most effective way of housebreaking your puppy, but you will need to be constantly vigilant and available to take him out regularly.
Newspapers	Sheets of newspaper placed on the floor are effective in the short term for initial training, especially at night, but it is better introduce your puppy to his outdoor place as soon as possible.
Training pads	Specially designed absorbent training pads can be used in the same way as newspaper, but they are more expensive.
Crate training	If your puppy sleeps in a crate at night, make sure it is near a door with pads or paper close by – dogs hate to soil their own area.

Suggested daily routine

Establishing a daily routine can help a dog to develop a sense of security and confidence as well as helping with housebreaking.

7–8 am	Go outside with your puppy. Use a keyword or phrase such as "hurry up" and wait for him to relieve himself. Praise him immediately.
8:15 am	Feed him.
8:30 am	Go outside and praise him when he goes.
9–11am	Rest period.
11am	Take him outside again and repeat your keyword. Wait patiently for him to perform and then praise him as before.
11:15 am	Feed him and take him back outside.
11:45	Rest and play – with half-hourly trips outside, more often if signs of him wanting to go.
4 pm	Feed him and take him outside immediately.
4:15 pm	Play and rest time.
7 pm	Last feed of the day and then back outside, with lots of praise if he goes.
7:15 pm	Sleep and some light play.
10 pm	Last trip outside before settling down for the night in his bed.

Wait patiently while your puppy sniffs the ground before relieving himself – trying to hurry him up may prove counterproductive.

Housebreaking is easy if you are vigilant

Choosing a diet

ENSURING THAT IT IS NUTRITIONALLY BALANCED

Starting at between 4 and 6 weeks, your puppy will be weaned from his mother's milk onto solid foods. He will require a carefully balanced diet as he will grow rapidly throughout his first year, and if the correct nutrition is not provided his health and development may be compromised. The development of both his physical and immune systems is dependent on the ingestion of the right amounts of proteins, carbohydrates, fats, vitamins and minerals.

The appropriate diet

Ideally, the breeder will have selected a high-quality puppy food to start your puppy off and will advise you in advance about what to buy. If you have concerns about the quality of his diet, or the ingredients, discuss this with your vet. A breeder may have the best intentions but many old-fashioned weaning plans are still practiced despite being nutritionally inappropriate.

Choose a diet that is appropriate for your puppy's age and breed size. If it is "complete" or "balanced" you won't need to supplement it with additional vitamins, which can cause serious health problems.

Check the labels

Always read the labels. If the diet is "complete" it contains everything your puppy needs. If it is "complimentary," then you must offer additional food to provide the required nutrition. Be aware that it is never appropriate for a puppy to eat a diet that is designed specifically for an adult dog or to be on the same schedule as an adult for meals.

Large and giant breeds

Excess energy and calcium intake can cause an increased likelihood of orthopedic disease. Choose a diet designed for puppies of this size as specialized diets have been adjusted to ensure the right nutrition.

Diet options

Dry food	This is the easiest way for most owners to feed a measured, balanced diet. Quality varies significantly across the brands, so pay attention to the ingredients. Choose one designed specially for puppies that lists a specific type of animal protein, such as "chicken" or "lamb," rather than a vague "meat" description. "Premium" diets are usually of higher quality than other types, although checking the ingredients is the only way to be sure. High protein levels are commonly linked to problem behavior in dogs, although scientific evidence for this is scarce. The protein quality, rather than the percentage, is probably most relevant.
Wet meat (canned) or semi-moist food	The quality will vary, so be sure to choose a recognizable brand that is designed specially for puppies with clearly listed ingredients on the label.
Homemade food	A perfectly balanced diet is hard to create, so, unless you have experience or have specific advice from a canine nutritionist, this may not be advisable during this critical period of growth and development.

Your puppy is likely to feel hungry after energetic outdoor play or walks.

Choose a quality diet that suits your puppy's needs. Make sure that it the right one for his size, weight and age – puppy foods vary immensely.

Feeding your puppy
A REGULAR ROUTINE IS IMPORTANT

Initially, your puppy's digestive system will only be able to cope with small amounts of food at a time. To keep up with the demand from his growing body, he will need to be fed several small meals daily:
• Four meals per day up until he is about 4 to 5 months old
• Three meals per day up until he is 6 to 7 months old
• After this time, if he is healthy, he can be fed just two meals per day, and this feeding schedule can continue throughout his adult life.

Foods to avoid

Don't feed	Reason
Chocolate	Contains theobromine and caffeine, which are both potentially fatal.
Tea and coffee	Contains caffeine.
Cooked bones	High risk of splintering, internal blockages and perforations.
Onions, garlic, raisins, grapes	Highly toxic if consumed in high quantities.
Sugary treats	Tooth decay, obesity, hyperactive behavior and diabetes are all a risk.
Products containing sweetener	Liver damage.
Avocado	Contains persin, which can be fatal.
Peaches, plums, apricots	The stones contain cyanide and pose a choking and internal blockage risk.

Changing from one diet to another

If you decide to change your puppy to another diet you should introduce it gradually over a period of a week to 10 days to allow his system to adjust without upset. If possible, wait a few days for your puppy to settle in to his new home before making changes, as the anxiety related to a change in environment may cause a digestive upset.

Puppies often go through apparently picky stages, but if your puppy's diet previously suited him, resist changing it as you risk creating a fussy adult. In most cases, puppies will resume eating within a few meals, but if yours is not drinking any water either or is lethargic, seek veterinary advice.

Mealtime routine

Try to spread your puppy's meals evenly throughout the day. Having a regular meal schedule will benefit his housebreaking as he will be more predictable.

• Use a measuring cup to ensure that you offer the correct portion size.
• Call your puppy to you and use a tasty morsel of his meal to encourage him to "sit" before you put the bowl down for him to eat.
• Prevent other pets or children trying to interact with him while he eats.

Adapt as he grows

Your puppy's requirements will change as he gets older and grows, so adjust the amount you feed

Encourage your puppy to "Sit" politely before placing the food bowl down on the floor. He must learn good manners and to wait to be fed.

Using treats

Treats are the ideal way to encourage desirable behavior, but ensure that they do not account for more than 10 percent of your puppy's diet or you risk causing an imbalance. Reduce his main meals to accommodate the extra calories. Be aware that many treats contain colorings, sugars and fats, so opt for healthy ones. Treats can be broken into tiny pieces, meaning that a small amount can go a long way. If you are sensible, using food during training will not lead to obesity or cause a begging problem.

Placing extra kibble in your puppy's bowl while he eats will get him accustomed to hands bringing good things and make him less possessive.

him once every 2 weeks. Slow, steady growth is required in puppies of all breeds to prevent bone or other growth deformities. The portion advice printed on the packaging is relevant for an average puppy and is certainly not a fixed rule, so do not panic if your puppy tends to eat a little more or less than is recommended. As long as he appears well and is a healthy weight, he will be eating enough.

Water

Making a free supply of fresh drinking water available at all times is critical to your puppy's healthy diet, even if he is fed a wet meat one.

Diet checklist

By the time your new puppy comes to live with you, he should be fully weaned and will almost certainly be eating four small meals a day. A puppy's stomach is very small, which is why he cannot cope with one large meal. It also gives you the opportunity to take him out after each meal.

Food sensitivities and intolerances

Some puppies appear to be sensitive to or even intolerant of certain ingredients and additives in manufactured food, which can result in a variety of health problems. Common symptoms include:

- Lethargy
- Aggressive or hyperactive behavior
- Chronic skin and ear problems
- Light to mid-brown loose bulky stools or diarrhea
- Slime and jelly being passed with the stools
- Flatulence, bloating and weight gain or loss
- In extreme cases, colitis (slime and blood in the stools) – consult your vet if this happens.

Monitoring weight and health

Keep a close eye on your puppy's weight and general health. These will give you pointers as to whether his food suits him or not.

- He should be growing well with a healthy-looking, shiny coat.
- His stools should be dark brown, solid and well formed.
- Watch out for weight gain as a result of feeding too many treats.

Top diet tips

- Read the labels carefully on dog food, so you measure out the right amount.
- Be guided by the ingredients rather than the packaging.
- Feed age-related puppy foods to meet the specific needs of your growing dog.
- If your puppy normally eats well but loses his appetite, consult your vet.
- Don't entice him to eat by feeding unsuitable, high-calorie foods.
- If he is underweight or overweight, seek veterinary advice.
- If you are worried that he may have a food intolerance, talk to your vet about this.

Feeding guidelines for a puppy

Age	Meals
8–12 weeks	4 meals per day
3–6 months	3 meals per day
6–9 months	2 meals per day
9 months +	1–2 meals per day

Treats

Treats are a very useful tool in reinforcing reward training, but too many can lead to obesity, so opt for healthy ones that are meat- or cereal-based and formulated specially for dogs. They should form no more than 10 percent of a dog's daily food intake. There are so many varieties and flavors, and it is incumbent on you to find the ones that your puppy enjoys and that motivate him in training.

- **Chews:** These are generally dry or semi-moist and come in a wide range of flavors, shapes and sizes.
- **Pigs' ears:** A great favorite with most puppies and a longer-lasting treat.
- **Raw marrowbones:** You may be able to get these from a butcher. Most dogs love them, and they will not only clean your puppy's teeth but also give him nourishment at the same time.
- **Dog chocolate drops:** Dogs love these, but you must only buy special dog chocolate ones as human chocolate is poisonous to canines.

Caution! Don't offer your puppy fatty or sugary human snacks, such as cookies or potato chips. Tiny pieces of cheese or cooked liver are acceptable as occasional high-value treats.

Make sure that your puppy has access to fresh water at all times by regularly refreshing his bowl.

Your puppy's diet makes a difference in his health and behavior

What should you feed?

There are so many dog foods available and what you feed your puppy will depend on a combination of what is convenient for you and what suits him. Try not to change his diet too much or too often, as this can cause digestive upsets. However, it is perfectly normal to try out different foods until you find one that suits him.

Dry food	There are many specially formulated dry foods for puppies. They contain all the nutrients a growing dog requires and are very convenient. The water content is approximately 10 percent, so you must provide fresh water at all times.
Semi-moist food	Generally, these foods are available as treats in the form of "bacon shapes" or "pork chops." They are not a substitute for a meal.
Wet/ canned food	This is not only higher in moisture than dried food, but tends to be contain more protein and fat, too. It is made in a sterile environment and usually canned as it is cooked.
Natural diet	Many people like to feed their dogs a natural diet, which usually involves cooking cheap minced meat, tripe and organ meats for your dog. If you have the time, this is a great way to feed him but make sure he is getting all the nutrition he needs.

Setting boundaries

ALWAYS BE CONSISTENT

Your puppy is continuously learning about his new environment. For this reason, it is helpful to be consistent with the things that you allow him to do. This is much easier than having to retrain bad habits once they have become a nuisance. It is useful to remind yourself regularly of the agreed house rules in order to help your puppy to follow them.

Make a point of encouraging your puppy to sit calmly beside you before making a fuss over him.

Bad habits form easily

Puppies have a wonderful enthusiasm for life and will be led astray easily without the care of a sensible owner. They learn through experience, and even a single incident in which something happens that your puppy enjoys can lead to him repeating the behavior he associates with the reward. You may think that "one time won't hurt" and offer a scrap from your plate, but while you know that it was a "one off" your puppy has no way of understanding this and he will be confused if you reprimand him next time for the same behavior.

Mistakes happen

You and your puppy will both make some mistakes over the coming months. You need to practice communicating with him just as he needs to learn about you and your expectations of him. Start early by establishing the ground rules now, and you will be rewarded later on by his good behavior.

A child safety gate is useful for containing your puppy within agreed designated areas of your home while he settles in.

Correction methods

It's counterproductive to use heavy-handed or even excessive verbal reprimands for puppies as they will usually become confused and fearful. When a dog corrects another it knows:

- Exactly when to do this
- How strong the message needs to be
- How to interpret the reaction.

Human beings, on the other hand, are:

- Never able to mimic a real dog
- Usually too slow in responding
- Too harsh and bad at knowing when to stop.

Interrupt undesirable behaviors, but praise your puppy as soon as he stops. Preempt problems and create good habits by asking him to do something (such as "Sit" as a friend approaches) before he has a chance to do the wrong thing, such as jump up.

Useful reminders

- Keep your puppy within his own secured area during the early days of settling him in to your home, so he can familiarize himself with it.
- Take him out to relieve himself regularly – he will need to do so at least once every hour initially (although, of course, he will manage longer while he is sleeping).
- Gradually permit him access to other areas of the house, if it's agreed by everyone in the family that he is allowed.
- Pay extra attention to him when you introduce him to new areas, as he is more likely to relieve himself there since he's further from his familiar sleeping and eating areas.
- Always praise him when he does something good. Remember that simple actions, such as settling down quietly, are as worthy of a reward as following a training command.
- Your puppy is cute but do not take him into your bed or cuddle with him on the sofa unless you want this to become part of your daily routine as he grows up and gets bigger.
- Work together with your puppy to maximize his progress and minimize any confusion in your training program.
- Strictly adhere to his normal diet and treats. Offering him scraps from the table while you are eating will only encourage him to beg, and many human foods are not safe for him to eat.
- Start as you mean to go on – if you let him jump up now, he will do so when he is bigger.

Think and plan ahead to prevent your puppy from making too many mistakes

4 SOCIALIZING YOUR PUPPY

When to start

WHAT IS SOCIALIZATION?

Nobody imagines the prospect of owning a terrified dog when they pick up their puppy. While some anxiety problems are unavoidable and stem from traumatic experiences or illness, the majority can be attributed to a dog's early life and the amount of socializing he receives as a puppy. Socialization is the process whereby your puppy learns how to interact with people, dogs and other animals. These lessons will influence how he responds throughout his life and will therefore play a critical role in the creation of a robust temperament and friendly disposition.

Don't delay socialization

After 12 weeks your puppy will be significantly less able to cope with novelty, thereby making it more likely that fear or anxiety behavior patterns will develop. A puppy that can respond appropriately during social encounters will make a safer and more reliable pet in the future. Socialization is very important and it cannot be missed or delayed until another time. The window of opportunity is very short – between 3 and 12 weeks is the duration of the initial "sensitive period."

Preventing problems is important

"Reprogramming" a puppy or an adult dog via behavioral modification later on can only achieve a certain amount of improvement. Computer users can understand this: if you have a basic computer you may add new programs or extra memory but the potential for improving it is limited before unavoidable "error" messages pop up and the system crashes. Similarly, an undersocialized puppy may improve through a desensitization and counterconditioning program, but he may only ever cope under controlled circumstances before fear and panic occur and "crash" your progress.

As part of his socialization, your puppy will need to meet adult dogs.

Breeders have a responsibility for the development of the future good behavior of their puppies

Poor potential

Puppies raised in completely barren environments, as in the case of many puppy farms, will often fail to adapt at all, despite the most dedicated owner. Studies have shown the disastrous impact of limited experiences before 12 weeks, but, of course, early experience alone cannot ensure an ability to cope if the puppy has no further contact during the later juvenile stage of development.

Owner concerns

A common reason for owners delaying their puppy's socialization experiences is due to the fear of disease. Waiting until he is fully vaccinated would mean missing out on the critical "sensitive period," which will impact on his entire behavioral development. In fact, statistically, a puppy is more likely to be euthanized due to a behavioral problem than a disease that can be vaccinated against. Luckily, a healthy puppy will have derived a good level of immunity from his mother and this means that it is possible to safely socialize him before the age of 12 weeks by taking particular precautions, as listed in the box (below right).

Socialization guidelines

As a responsible owner, you should:

- Start training your puppy
- Encourage him to explore
- Introduce him to all sorts of people
- Meet other dogs
- Take him to different places
- Expose him to household noises
- Let him interact with the world
- Go to puppy socialization classes.

Your puppy needs to encounter other people and their dogs when they visit his home or you take him to meet them.

Early socialization

Before your puppy is 12 weeks old, you must do all the following things with him:

- Carry him on short walks to visit neighbors and friends, experience road traffic and if you live in a rural area, view poultry, horses or livestock
- Allow him to meet a variety of dogs that have been vaccinated
- Invite friends and their children or vaccinated pets to visit your home
- Let him walk and explore in safe areas that are free from dogs that have not been vaccinated
- Take him for regular car trips.

Start socializing

Imagine the sort of life that you would like your puppy to lead and then you can try to prepare him for this. Your current situation may not last for the lifetime of your pet, so ensure that you include all other animals, people, children and varied environments in your plan. Many owners have good intentions but they probably do not socialize their puppy as thoroughly as they should. The socialization countdown has already started, so try to arrange different experiences for him each day.

How to start

As a responsible dog owner, you should always approach socialization systematically as this will help you to avoid overwhelming your puppy. For example, although taking him to the school gates where he can meet 50 children may seem like a great opportunity, it is better to build up gradually to this level of interaction through one-to-one introductions and, later, small groups before progressing to larger ones. Your aim is to expose him to the experience without causing him to feel stressed – this means taking it at his pace.

Introduce your puppy to new people in the security of his home.

Relaxed

Allow your puppy to see a person at a distance, and then, if he is happy to do so, let him approach. Observing how he responds to this experience will help you to understand how well he is coping. If he is relaxed and enthusiastic about meeting new people, then continue socializing him in this way and introduce new experiences.

Too intensive

If your puppy is tense, trying to move away, refusing to approach or showing stress signals when meeting someone new, you must reduce the intensity of the experience immediately by allowing him to move away or asking the person to move or turn away, thereby diminishing contact and slowing down any

Genetics and socialization work together

Good genetic influence	+	Adequate socialization	=	Maximum potential for a good temperament.
Good genetic influence	+	Poor socialization	=	Temperamental weaknesses are likely.
Poor genetic influence	+	Adequate socialization	=	Temperamental weaknesses are likely.
Poor genetic influence	+	Poor socialization	=	Minimum potential for a good temperament.

If you have children, they will enjoy playing with your new puppy, but ensure you supervise them initially to prevent him feeling overwhelmed.

movement. If your puppy feels that he can control his exposure to a stimulus he will naturally be more relaxed and therefore will cope better.

If your puppy is worried the first time he encounters something new, don't take a decision to avoid this experience in future – just try to arrange it in such a way that he is exposed in a gentler manner next time, and then build up to the full-blown experience as his confidence grows.

Puppy parties

Many veterinary clinics provide puppy parties for owners with young, partly vaccinated puppies. You may be invited to attend one or several of these sessions where puppies can mix while their owners are given advice. Well-run parties are a good way to provide essential early contact, but less well-organized ones can initiate a lifetime of fearful or bullish behavior. Look out for:

- Experienced staff
- Low numbers
- Age limits
- Controlled play.

As soon as you bring your puppy home, you must start introducing him to as many new people and experiences as possible.

Habituation

EXPOSING YOUR PUPPY TO OTHER EXPERIENCES

Habituation is the term that is used for the learning process whereby a puppy becomes accustomed to all manner of nonliving experiences, such as sounds and textures, and, gradually, via repeated exposure, stops reacting toward them. This is an integral part of development, which is observed across different animal species. Habituation allows us to filter out the events in our environment that pose no threat and therefore we do not need to waste time or physical energy responding to them.

Benefits to your puppy

Your puppy must also learn which stimuli are safe and can be ignored or accepted, and which ones should be approached with caution. Therefore it is helpful for him to learn not to startle at the sound of passing traffic or noisy fireworks, or when he sees or encounters specific items, including rustling plastic bags or a changing floor surface, such as when a carpet ends and gives way to ceramic tiles. Repeated exposure will be needed for thorough and durable habituation, so it is essential to provide lots of experiences for him as early as possible.

Intense fear reactions: These may be triggered by noisy vacuum cleaners, electric blenders, washing machines and hair dryers.

Give it a try

Experiencing everyday home electrical equipment and domestic appliances is of great importance. You can start off by exposing your puppy to the sounds in an adjoining room.

1 Turn the vacuum cleaner on in a next-door room but keep the doors closed in between. If possible, ask someone to do this for you to free you up for playing a game or offering your puppy his dinner and observing his reactions.

2 Gradually increase the intensity by opening the doors between the two rooms and allowing your puppy to explore if he feels confident enough.

3 Always make a point of praising him when he remains calm and settled.

Get your puppy accustomed to noisy household appliances, such as a vacuum cleaner, from the earliest possible age.

Best avoided: Suddenly turning on the vacuum cleaner while your puppy is standing nearby, or moving it toward him, could create an associated fear response. But once a dog has been habituated to noises, he is likely to recover after such a startling experience should it occur accidentally.

Audio sound tracks

It is possible to desensitize your puppy to noises that may trigger anxiety while avoiding the genuine event. Audio sound tracks can be very helpful, and there are several excellent brands of CDs that are designed specifically to expose young puppies to different sounds. A conscientious breeder may play these to their litter daily during the early weeks for maximum benefit. However, it is never too late to start, so you could buy one to play to your new puppy from the time you bring him home – this can be extremely effective and successful.

Although audio recordings are never going to replace the need for the genuine experience in real life, they can be very useful, and they have been shown to increase a puppy's steadiness when he is faced with these sounds later on in life as an adult. Individual tracks that may be relevant to your lifestyle can be downloaded or personally recorded.

Commonly used sound tracks: These include fireworks, traffic noise, barking dogs, children and babies, vacuum cleaners, thunderstorms, kitchen noises, gunshots and bird scarers. Listening to them regularly will help to desensitize your puppy.

"Escape" options

When you have to be noisy or perform an activity your puppy may find concerning, make him feel safer by providing an "escape" option, such as going to his bed or outside in the yard or another room within the house.

Pheromone therapy can aid your puppy's relaxation during noisier times

Audio guidelines

If you use audio sound tracks to desensitize your puppy, ensure you:

- Play the tracks at a low volume
- Gradually increase the volume
- Distract your puppy by playing one of his favorite games or by offering him his meal.

You can use audio sound tracks to habituate your puppy to the noise of traffic but it is also vital that you walk your dog beside busy roads.

New locations

EXPOSING YOUR PUPPY TO NEW PLACES

Taking your puppy to a wide range of new places and environments will provide some of the necessary experiences he requires for his general socialization and habituation. Don't delay – start this as soon as possible.

Timing

Where you decide to take your puppy will depend, to some extent, on his age.

- **Pre-vaccinations:** Visit the homes of friends and family and your veterinary clinic.
- **Post-vaccinations:** Attend puppy classes; walk to the park and over bridges; travel on buses and trains; visit cafés, shops and dog-friendly venues.

Locations

In each new location, your puppy will experience new sights, sounds and smells as well as social encounters with people and other dogs. If you can create safe and enjoyable experiences for him, these will combine to provide him with the very best of developmental opportunities. Where it is safe and appropriate to do so, allow your puppy to explore the area, taking his time to approach and sniff or investigate things that are unfamiliar. Never force him to approach something that causes him concern. Instead, let him see you approaching, touching or looking at it. Drop some treats around the item or in the area, so that he will be rewarded

If you introduce your puppy to a wide range of new locations, he will not be fazed as you gradually work up to crowded ones.

as he finds the confidence to explore. If he does not approach, he is not ready, so don't force him but try repeating this or a similar encounter again in the near future. Puppies glean a lot of information from their pack members, and the way in which you behave will influence his choices.

Confidence around traffic

Normal traffic can pose a challenge to some dogs. Understandably, puppies can be overwhelmed by heavy vehicles, squealing brakes and noisy motorbikes. They often freeze or pull away initially, and, depending on their temperament and breed type, they may either begin to refuse to walk near roads or may start to lunge at passing traffic.

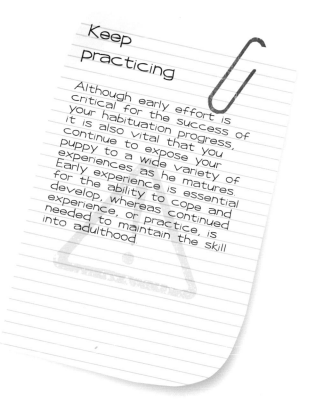

Keep practicing

Although early effort is critical for the success of your habituation progress, it is also vital that you continue to expose your puppy to a wide variety of experiences as he matures. Early experience is essential for the ability to cope and develop, whereas continued experience, or practice, is needed to maintain the skill into adulthood

Traffic guidelines

- Begin your puppy's experiences on quiet roads where he can get accustomed to the noise, smell and vibration without sensitization.
- Some puppies benefit from walking toward oncoming traffic, so that they have the chance to observe rather than being taken by surprise.
- Keep him on the inside, away from the road, with you positioned between him and any cars.
- You can desensitize a fearful puppy via audio recordings and by walking in an open field or park where he can see and hear cars from a safe distance while you encourage him to play.
- Praise him and offer rewards each time he remains calm and ignores the passing cars.
- As he relaxes, you can reduce the distance between him and the road.

This puppy is being fed a reward as a car passes by, helping to distract him and build good associations.

Always create a safe and enjoyable experience for your puppy

Meeting people

ENCOURAGING RELAXED INTERACTION

No matter what your lifestyle, your puppy should be sociable with your family, friends, postal workers and delivery people, members of the public and, of course, veterinary staff. Although dogs are a social species and their ability to interact with humankind has led to their incredible success, relaxed interaction is not a certainty, so the more people with whom your puppy becomes familiar, the more readily he will accept strangers. A puppy used to a quiet owner can be startled by a loud talker who uses exaggerated gestures – if this is the case, incorporate different gestures and ways of talking and walking into games, so that your puppy becomes accustomed to a variety of interaction styles.

Timescale

Although the sensitive period for socialization finishes at 12 weeks of age, when interacting with humans it is important to continue socializing your puppy throughout his first year in order to develop the best human-interaction skills.

Humans are unusual

An experienced puppy learns to understand that humans interact in ways that may not be in line with canine social etiquette. For example, humans often use direct eye contact. We lovingly gaze at each other and our puppies and directly look at them when we call to them. However, continuous direct eye contact is used as a threatening gesture between canines. These distinctly different messages could cause your puppy to feel stressed or confused if he does not learn to interpret them correctly, so the more contact he has with humans, the better his understanding will be.

Adult interaction

Family and friends will want to meet your puppy. Ideally, you should prepare in advance and advise people as to how you want the interaction to go. For example, you might like them to crouch down and allow your puppy to approach, or you may prefer them to wait until he is sitting before they greet him. Provide them with treats and a toy to make the encounter pleasurable for your puppy.

Forward planning

Think about the behavior you want your adult dog to exhibit and try to guide your puppy toward this goal. Do not expect him to get it right immediately.

This puppy has been invited to come and say hello, and his choice to do so indicates he is comfortable with the encounter.

Making mistakes and finding out what works and what doesn't are part of the normal experience for a baby of any species. The important message from socialization is that new people are nothing to be fearful of, so if your puppy makes a mistake try not to get upset. Instead, follow the techniques outlined in Chapter 7 (see page 184) and continue to make the encounter a positive one.

First impressions

Many adults will have prior experience with dogs and will be extremely confident around them. However, they should remember that this is your puppy's first experience and they will leave an impression. Soothing tones of voice, slow movements and avoiding rough play or physical reprimands will create a positive learning experience for him.

Settling down quietly

No time to say hello? Not all visitors will have the time or the desire to meet your puppy, so put him away in his secure place. This is a good lesson in itself since it will not be appropriate for your dog to meet absolutely everyone who comes to your door. Get him accustomed to settling down quietly in his bed or distract him with a toy or chew.

To your puppy the human shape is altered by hats, glasses and coats, so it's important you allay their fears at an early age and "stage manage" meetings.

Involve people of all ages, sizes, skin and hair color, clothing styles and mannerisms in your puppy's socialization process

Babies

Unless there are babies within your family or circle of close friends, regular encounters are highly unlikely. However, including these in your puppy's socialization program creates a reference for his future experiences. When introducing babies to him, always:

- Try to appear calm and confident, so that both your puppy and the baby's mother remain relaxed, too
- Familiarize your puppy with baby scents with blankets or toys to reduce his excitement during the actual meeting
- If you have permission, allow him to approach and sniff the baby. Then call him away for praise and offer a different game
- You can teach him what an infant sounds like via sound tracks and what it looks like using a baby doll (ideally dressed in some clothes and blankets from a real baby). Carry the baby doll during some training exercises and extend the experience by including borrowed baby toys and a stroller.

Safety tip: Your puppy should wear a training line, so that you can gently prevent him from rushing forward or jumping up at the baby.

Children

A child is not just a mini-adult. From a dog's perspective, children look, move, smell and sound

Parents should supervise all initial encounters between children and a new puppy and ensure that these are positive, friendly experiences.

If supervised, children can be involved in your puppy's training routine. Introduce him to children of different ages as part of his socialization.

different from an adult. They are notoriously unpredictable and use sudden high-pitched noises that can startle and excite a dog. The more positive experiences your puppy has with children, both male and female, the more likely he will be to behave well around them.

- Ensure that the child is sitting either on the floor at puppy level or a low chair beside a supervising adult when the puppy is introduced.
- Allow your puppy to calmly take some tasty treats offered by the child and enjoy the gentle petting and then encourage him to come away calmly.
- Repeat this short exercise a few times, so that the child and your puppy both have an enjoyable time without either being overwhelmed.
- Repeat the exercise with the child standing and in a range of different locations.

Safety tip: Ideally, during the first meetings, your puppy should wear his house line or leash to allow you to control the speed of his approach. An enthusiastic puppy may overwhelm a small child, no matter how friendly his intentions are. A frightened child is likely to squeal, leap up and wave their arms. All these events could cause your puppy to feel scared or trigger overexcitement.

Outdoor opportunities

It is helpful if you walk your puppy in a range of different locations where he can see children playing. Always make sure that you are ready with praise and rewards whenever he responds in a calm manner around children.

Caution! Do remember to ask permission from parents before you allow any interaction between their child and your puppy. Equally, feel free to say "No" to children who ask to stroke your puppy if you think that he may be overwhelmed by the attention.

Meeting different people

Introduce your puppy to as many new people as possible, not just close family members, friends and neighbors. He needs to feel comfortable around all sorts of people of different ages, personalities and appearances. This involves meeting:

- Tradespeople and delivery people who visit your home, such as garbage collectors, postal workers
- People in uniforms, e.g., police officers, the military
- Elderly people
- Men as well as women
- People with beards or glasses
- Strangers in the street or park
- Babies, toddlers and young children
- Teenagers and young people.

Encourage your child to be gentle with your new puppy and not to overwhelm him or tease him – they can form a special relationship.

Postal Workers

Take your puppy outside to meet the postal worker as often as possible in the early days. Keep some treats on hand, so the postal worker can offer him a tasty morsel each time. This will reduce the likelihood of territorial barking or aggression when your mail is delivered, which could even lead to the withdrawal of your mail service.

Your puppy must always be handled gently - never allow children to chase, grab or tease him

Socializing with dogs

A VITAL PART OF SOCIALIZATION

Making sure that your puppy grows up to be sociable with other dogs is very important, yet this can be difficult to achieve. Due to the potential health risks that arise from mixing with other dogs, many puppies do not receive adequate socialization at an early enough age. Waiting until your puppy is 12 weeks or even older before resuming this process at classes or out on walks is not ideal. As you have already learned, the sensitive time for socializing him is extremely short, so every week is vital.

Introducing your own dog

If you already have an adult dog at home, you must observe some simple guidelines when introducing your puppy to him. Most sociable dogs will tolerate a puppy's clumsy ways with great patience.

Social problems: If your original dog already has social problems with unfamiliar dogs, be extra cautious during the introductions. Allow visual contact through a child safety gate or use leashes on both to give you extra control. Aim for short, enjoyable meetings. Once they have had time to become accustomed to one another, dogs usually find their own pattern and work out their relationship with minimal human intervention.

Don't...

· Shout at your adult dog as this will worry both dogs.

· Allow play to build up to a point where it starts getting out of hand and the fun begins to turn into tension.

· Allow the adult dog to play roughly as this could cause damage to the puppy's soft bones and joints.

Do...

· Introduce your puppy to older dogs in an open area, such as your yard.

· Make the experience enjoyable for the adult dog and your puppy.

· Supervise tiny puppies during play with boisterous adults.

· Crouch down and invite your puppy to come away if he seems to need a break or safe refuge from a bigger, bouncier dog.

Learning to be gentle

Bite inhibition, whereby a dog learns to use little or no jaw pressure during play or minor scuffles, is incredibly important for puppies to learn. Unfortunately, this lesson is usually acquired in the weeks after they are homed and when contact with other dogs is low. It's normal for an adult dog to correct a youngster that crosses the line of acceptable play. While they are young, this lesson may involve vocalization and possibly noncontact snaps toward the puppy. Later on, when the puppy is older than about 18 weeks, the reprimand may become more intensive, although a sociable adult dog is unlikely to cause damage.

Time apart

Create separate areas for your dogs to prevent them from being together all the time. In multidog households, puppies can learn that the adult dogs provide play and interaction and, as a result, they are often less responsive to their owners. Make sure that every day you have some one-to-one time with each of the dogs for play and training in order to establish good relationships.

Puppies will naturally offer polite, appeasing signals to less familiar adult dogs, but always ensure you supervise these encounters.

Preventing bad habits

If your puppy is particularly confident and he appears to pester your softer adult dog, you must step in to stop this before the unruly behavior becomes established. Allow your dogs to interact but when you see your puppy getting excited, call or guide him away for some quiet time.

Acceptable play: Your puppy will soon learn that certain types of play – with toys or chasing one another – with adult dogs are acceptable, whereas other actions, such as mouthing, will result in the end of play time.

Constant rough play may eventually lead to social problems if a puppy never learns to play nicely in an acceptable way.

Meeting unfamiliar dogs

You may be apprehensive about letting your puppy meet an unfamiliar dog, and initially, it's better that he mixes only with socially reliable dogs. First encounters are important in how he perceives other dogs. Once he has had lots of good experiences, one negative incident won't have such an impact.

Puppy classes or parties

These are a safe way to introduce your puppy to others – mixing with puppies of a similar age minimizes the risks. The controlled playtime, under supervision, will allow him to develop his social skills. Find out about puppy classes in your area.

Dogs come in all shapes and sizes

If your puppy meets other dogs on walks in the park and at training classes, he will encounter a wide range of breed types and personalities. This is particularly important as he learns that all dogs do not look like his mother and siblings. Even puppies from multidog households should be taken out regularly to meet unfamiliar dogs in order to learn good social skills outside their "family" unit.

Positive interactions

Never introduce your puppy to adult dogs that have not been socialized and are unaccustomed to meeting young dogs. You do not want to expose him to potentially bad experiences. It is important to keep all dog-to-dog interactions positive.

Assess the situation

When you see a dog approaching it is good practice to think ahead and make an assessment about whether it appears to be under control, how boisterous it is, and whether your puppy is able to cope. If you feel greatly concerned, change direction without any fuss and walk away.

Friendly dogs: Many puppies are excited when they meet another dog, although they may also become frightened if this excitement is reciprocated. If the other dog is friendly, crouch down and invite your puppy to return to you for safety.

Unfriendly dogs: If the other dog appears to be aggressive, ask its owner to hold their dog while you and your puppy move away. While it may be necessary to carry a tired or a very scared puppy, try not to get into the habit of picking him up whenever a new dog appears. This may result in him growing into an adult dog that has never learned to cope with the arrival of a new dog and is forever pestering you to pick him up.

Handling an encounter

- Speak to your puppy in a friendly voice and always try to appear calm and relaxed.
- Avoid crowding the dogs since this can add pressure to the experience.

Puppies should play with adult dogs to learn appropriate behaviors.

- Be sure to keep the meeting short and positive.
- Use a chirpy voice to encourage your puppy to come away rather than pulling on his leash.

It's not always playtime

Socializing is very important but it should not mean that your puppy gets to meet every dog he sees. Many owners complain that their pet pulls or gets frustrated if it sees another dog when out on a walk. You can avoid this by teaching your puppy to "Sit" or to focus exclusively on you when other dogs pass by. Always be sure to praise and reward him well for his good behavior and then, if appropriate, allow him to meet the other dog.

Meeting other dogs

It is sensible to take precautions when you are walking your puppy in open spaces where adult dogs could be running loose off leash.

- Keep your distance from potential encounters with unsupervised dogs.
- Distract your puppy by playing a game with him.
- Avoid experiences with other dogs that are out of your control.

While talking to other owners, always encourage your puppy to sit and offer him praise and a treat to indicate that he is behaving well.

Minimize interventions

If you intervene too much during puppy-dog interactions, your puppy may never learn to read the body language and signals given by other dogs and this will cause problems in the future.

- Be cautious and watchful but not over-protective of your puppy in these situations.
- Try to remain calm to minimize the impact of an imperfect encounter on your puppy.

If an interaction does not go as well as you hoped, meet up with a friendly dog your puppy already knows the same day, so his overall experience is positive

Meeting other animals
TEACHING YOUR PUPPY HOW TO BEHAVE

It is really important that your puppy learns how to act around other species for his and their safety. Introductions to any other animal should be performed calmly under carefully controlled conditions to minimize stress to both parties. It is usually best to avoid making any introductions during the first few days while your puppy settles in to his new home.

Cats

Introductions must be performed carefully since experience of chasing or being chased could cause both animals to develop permanent bad habits. A cat, of course, also has the potential to cause significant injury with its sharp claws, should your puppy irritate or stress one enough. You must take considerable care, even with tiny puppies or very confident cats, to prevent future problems developing. Introductions can be made:

• Through a safety gate
• With your puppy inside a puppy pen
• With your puppy on a house line
• While your cat is in his carrier.

Small animals

Small animals, such as rabbits, guinea pigs and birds, are likely to resort to their instinctive desire to run or hide when they meet your new puppy. They are best introduced:

• With a cage or fence separating them
• From afar initially, with the puppy on his leash
• By slowly reducing the distance between your puppy and the other animal(s).

Caution! Stop and walk your puppy away if, at any time, he becomes overexcited or vocal. Never allow him to run around a rabbit's hutch or jump on top of it, even if it is secure, as this will cause intense stress for the animal(s) inside.

While your cat is in the same room, distract your puppy with alternative games and be sure to praise him for interacting calmly. Even if you are introducing them through a cat carrier, you must be careful since your cat could feel vulnerable while he is confined to this space, especially if you let your puppy sniff and approach the carrier.

Always praise and reward your puppy with a treat for behaving well when he encounters other animals, such as these hens.

- Always walk your puppy on a leash or a long training line when near livestock
- Call him back when his interest in them begins to build up and offer exciting rewards and praise.

Horses

Practice your training when you are near horses – if your puppy were to startle a horse, it could lead to injury or even the death of the dog, horse or rider.

- Call an off-leash puppy back to you and attach his leash to his collar.
- Walk to the side of the path to make room for the horse to pass by safely.
- Ask your puppy to "Sit" and quietly praise and reward him while the horse passes by.

Large animals, such as horses, cattle or more unusual livestock like these llamas, can be intimidating to a small puppy, so keep him on a leash.

Horse socialization

If you live in an area where there are a lot of horses, practice the procedure outlined below. Start doing this as soon as your puppy can be taken out on walks. He needs to become socialized to their presence as quickly as possible.

Livestock and poultry

Early experience of livestock will be helpful for future walks in the countryside or in parkland. Instinctive predatory behavior is stronger in some breeds but all dogs may learn to chase and bark when they see animals unless they are taught to behave appropriately. Your puppy will be curious and want to investigate, but some animals are likely to startle and run, which can lead to a chase game with a potentially disastrous ending. It is sensible to:

Signs of problems
RECOGNIZING THE SIGNS AND ACTING QUICKLY

Always being vigilant will allow you to detect how well your puppy is coping with the situations he encounters during his early socialization and habituation. Understanding his emotional condition will enable you to adapt your approach and prevent any unwanted patterns from developing. Typical socialization problems will involve fearful reactions, but early detection will give you the biggest advantage in helping your puppy to recover and develop alternative coping strategies.

Recognizing the responses

Your puppy can respond to stimuli that he finds frightening in one of the following four ways.

Freeze: A very young puppy or an intensely frightened one will "freeze" – this is when he crouches down and hopes that the scary thing will move away without noticing him.

Flight: Some dogs will choose "flight" – they turn away, back away or run away, depending upon how frightening they perceive the stimulus to be.

Fight: This category includes all the overtly defensive reactions, such as barking, growling, lunging, snapping and biting.

Acting erratically: This reaction is commonly observed and it involves the frightened dog displaying a range of unconnected behaviors, such as scratching or jumping, which may serve to appease the individual they are worried about, displace some of their own stress, or distract from the intensity of the situation. Unfortunately, many owners misinterpret these actions as disobedience and their subsequent reactions to regain control only serve to further intensify the anxiety felt by the puppy, which is, ultimately, counterproductive.

Jumping up may signal a need for reassurance rather than naughty behavior – prevent it happening, especially with giant breed puppies.

"Fear imprint" stages

Puppies have two "fear imprint" stages during their development. The first one occurs at between 8 and 11 weeks of age.

The second one occurs during adolescence at between approximately 6 and 12 months, and it lasts for a few weeks.

Desensitizing to something scary

Your puppy may require several exposures to a stimulus at very low-level intensity before he desensitizes and can cope with it getting closer or louder again. As he appears to relax, you can gradually increase his exposure. You must do this at his pace, although you should be prepared to practice regularly rather than avoiding the situation completely – otherwise the sensitivity is likely to reappear at a later date, at which point it will be even harder to overcome.

Ideally, your puppy should be unfazed by most experiences, but try to preempt them by introducing him to new people and situations.

What to do if your puppy can't cope

If, during one of your socialization or habituation exercises, your puppy becomes worried, you must try to remain calm. If you appear to panic, you will only reaffirm his anxiety as he will think that you, too, are concerned by the situation.

You should...

• Allow him the freedom to move away.
• Where applicable, reduce the noise, or the amount of visual exposure.

These actions reduce the intensity of the stimulus and thereby will increase your puppy's ability to cope with it in a more confident way.

Try not to: Compensate for the upset by soothing or consoling your puppy – by doing so, you may accidentally reinforce his fearful response as it's difficult for him to correctly interpret your intentions to make him feel better.

Socialization checklist

Early socialization is probably the most important aspect of bringing up your puppy to be a confident, friendly and well-trained dog. He needs to be subjected to as many new people, experiences, sights and sounds as possible – a wrong turn in his behavioral upbringing can trigger potential behavior problems later on in life as an adult.

Keep a chart

As you start introducing your puppy to more new experiences, it's a good idea to keep a record of exactly what he has been subjected to and how he has coped. Things you can list include:

- Cars, motorcycles, trucks, tractors
- Buses, boats, trains
- Traffic, busy roads, crowded places
- Parks, stores, cafés
- Children, babies
- Elderly people, adults, teenagers
- Joggers, cyclists, horse riders
- Vet, groomer, pet sitter

- Vacuum cleaner, television, washing machine, hairdryer, lawn mower
- Telephone, doorbell, fire and smoke alarms
- Steps, flights of stairs
- Shiny and tiled floors, grass, gravel, sand
- Mailboxes, traffic lights
- Fireworks, thunderstorms
- Other dogs
- Other animals – cats, small pets, livestock.

Top socialization tips

- Set a routine from day one and stick to it.
- Use positive reinforcement by praising and rewarding good behavior and ignoring undesirable behavior.
- When your puppy starts going out on a leash, gently expose him to as many different things as possible.
- Remember the "fear" periods and reassure him – take care never to inadvertently praise fearful behavior.
- Make sure he meets a range of different people – of different ages with glasses, uniforms, hats and beards.
- Socialize him with other dogs and animals.
- Do not introduce more than two or three new experiences per day.
- Habituate him to noisy traffic and household appliances.
- Learn to read his body language, which is his way of telling you how he feels.

Your puppy needs to meet as many people as possible from the earliest possible age – make these encounters enjoyable and fun for him.

It's your job to provide a wide range of good experiences for your puppy

Leaving your puppy alone

It is important that your puppy also gets accustomed to being left alone. As a pack animal, he naturally enjoys being with people and other dogs, but he also needs to learn to tolerate being left on his own sometimes. Begin with very short sessions at a young age, and gradually build on them, making them longer, as he matures.

Introduce your puppy to other dogs under your close supervision in situations and locations where you are in control.

Body language signs

Normal	Ears pricked, mouth closed, tail gently wagging, body relaxed.
Playful	Tail high and wagging, eyes wide, soft and looking sideways, body crouched forward and resting on front legs in play bow.
Fearful	Back flat and head low, tail down or between legs, licking lips and swallowing.
Aggressive	Ears held flat back to head, eyes wide, lips pulled back exposing teeth, standing tall on toes, hackles risen.
Submissive	Can be similar to fear – may roll onto back or even urinate involuntarily.

Stay calm and reassuring when you expose your puppy to unfamiliar animals and experiences – this will give him confidence.

Choosing the right toys

PROVIDING A VARIETY OF PLAYTHINGS

Play may appear frivolous but it is an important part of your puppy's development and natural behavior. As well as enabling him to develop the skills he needs for adulthood it is also critical for teaching him how to communicate effectively, bond socially and learn about cause-and-effect as well as improving his motor skills and physical coordination while burning off excess energy. Providing a variety of playthings for your puppy is viewed as an essential part of responsible puppy ownership and can help to minimize potential problem behaviors.

Choice of toys

The dog toy industry is immense and constantly growing, reflecting the diversity of play and our commitment to keeping our pets happy. There is a fantastic array of toys to suit all breeds and personalities. While there are different uses for most toys, they can be split into groups according to their main purpose (see the chart opposite).

Your puppy's purpose and preferences

Each breed was originally intended for a particular role and this has influenced the strength of their various instincts. Understanding your puppy's breed type will give you clues about the type of toys he might enjoy playing with. However, his temperament will dictate which he favors most. Begin with a selection of toys for him to explore. As you get to know his preferences, build up his toy box with the types he is most interested in. When picking a toy consider its size, design, safety features, purpose, durability and what motivates your puppy.

Teething relief

While your puppy is teething his desire to chew will be particularly strong and, as a responsible owner,

you need to offer him suitable items to chew. Each puppy will have his own preferences, but specially designed dental toys are shaped for maximum benefit and many can be cooled in the fridge to soothe sore gums. Provide your dog with a range of different styles to ensure that he can find something he likes rather than turning to your belongings for relief – keep shoes and children's toys out of reach.

A filled food dispenser can encourage your puppy to play without your participation, and will keep him entertained when you are out.

Benefits of toys

Type	Benefit
Chewing toys	Tough and fairly durable.
Retrieving toys	Promote exercise and interactive play.
Food dispensing toys	Encourage activity and provide mental stimulation.
Dental care toys	Help maintain a healthy mouth and can soothe teething gums.
Tugging toys	Exciting and use energy.
Plush toys	Enjoyed by puppies and can provide comfort, too. Often involve a noise that can excite.
Rope toys	Can be chewed, retrieved, and tugged, and aid dental hygiene. A good all-around toy.
Soft rubber squeaky toys	Exciting and easy to handle.
Water toys	These toys float on water.

The opportunity to play with toys from an early age influences your puppy's future ability to play

A moving toy, such as a ball on a rope, can engage your puppy's interest, encouraging him to join in the game.

Different types of play

Independent play: When your puppy is left alone or while you are home but not involved, food-dispensing or chew toys are perfect for this.

Interactive play: Each member of the family should invest in fun-time with their puppy - retrieving and tugging toys are good and require your involvement.

Safety in play
MAKE THIS YOUR PRIORITY

While play should always be enjoyable, many dogs are injured during playtime. It will be your responsibility to make sure that the items your puppy is playing with are safe, and remain so over a period of time.

Dangers from toys

Problem	Risk	Action
Too small	Choking risk. Internal blockages may require surgery.	If you are in doubt about the size of a toy before you buy, opt for the next size up. As your puppy grows many of his toys will become a choking hazard and should be replaced.
Contains toxins and dyes	Poisoning risk.	Avoid cheap imports that have no quality assurance or guarantee.
Damaged toys	Parts may be broken off and swallowed. Sharp edges may cut his mouth and soft tissue. Internal squeakers or stuffing may be ingested.	Examine regularly and replace toys that are damaged and those showing wear.

Careful supervision will ensure that both your child and your puppy enjoy getting to know each other and playing gentle games together.

Safe options
Special puppy-proof soft toys without internal stuffing are available – these are the perfect alternatives for puppies that love to chew and take their toys apart.

Caution! If a toy can move to the back of your dog's mouth, then it is too small and you must remove it.

Children's toys
Toys that are safe for children are not necessarily safe for your puppy, as buttons, ribbons, doll's clothing, teddy bear eyes and stuffing may all fail to stay intact during puppy play. Encourage him to play with his own things and take measures to keep him out of your children's bedrooms.

Best friends
Children and puppies often create wonderfully exciting games together. However, you must always supervise young children and take care to ensure

Never play with...

Objects	Why?
Small rubber bouncing balls	They can easily slip down the throat and stick in the windpipe or block the intestine.
Sticks	Risk of impaling; ingestion of splinters.
Balls with single air holes	A vacuum may arise, trapping the puppy's tongue.
Stones	Choking hazard, tooth damage, head trauma, internal blockage; attracts puppy to stones and pebbles.

that neither they nor the puppy become overexcited. This may lead to a child becoming too noisy, tripping over the puppy or accidentally teaching him bad habits. An excited puppy is more likely to jump up, play bite, grab onto clothing or chase and nip small feet and legs.

Physical limitations

Your puppy may be eager to play, but during his first year do use caution before trying anything too physically demanding. He can easily become over-tired or strain his growing body.

• Prevent your puppy from leaping around and take care during enthusiastic chase games.

Supervising play

No matter how safe your choice of toy may appear to be, always try to supervise play. Only leave toys that you are absolutely sure pose no risk with your puppy when he is alone.

• Keep toys fairly low to the ground to prevent the need for jumping.
• Enjoy playing tug-of-war games together but don't shake or pull too hard.
• Allow your puppy to rest regularly.
• Select a safe area since an excited puppy may not pay attention to where he is running.

Strong chewer? If your puppy has especially powerful jaws, always opt for strong toys and closely supervise him at all times while playing. Swap non-chew toys for a safe toy or treat if he begins to chew it rather than play with it.

Caution! If you own dogs of different sizes, you must always use larger toys. Keep the smaller puppy toys for those times when he is separated from the bigger dog or you are available to closely supervise them playing together.

Ground-level games can help to prevent physical strain in young puppies.

Always make sure that your puppy only plays with safe toys

Styles of play
TEACHING YOUR DOG GOOD MANNERS

Your puppy will engage in several different types of play, which include social play, predatory play, oral play and sexual play. They are all part of normal puppy behavior and nothing for you to worry about.

You should get to know your puppy's preferred play style as this will be helpful during later training sessions – some love chasing balls.

Types of play

- **Social play:** In this type of play, your puppy romps and wrestles with another dog, taking turns to be the jumper or jumped-on.
- **Predatory play:** He chases a moving object.
- **Oral play**: This involves chewing, mouthing and tugging on objects.
- **Sexual play:** This includes mounting behavior toward other dogs, humans and inanimate objects, such as cushions and soft toys.

Playing nicely

In order for social play to be successful dogs use a process called "self-handicapping." This means that they don't use their full strength in order to avoid frightening or injuring their playmate. Fathers use similar techniques when play-wrestling with their young sons. Experience will teach your puppy the skills for doing this. Some inexperienced puppies forget to "self-handicap" and play too hard. If they don't learn early on that this behavior stops play, they continue this bullish behavior as adults and games often turn into real conflicts.

Breed influence

While there is no way of knowing for sure what game your puppy will love playing best, his breed instincts will give you a good idea of his play style and where to begin.

Sight Hounds	Love to see and chase moving targets (and often lose interest when the toy lands and stops).
Terriers	High-energy games with soft toys.
Collies , German Shepherds	Chase and herding games.
Bull breeds	Physical contact and wrestling.
Spaniels	Love to follow scents, find things and play with objects.
Retrievers	Adore mouthing, carrying toys and social play.

Play bow

Before starting a game, your puppy will give a "play bow" signal, which indicates to his playmate that his intentions are nonthreatening and "this isn't a real attack." He will use play bows toward you when he is trying to solicit play and during the games themselves. The bow itself may be a full gesture with his chest on the ground and rear in the air, or a quick dip with bent elbows, depending upon the situation. Well-balanced play by a skilled puppy will involve lots of pauses and play bows to ensure the encounter remains a friendly one.

Building confidence

Timid puppies and those that have not had the opportunity to learn at an early age may not play instinctively with toys. Patience and persistence can have fantastic results and open up the world of play for these pups. Don't expect too much at once – any pressure will be off-putting. Puppies differ in what they like but timid ones often respond well to small toys that can be wriggled at floor level. Get down on the floor with your puppy and move the toy around or try rolling it to trigger some interest. Praise and reward him for paying attention to the toy. With practice, he will usually start to move toward it, nose it and paw it, and the beginnings of play have been achieved.

A raised paw is used to confirm that the puppies are just playing.

Playing with your puppy

When you are playing with your new puppy, it is sensible to:

· Begin in a familiar place where he feels relaxed

· Get down to his level

· Use an excited tone of voice

· Let him explore new toys in his own time

· Don't expect too much at once

· Reward him for joining in.

Play biting

STOP THIS EARLY ON

It can be a concern to discover how keen your puppy is on play biting during the early weeks. His milk teeth are needle sharp and designed to get a reaction from his playmates. It's very important indeed that he learns to minimize pressure now before his adult teeth come in when he could inflict a severe bite on another dog or a member of his family.

Tackling the problem

Thankfully, dogs have developed their own clear lesson to encourage appropriate play. If a puppy play bites too hard the victim will yelp very loudly, possibly stopping play entirely. This causes the biter to let go and pause to assess the situation. Experience teaches the puppy that it's better to play nicely than to have his fun cut short. You can use this principle, too, when you are teaching him.

- As soon as your puppy's teeth touch you during a play session, you must yelp or say "Ouch!" loudly as though he has hurt you.
- If he lets go, praise him for his behavior and redirect his focus onto a toy.

If your puppy continues to bite at you, how you manage the situation will depend on his size and how hard he is biting. However, if you start this lesson very early on, he should never reach the stage where the bites are serious.

- Stop playing, fold your arms and turn away (stand if necessary). Ignore your puppy.
- Stop playing, stand and walk away from him. If necessary, leave the room, leaving him alone.

Enjoying interactive play

Not sure if your puppy is enjoying a game with another dog? Split them up for a minute and then give him the opportunity to go back to the game. His response will give you your answer.

Losing his playmate is not your puppy's intention, so this is a negative result. Play and your attention can resume when he is calm and interacting well. This way he will quickly begin to learn about the types of play that are rewarding for him and those that are best avoided. The entire household must work together on this lesson.

Terriers love squeaky toys and enjoy biting them but they can be very destructive and you may need to provide stronger, more durable playthings.

Useful equipment

- **Large toys:** These will reduce the likelihood of play bites to your hands.
- **A house line:** This will give you control without having to grab or push at your puppy (which can incite further mouthing).

Puppy play can be noisy

It often involves vocalization, such as growling, and play biting (inhibited in strength). During normal play, the dogs may bump into each other, jump on one another, mouth at the other's body, legs and neck. This is all normal and nothing to worry about. However, if you hear deeper growling noises, if bites focus on the head and neck of the other dog or they appear harder than a play bite, then it is definitely time to break up the encounter as things are getting out of hand.

Destructive play

It can be really frustrating and expensive when numerous toys are chewed up, one after another. When this happens some owners decide not to buy any more until their puppy learns to play nicely. However, the truth is that without the provision of appropriate playthings your puppy will have to search for alternatives, which are often items you really don't want to be damaged.

- Search for toys designed for hard chewers.
- Select larger sizes as these are usually more difficult for a puppy to destroy.
- Supervise play with other items and swap them for tough toys as soon as your puppy shows signs of settling down to chew.

If your puppy persists in play biting, stop playing and walk away

A soft rope toy is great for playing energetic tug of war games with your puppy but a stronger activity toy is more suitable for chewing games.

If your puppy play-bites you when you are playing together, say "Ouch" loudly as though he has hurt you and stop the game immediately.

Good behavior

ENCOURAGING IT THROUGH PLAY

Play uses up energy that your puppy might otherwise spend on getting into mischief. It also satisfies instincts that may have led to undesirable behaviors and it helps him to develop a strong social bond with you, his owner. While he is enjoying a game he is also less likely to find his surroundings scary. Games can help him cope with a range of situations in which he might normally be wary or apprehensive.

Good play habits

You can teach your puppy good play habits by avoiding the following types of games.

- Rough and tumble games involving mouthing and growling.
- Using your hands or feet as playthings.
- Letting your puppy tug or chew on any clothing.
- Chasing after him to get him to give you a toy. Instead, always encourage him to bring it back to you and release it on command. You can do this by switching it for another toy that is equally interesting to him or by offering him a tasty treat in exchange for the toy.

If your puppy enjoys playing tug of war games with you, stay in control and encourage good manners by not allowing him to play bite.

Play and training combined

To maximize your control during playtimes, you should practice your basic training commands (see Chapter 7). A puppy that can "Sit," "Stay," "Leave it," "Fetch" and "Come" on command can play many more games that are fulfilling for both of you. In addition, using the basic commands in the course of playing games will make training more fun and your puppy will learn more quickly and easily.

Recall and play

This is a good way of diverting your puppy from performing unwanted chase behavior or being tempted away from you by other dogs. If he knows that being close to you is fun and rewarding, he will choose to stay nearby and come quickly when you call. You can make returning to you exciting by:

- Running away from him for a short distance
- Dragging a soft toy attached to a line along the ground for him to chase
- Throwing his toy in the opposite direction, away from the distractions.

To teach your puppy basic recall, see the training sequence for "Come" on pages 194–195.

Tug of war

Tug of war games are loved by many dogs, particularly terriers and the bull breeds. However, teaching and insisting on good manners is always very important. It is essential that you teach your puppy to let go of the toy mid-game on cue. This is a particularly helpful lesson for him to learn if you need him ever to stop and back away from something that excites him in a real-life situation.

1 Sit on the floor and start a game with a toy that he will happily grab and tug on.
2 While he is tugging, stop moving the toy and hold it close to you, or on the ground. Do not speak to him. He'll continue to pull on it for a while but, since this game needs dual participation, he will eventually open his mouth and let go.
3 Immediately, respond by firmly saying "Drop" and praise him profusely when he does so. Offer him a treat from your other hand.
4 Practice until he lets go very quickly when the toy movement stops. Repetition will start to teach him to associate the cue "Drop" with letting go.

5 Begin to add in the verbal cue "Drop" while the toy is still moving slightly. Always reward your puppy for choosing to do so.

If your puppy really adores toys, you can reward the "Drop" by restarting the game or by offering a different toy instead of a treat.

Using games as a distraction

You can gradually build up the amount of toy movement, and hence the difficulty, over a series of many games to teach your puppy how to come away from the most enticing distractions.

You can reward your puppy with a game when he performs the desired behaviors during your training sessions together.

Playing safely

While your puppy is still growing, it is sensible to play gentle tug of war games with him since his jaw is still developing. Follow these simple guidelines for safety:

· Don't swing him around while he bites onto a toy.

· Never lift him up into the air off the ground through his hold on a toy – this should always be avoided.

Teach your puppy good manners, training commands and habits while he plays

6 CANINE BEHAVIOR

Body language

READING YOUR PUPPY'S BODY LANGUAGE

Owners with their first puppy or with a different breed of dog from the ones they previously owned may find themselves asking many questions about the behaviors they witness. Some puppy reactions cause concern but may be entirely appropriate for a canine or, in particular, for that breed. Domestication has altered dogs' physical shape and purpose, but canine communication is universal. Learn to recognize your puppy's signals and you will be able to detect and prevent many problems.

Body language

Numerous emotional conditions are expressed by a dog through a combination of clear and subtle signals. How your puppy responds is dependent not only on the situation but also his previous experiences and inherited characteristics.

Interpreting the signs: Each signal, such as ear movement and tail posture, is a little like an individual word within a sentence. It's important to recognize the implications of that signal, but your puppy's entire response should be considered in order to reach the true interpretation.

Look at all the signs: A lifted front paw might appear as a fun "shake paw" gesture. However, if you observe the rest of your puppy's body language the interpretation may be very different. A raised paw is an innate appeasing gesture, so if it occurs along with other signs, such as a dipped head, furtive glances, low tail carriage with a little wag and lip-licking, then he is feeling uneasy rather than playful.

Head

The way in which your puppy holds his head gives you some idea of whether he is feeling confident or stressed. Turning his head away (without directly looking at something else) usually signals he feels uncomfortable. A dog showing assertive behavior will be turned directly toward you or another dog.

Ears

Physical differences may make the detection of small movements difficult but learn to recognize even subtle changes in your puppy (see below).

Mouth

Your puppy's mouth can express much more than just aggression and you need to learn to recognize these signs (see the table opposite).

Ear language

Signal	Interpretation
Natural ear position	Calm and relaxed.
Flattened backwards against head	Fearful.
Slightly turned back when approaching	Signals nonthreat; friendly.

The ears will prick up when your puppy is showing an interest in what is going on or perhaps your training command or a toy you are offering.

Mouth language

Signal	Interpretation
Partially open, relaxed jaw	Relaxed.
Tightly closed, possibly drawn back at the corners; the tongue may flick out and up toward the nose	Tension, fear or appeasement.
Lips drawn upwards to expose the large canine teeth. Muzzle is wrinkled. Tongue pulled back inside mouth.	Threat signal; intention to bite if signals are ignored.
Tight muzzle, creating a "small" mouth; may puff cheeks while breathing heavily	Stress; warning signal indicating "stay away."
Lips pulled back in a wide gape, exposing all of his teeth and tongue	Fear.
Yawning	Stress and appeasement.

Eye language

Signal	Interpretation
Appear "soft"	Relaxed.
Rounded eye with a crescent of white exposed, usually turned away slightly	Anxiety, fear and stress.
Rounded but with direct gaze, wide pupils with little if any white on show	Threatening gesture.
Squinted eye	Pain, extreme fear or threat.

Eyes
You may be surprised to know that your puppy's eye shape will alter with his mood. Here are some guidelines (in the panel above) as to what signals to look out for and how to interpret them.

Body
A confident puppy will stand tall, but as a puppy's confidence drops he will make himself smaller, to the point of crawling on the floor or lying and rolling over to expose his stomach, neck and genitals. Clearly, this is not to be confused with a puppy that is lying down during a rest or while responding to a training command.

Try to observe where your puppy is looking and how relaxed he appears. This is very useful when you are socializing him, as you will get a better feel for how confident he is.

Dogs turn away when trying to appear nonthreatening

Tail

A wagging tail is often thought to be a friendly signal. However, unless the tail is loose and wagging generously from side to side, it may actually signal a very different intention. Wagging can be taken as intent to respond in some way – positively or negatively. The lower your puppy's tail, the less confident he is feeling. A relaxed tail will usually rest somewhere in the middle. The natural tail position is dependent upon the breed but the movement can be easily detected in most dogs, although some breeds, like the Samoyed or Pug, have tails that curl up and over their back, and some sight hounds have tails that hang low while relaxed, while others have natural bobtails (Pembroke Welsh Corgi and Australian Shepherd).

Coat

You may occasionally see the hair along your puppy's neck, shoulders and possibly his back rise, or bristle. These hackles, or "piloerection," indicate

Your puppy's tail position and movement can signal his emotions.

arousal and, contrary to assumptions, may be a sign of many emotions other than aggression, including:

- Fear
- Agitation
- Nervousness
- Great excitement.

Groups of signals

Observe your puppy when he is experiencing different emotional conditions, but never focus on interpreting just one signal; you need to look at his overall body language.

Happy, relaxed puppy

These signs are observed when your puppy is contented and relaxed.

- Relaxed face with open mouth.
- Head held upright facing events of interest.
- Eyes appear "soft" and natural.
- Relaxed tail, held midway, probably wagging in wide sweeps.
- Shows interest in toys, people, smells.
- May lie down and relax completely, emitting big sighing breaths.

Tail language

Signal	Interpretation
Relaxed, horizontal tail, possibly a slow wag	Interested but still assessing the situation.
Held higher than usual and still	Assessing a situation and alert.
Held low, with a fast wag	Feeling vulnerable and trying to appease.
Upright and stiff tail, possibly with a slow wag	Suggestive of assertion and confidence.
Upright, stiff tail, wagging or "vibrating"	Sign of agitation with the confidence to respond.
Fast, enthusiastic wag, side-to-side or in a circular pattern	A happy greeting or playful response.

Excited puppy

These signs are observed during play or greetings.

- Lots of movement of the body and head, possibly "bouncing."
- Wagging enthusiastically, in large arcs or circular movement.
- Play bowing to the ground with rear in the air, or lifting paws to bend the elbows.
- Tries to nudge, bump against, mouth, jump on a person or another dog after the play bow signal.
- Pawing the ground or grabbing a toy.
- May emit a little playful growling or barking.

Appeasing puppy

These signs may be observed during greetings, when being reprimanded or when a puppy is anxious during a social encounter.

- Head dipped low.
- Upward lick of the front lip toward the nose.
- "Submissive" grin – wide gaping mouth displaying all teeth.
- Ears held back.
- Yawning.
- Low body carriage.
- Raising a paw.
- Tail tucked low with a fast wag.
- Urination.
- Rolling over to expose belly and throat.

Watch your puppy

Get to know his body language by observing him in different situations. Make a note of how his body reacts to different things, including going for walks, playing games, meal times and treats.

Never focus on just one signal - observe the overall body language

The puppy lying on his back is displaying many appeasing signals during this meeting with his larger and more confident sibling.

Vocalization

INTERPRETING THE SIGNALS

Canine communication relies predominantly upon physical bodily movement, but this can only be effective when the dogs are close together. Vocalization (barking) is perfect for signaling across greater distances, although a dog can create many types of sounds that occur in different contexts, including when he is in close contact with another dog, animal or human. Learn to recognize your dog's vocalizations.

Why do dogs bark?

Dogs have developed a far greater vocal repertoire than observed in their ancestors. This change has come about through the process of domestication. One theory explains that dogs needed a group signal to alert them to the presence of a predator or danger. Since scavenging dogs needed to stay close to human settlements they frequently encountered danger. Those that stayed close and opted to bark to keep the danger away were successful; those that were quiet and ran away were not. Over time, the successful ones, with the predisposition to bark, were domesticated. Humans then bred particularly vocal individuals to perform certain jobs for them.

Above: Some breeds, such as the West Highland White Terrier, tend to be more vocal than others, and you should expect them to bark.

Left: Small toy dogs, including the Chinese Crested Dog, have a reputation for being "yappy" and should not be encouraged to bark by their owners.

Interpreting barks

Type	Reason	Signs
Alarm bark	Particularly common and used to alert the pack to possible danger; typically used when someone approaches the front door.	Characterized by short, rapid bursts of loud barks.
Excitement	Often during play or in the buildup to an event, such as a walk or a turn at agility.	Repeated yip-yip sounds, usually higher pitched.
Request for company	When alone and distressed.	Long bouts of steady barking, broken by periods where dog listens for a response before resuming.
Demanding bark	Used to gain access to a resource; may be fueled by frustration.	Steady, persistent barking directed toward you.
Aggressive bark	In any situation where a direct threat is perceived.	Tone is lower, often accompanied by growling.

Barking as a signal
Dogs are quick at making associations between their actions and the result. Your puppy will soon learn that if he barks at a certain time, or in a particular way, you are likely to respond to him. This will then become his "signal" for a game or to be fed, let out or walked.

Other vocalizations

Type	Reason
Whining	One of the first vocalizations, this alerts the mother to a puppy's needs. If you hear whining or whimpering, your puppy may feel hungry, cold, frightened, in discomfort or need to go out to relieve himself. Be careful that whining doesn't become a way of getting your attention.
Howling	May occur if your puppy has a need that has not been met when he signaled by crying or whining. Typically occurs when left alone as natural signal to bring the pack back together.
Growling	Although we associate this with aggression, growling can also occur during play. Identify the meaning by assessing the physical body language of your puppy.
Grunting	Sometimes mistaken for a short growl, a grunt indicates pleasure and may often occur when your puppy is very comfortable and perhaps being petted.
Yelping	Indicates pain or a sudden surprise. If your puppy yelps continuously he may be in considerable pain. Some fearful puppies will yelp or "squeal" before another dog has even made contact.

Howling and yodelling
Beagles and Siberian Huskies are prone to howling. Basenjis "yodel" instead of barking.

Your puppy's senses

SCENT IS PARAMOUNT

Unlike human beings, your puppy's perception of the world around him is dominated by his incredible olfactory ability, which is probably his most highly developed feature. Indeed, a dog's nose is actually so sensitive that a male can detect a female in season several miles away.

Scent detection

This is different from relaxed breathing. When your puppy really wants to assess an odor he:

- Will become focused, drawing air in quickly
- Might appear to be almost tasting the air.

The air swirls around in his specialized nasal cavity across his large olfactory bulb, which is connected to his brain by up to 220 million scent receptors. Even those breeds of dog where a keen sense of smell was not specifically selected have about

120 million scent receptors. This is hard for us to imagine as we humans only have five million scent receptors and we rely on our sight rather than scent to learn more about the world around us. Your puppy will be better at detecting smells than you.

Wet nose: Your puppy's nose is ideally slightly moist to enable maximum odor detection. You might observe him licking his nose to keep it wet.

Your puppy exists in a complex world of scent in which a variety of different odors provide information all around him.

Sight hound puppies have excellent long-distance vision, which is tuned to detect movement.

Specialized feature: Your dog has an area up in his palate called the Jacobson's, or vomeronasal, organ, which enables him to detect specialized pheromones emitted by others of his species. This can result in a changed emotional state. It is this area that also detects the chemically synthesized pheromone used in calming canine products.

Caution! Your puppy's extremely sensitive nose will often lead him into mischief. He will be attracted by food wrappers in the garbage and crumbs on the floor. Treats left in coat pockets might entice him to lick and chew, so invest in a special treat pouch.

Hearing

Your puppy has a far greater range of hearing than a human, explaining why he will sometimes react to apparently nothing. Whereas humans can detect sound frequencies between 20 Hz and 20,000 Hz, dogs can identify them up to 60,000 Hz.

Adapted for sensitivity: Your puppy can swivel his ears to maximize the detection of noises and to accurately locate them. It's estimated that he can hear sounds four times farther away than you can.

Taste

It's hard to believe that your puppy can possess taste buds after you've seen him devouring a whole range of unmentionable things. He cannot detect the same range of flavors as a human (sour, sweet, salt and bitter) because doing so gave no advantage during dogs' evolution. Early experiences will influence his likes and dislikes when it comes to taste.

Vision

A puppy's eye has many similarities to a human's but it has become especially adapted for his survival. To create the perfect predator, a dog's eye is:

• Adapted to work in low light
• Adapted to detect movement.

Color vision: Your puppy has little need for complex color recognition and he does not see red or green – his vision consists of blues, yellows and shades of gray. However, he can easily detect contrasting shades and tones and his other senses will provide all the information he needs.

Vision differs between breeds: The shape of your puppy's skull alters his range of vision. For example, flat-faced breeds like the Pug were bred as companions and have a similar visual field to that of a human, whereas long-faced breeds, like the Greyhound, have a wide peripheral view, so they can spot prey without turning their heads.

Your puppy will need to be fairly close to an object to detect its detail

Natural behavior

WHAT IS "NORMAL"?

Dogs fit into our human lives very well, and this is the reason why their domestication was so successful. However, there is sometimes a fine line between the canine behavior that we find acceptable and that which we do not. Knowing about your puppy's natural behavior and development (often linked to selective breeding) will help you recognize what is "normal." Two areas of canine behavior that are often wrongly interpreted as abnormal include aggression and predatory behavior.

Aggression

Canine aggression is almost always unacceptable, but however uncomfortable it makes you feel, in the majority of cases aggression is a "normal" canine behavior. All dogs have the potential to express aggression and will do so in contextually appropriate situations.

Labeling a dog "aggressive" is often unhelpful, and it is more accurate to say that he exhibits aggression in a particular circumstance, such as toward strangers or when encountering non-neutered male dogs. Aggression is an emotional state that arises from a situation in which the

Digging is a completely natural behavior for many dogs, so if your puppy likes to dig provide him with acceptable outlets to do so.

dog finds himself. Some puppies have a higher tolerance to events than others (due to genetics and good socialization) and will therefore endure more before they feel that aggression is warranted.

Identifying the triggers: If your puppy displays aggression it is very likely that he is either in pain or fearful. A young puppy will not be "dominantly aggressive" toward you. By paying attention to the exact circumstances and his body language, you can identify the trigger and seek professional advice to help overcome the problem.

Careful management

Together with behavioral modification involving positive reinforcement, this can help to change your puppy's responses to specific triggers, reducing the likelihood of an aggressive reaction. Negative training methods are likely to increase anxiety levels and therefore worsen the problem.

Predatory behavior

It often comes as a surprise to learn that all dogs retain some level of the innate prey drive that helped their ancestors to survive. We are comfortable with our pets playing with toys – searching for, chasing, grabbing, shaking and chewing – yet it's often forgotten that these sensory and motor skills are part of the repertoire for normal predatory behavior. Since our puppies don't need those skills to survive, when they do emerge, the behavior is considered abnormal.

Breed-type behaviors

Breed type	Typical behavior patterns observed
Terrier	Chasing and digging where small animals can be seen, smelled or heard; instinctively bite and shake.
Herding	Herding people and other animals, occasionally nipping to move them on or to keep individuals within the group.

Selective breeding: Over several centuries, this has exaggerated particular hunting traits while significantly inhibiting the expression of the "kill and consume" phase in most dog breeds. Whether your puppy expresses predatory behavior is influenced by genetics, opportunity, social influences, experience and motivation.

Acceptable outlets

Although you cannot expect your puppy not to perform innate canine activities, you can take action to provide appropriate outlets for instinctive behaviors to make them acceptable.

Unacceptable responses: Whether it is normal or abnormal, predatory behavior expressed in particular ways should be taken very seriously. Unacceptable responses include:

- Chasing and catching pets, livestock or wildlife
- Chasing cars, bicycles, skateboards or joggers
- Biting feet or legs as people move past
- Chasing and grabbing at running children
- Working as a group to capture prey
- When a baby or toddler is targeted.

You can channel your puppy's chasing instincts into more appropriate behavior by throwing exciting toys for him to chase.

If your puppy lunges at passing cyclists, desensitize him from an early age and reward him with praise and a treat for ignoring them.

Although it's normal canine behavior, always take signs of aggression seriously

Abnormal behavior

WATCH OUT FOR THE SIGNS

While many dog owners often report "abnormal" behavior, thankfully, in most cases, they are actually describing a normal but unacceptable behavior. However, true abnormal behavior can occur in puppies and adult dogs and should always be taken very seriously. Seek professional help if you believe your puppy is exhibiting signs of abnormal activity.

Why do abnormal behaviors occur?

There are many scientific studies on this subject and the most common causes involve the following:

An unsuitable environment: When a puppy's basic emotional and behavioral requirements are persistently not met he will become more susceptible to the development of a range of possible abnormal behavior patterns as a form of release for these frustrations. This is classed as Functional Abnormal Behavior.

Health problems: Where disease or a parasite burden impacts on the expression of behavior in a puppy, Organic Abnormal Behavior may develop.

What you can do

Health	Maintain a good diet, regular parasite control and vet checks.
Genetic factors	Check the breed line where possible as certain problems are inherited.
Select your puppy carefully	Avoid puppy farms with barren environments and limited experiences.
Early intervention	Address signs of stress or behavioral disturbance as soon as possible.

Breed-specific behaviors

Some repetitive behaviors are more common in particular breeds than others, including:

- **German Shepherd:** Tail chasing and excessive licking (causing a lick granuloma)
- **English Bull Terrier:** Tail and shadow chasing
- **Doberman Pinscher:** Sucking on their own flanks.

Abnormal behavior may involve...

- A reduction of the normal canine behavioral repertoire.
- The development of functionless behaviors or "stereotypes," which are repeated over and over again, using energy, causing the puppy physical harm or preventing the expression of other normal behaviors. These are often described as "compulsive disorders."

A self-perpetuating problem: When a compulsive behavior begins it provides the puppy with relief from the stresses he is experiencing. Usually the repetitive actions trigger the release of endorphins, which make him feel better temporarily. Over time, changes in the central nervous system may occur, which then fuel the compulsive behavior. It begins to be exhibited in other situations, too, particularly when the puppy is stressed or overexcited.

Caution! Owners can accidentally reinforce the behavior by offering attention, reprimanding or responding to it in some other way.

Providing your puppy with more opportunities for play will keep him busy and mentally stimulated, thereby reducing the risk of abnormal behavior.

Watch out for...

Canine behaviors that can cause puppy owners concern may include the following:

- Pacing and/or circling
- Excessive licking
- Repetitive barking
- Self-mutilation
- Shadow or light chasing
- "Fly catching" or air snapping
- Staring into space
- Tail chasing or spinning
- Flank sucking
- Toy or object fixation.

Note: It can be extremely difficult or impossible to distract a dog. Seek professional advice if so.

Prognosis

If it is left untreated, the impact of a repetitive behavior can be serious. Some dogs perform the activity endlessly and this eventually results in:

- Loss of weight
- Physical injury
- Exhaustion
- Dehydration.

Caution! Don't punish your puppy if he performs a repetitive behavior – the added stress could cause significant deterioration. Try to identify the problem instead, and offer alternative activities.

Solutions

Most abnormal behaviors are treatable if you:

- Avoid punishing your puppy.
- Try to identify the triggers for the behavior.
- Seek veterinary advice about recommended examinations or tests.
- Seek professional behavioral advice.
- Enrich your puppy's environment with more toys, play opportunities, social time, physical exercise and mental stimulation.
- Provide a consistent routine as this will reduce any frustration or conflict.

Sometimes puppies may get fixated on a soft toy and carry it around everywhere.

Adolescent changes

ONLY A PASSING PHASE

Just as in humans, the stage before adulthood is often a troublesome one for puppies. This is the time when young dogs are at particular risk of being rehomed or when desperate owners may turn to punitive methods of training because their dog won't listen to them any more. Adolescence lasts roughly from 6 to 12 months but breed (and size) variances occur – larger breeds tend to mature later than smaller ones.

Hormonal changes during adolescence

Males	Mature earlier than females, often becoming fertile by 6 months of age.
	A surge of testosterone production occurs as your puppy enters adolescence, explaining why specific behaviors can suddenly become a nuisance (mounting, marking). Adult testosterone levels are significantly lower.
	Reach full sexual maturity by 15 months.
Females	Their first "season" may occur between 6 and 18 months. It may be irregular at first.
	A female's cycle is composed of four periods:
	1 Proestrus: This lasts approximately 9 days, and swelling of the vulva and bleeding occurs. Mating will not be accepted although males will show interest.
	2 Estrous: The fertile stage lasting approximately 9 days, when the female is receptive to mating.
	3 Diestrous: Whether pregnant or not, this lasts approximately 60 days. False pregnancy symptoms may appear.
	4 Anestrous: This is a quiet period without reproductive activity, lasting 3 to 5 months.

Body changes

During the important adolescent stage, your puppy will continue growing and developing physically until he eventually achieves his recognizably adult physique. Observe him closely throughout this period and you will notice the following changes:

- **Rapid growth:** Your puppy may experience spurts of rapid growth and these can occasionally cause him pain and lameness. Do not over-exercise him if this is the case – be patient.
- **Final adult teeth are moving into position:** This results in teething pain and the need to chew.
- **Adult coat grows in:** The texture of your puppy's coat will change and become less soft.

Testosterone plays a key role in triggering leg-lifting behavior in males.

Emotional changes

Due to the surge in testosterone levels and the advent of sexual maturity, adult male dogs will begin to respond differently to adolescent males, making challenges and intolerances far more common. Indeed, many forms of puppy behavior will become less acceptable to the adult dogs.

Fear-imprint stage: The second "fear imprint" stage occurs during adolescence. Your puppy will suddenly find some events that he could previously cope with seem startling and sometimes terrifying.

It is essential that you stay calm and reassuring at all times – this is just a passing phase and nothing to worry about – and that you continue to carefully socialize your puppy. Don't reward the behavior inadvertently by treating him when he is fearful.

In addition, you must try to avoid introducing any major new events in his life, such as neutering or kenneling. Just be patient and reassuring – this stage does not last forever and it will soon be over.

Helping your puppy

- Neutering can alleviate sexually driven behaviors but good timing is vital.
- Continue attending an age-appropriate training class that uses kind, reward-based methods. Persevere and the training results will be apparent as your puppy matures.
- Reintroduce his safe area or crate.
- Provide him with both increased physical and mental stimulation.
- Reward good behavior more frequently.
- Continue doing enjoyable activities together.
- Be patient.

Canine acne

Many owners are surprised to learn that during their puppy's adolescence, hormonal changes may contribute to canine acne. Check your puppy over when you are grooming him or just sitting quietly together. If you notice any spots or scabs on his face, chin or lips, make an appointment with your vet to investigate them – they can be treated.

Training often suffers during adolescence, making it even more important that you practice regularly and make it interesting for your puppy.

How puppies learn

TEACH YOUR PUPPY TO RESPOND TO COMMANDS

Puppies make excellent students as they are like sponges, enthusiastically and constantly absorbing new information about their surroundings. Take the time now to teach your puppy the appropriate behavior and responses to your requests. A well-trained puppy is likely to be taken out more often, allowed to meet and socialize with more people and dogs and, generally, will have a more enriched lifestyle. It is also very satisfying for you to have a better bond with him after all your effort.

Building result-based associations

Your puppy builds associations between events and their results. He remembers if an action brought a reward or something unpleasant and this influences his future decisions. He will need to practice an action or response many times before it becomes automatic. Maximize your training efforts by:

- Having rewards close at hand at all times – delay weakens the association
- Encouraging your puppy to repeat the action via luring and creating opportunities
- Responding as he performs a desirable action
- Limiting his opportunities for undesirable actions.

Timing: The timing of your reward or reinforcement is critical during training. Even a few seconds' delay may cause confusion in your puppy as to exactly which action you are encouraging.

Realistic expectations

You have to be patient and consistent while training your puppy. He will impress everyone by mastering some lessons within a few sessions, but you may need to work harder at achieving success with other activities – this is normal and to be expected.

Your entire family can be involved in your puppy's training routine, and it will be more effective if you all use the same commands and methods.

Low intelligence?

While there is some variation between breeds and specific individuals, all dogs have been shown to have a remarkable ability to learn and remember commands if they are taught properly. Some people believe that their puppy lacks intelligence because their training is taking more time than anticipated. However, this is unlikely to be the case; our puppies are usually a reflection of the amount of training we have put in, our own skills, and whether they have the opportunity to fulfill their basic needs at other times of the day. Your puppy's health will also play a role in his ability to process information and respond in an appropriate way.

Your puppy's failure to grasp a new training task immediately is not an indication of his low intelligence or bad memory. Repeat the lesson using a jackpot prize to make a big impression on him.

Reasons for slow responses

- Mistimed rewards encourage another movement or activity instead.
- There's insufficient consistency and repetition during the training.
- The correct behavior was not reinforced via praise or a reward.
- There was too much distraction.
- Using low-value rewards can reduce your puppy's interest and incentive.
- Punitive methods will interfere with his ability to focus on the lesson.

Be realistic

Your puppy cannot be expected to respond perfectly all the time. Young animals must explore and try new behaviors in order to understand how their world works. Sometimes this involves getting things wrong. If he fails to pick up the basic lessons, reassess your methods.

Be attentive

Try to focus exclusively on your puppy during short training sessions. Practice responding as soon as he does something you like. He is very bright and will soon begin to adapt his behavior to maximize the praise and rewards that you offer for the desired responses.

Offer a "jackpot" of several treats in a row, one larger treat or a higher value reward for a fantastic response

In training, offering your puppy a special "jackpot" reward of several favorite treats is an effective way to highlight a great performance.

Choosing a training method
THE RIGHT ONE FOR YOUR PUPPY

Deciding on the best way to train your puppy can be difficult. There are many different opinions on dog training, as well as techniques that involve slight variations on one another, or are radically different. Thankfully, we are now in a position where we can look to science to understand exactly how canine learning occurs and which methods get optimum results.

Which method is best?

Reward-based training (see the table below) is the most widely practiced method for training dogs today. Owners use a combination of food, praise and games to reward the correct responses and reinforce good behavior, thereby strengthening the bond between them and their puppy. Dogs are more likely to repeat rewarding behavior as they learn by their successes and want to please their owners. Clicker training enables you to "mark" desired behaviors and signals to your puppy that he will be rewarded.

Different training methods

Traditional	In the past we didn't fully understand the dog's brain and tended to use harsher techniques during training. Dogs were often physically maneuvred either by hand or via use of forceful training equipment. Punishment was used when the dog made a mistake and owners were usually blamed entirely for any misdemeanurs by their dog. Traditions are hard to change although most trainers and animal professionals now realize that there are better ways to raise puppies.
Reward-based	Modern knowledge about dogs and their mental capacity has led to an increase in "positive training methods." This involves the handler rewarding desirable behavior and avoiding any equipment that causes pain or discomfort. Rapid learning and good relationships can occur as a result. Trainers vary in the amount and type of punishment they use alongside their rewards so owners should always ask. While the use of "No" is still a punisher, it is very different to throwing chains or spraying water. Any method used on your puppy should be carefully considered.
Clicker training	A form of reward-based training, this technique is very popular due to its results. Clicker training allows you to "mark" desirable behavior very precisely, which helps your puppy to recognize which actions are worth repeating. The clicker is a small plastic box containing a metal tongue, which emits a unique "click" sound when pressed. This sound is paired to the arrival of a treat and therefore becomes a reinforcer in its own right. With clicker training you can wait for your puppy to perform a desirable action naturally, then "click" to encourage it, or you can lure him and then reinforce the response. Either way, results are usually achieved very quickly when the clicker is used correctly.
Alpha training	Based on the notion that all of a dog's behavior is influenced by his perception of pack order, this method relies on owners trying to emanate a dominant or Alpha dog. Despite having great popularity at one time, science has shown this concept to be seriously flawed and potentially dangerous.

Training can be fun for both you and your puppy if you make the sessions enjoyable and always praise and reward his good behavior.

Suitable equipment

There are many tools available to help you train your puppy but, initially, you will not need much equipment. However, it's a good idea to invest in the basic training kit and then, as you get to know your puppy's strengths and weaknesses, you can select specific items to help you make good progress. Your basic training kit should include the following:

Essentials

- A variety of tasty food treats and interesting toys for rewarding your puppy when he performs the desired behavior.
- A comfortable collar and leash.
- A long training leash.

Useful items

- A treat pouch.
- A clicker.
- A house line.

You will not need...

- Check/choke chains.
- Spray collars.

Equipment guidelines
- Examine your training kit regularly for any signs of normal wear and tear.
- Perform routine maintenance if and when it becomes necessary, and always keep all your training equipment scrupulously clean
- Replace any worn items or those that become too small as your puppy continues to grow.
- Commercial treats tend to have a long shelf life but you should never offer spoiled food to your puppy. Always check the "best before" dates.
- When balls and toys get old and battered, make sure you replace them with new ones.
- Motivate your puppy to perform better by occasionally introducing new interesting toys or tasty food treats. These will keep him interested and make him want to please you even more.

A clicker can be used to signal to your puppy that he has given the right response to your command, whether it's a hand signal or voice cue.

Using treats as rewards

REWARD-BASED TRAINING REALLY WORKS

Food is commonly used as a reward for appropriate behavior during puppy training. Many studies have shown this to be the fastest way to encourage, or train, a new action or behavior. Food rewards work effectively for the majority of puppies – after all, they all like to eat.

Why use food?

Food is a natural reinforcer, allowing you to quickly reward desirable behavior. You can control how much, how often and what you offer in order to gain the most from your training sessions. Most puppies require more motivation than just praise. Treats should be small, palatable and varied.

Suitable treats

Treat options	Foods to avoid
Commercial puppy treats	Chocolate
Meat	Sweets
Cheese	Chips
Kibble	Nuts

How many?

Initially, use lots of tiny treats as it's important to reward every correct response. Since your puppy will have a short attention span, each training session will only last a few minutes, so he won't consume too much. He can earn his entire daily food intake through his training program. However, treats should only make up 10 percent of the total, so you may wish to use his regular kibble, too.

Try mixing several treats together. High-value treats, such as cheese or meat, will rub against a puppy's regular kibble, making it more interesting.

Misconceptions about using food

• It encourages begging behavior.
• It leads to obesity.
• It creates lack of respect.
• It creates permanent need for treats.

If you use food rewards in an appropriate way, these problems will not occur.

Alternatives to treats

If your puppy is not particularly keen on food treats or he has a very sensitive stomach, you can reward him in other ways, including the following:

• Using enthusiastic praise
• Petting him
• Playing a game with his favorite toy.

Earning a tasty food treat for lying down makes it more likely that this puppy will choose to repeat this behavior again.

Using treats effectively

Improve the accuracy of your training by breaking the treats into small pieces and storing them in a treat pouch. A delay in the arrival of the reward will reduce success. You can overcome this by praise or using a clicker to "mark" the correct behavior and then following it up with a tasty treat.

Stage 1: Use a treat every time until your puppy is reliably performing the required task.

Stage 2: Gradually begin to fade out the treats by offering them on a more random basis. Continue to use praise to ensure that your puppy still finds the training experience a positive one.

Caution! Even if your puppy seems well trained, don't stop rewarding him. He will respond for a short while but is likely to ignore you eventually, particularly if another activity is more interesting.

Bad habits

Don't let your puppy demand treats. Use food to reward him for responding correctly or behaving well. He must "work" to earn rewards rather than having snacks offered for no reason. Increase his enthusiasm during difficult training tasks by:

- Increasing the value of the rewards – try using small pieces of sausage or cheese
- Asking him to earn all his food rather than feeding him from a bowl
- Using a selection of tasty treats to keep him really interested
- Pairing enthusiastic praise with treats and favorite toys for maximum impact.

Always be sure to reward the appropriate behavior by your puppy during training sessions with praise and a tasty treat or a game.

Teaching the commands
GETTING STARTED

Following the basic commands is the minimum you should aim for when training your puppy. Being able to respond appropriately improves his safety as well as that of those around him. Untrained puppies will grow up to be unruly and are more likely to end up in a rescue shelter.

Start as soon as possible

When your puppy comes to live with you he is already swiftly absorbing information about his world. Therefore, it is never too early to start teaching him the basic lessons. In fact, you'll be impressed at the speed with which he will learn during the early weeks. The commands, or training requests, that owners need differ but the main ones your puppy should be taught include: "Sit," "Down," "Come," "Leave it," "Stay," "Go to bed," "Settle," "Fetch" and walking nicely on leash.

Shaping an action

Your puppy won't know what is expected from him immediately. Help him to get it right by guiding him and breaking down a task into different parts if necessary. For example, some puppies find lying down on command quite difficult. "Down" can be shaped by rewarding him for:

- Lowering his head
- Lowering his shoulders
- Crouching down low
- Finally, his tummy touching the ground.

This gradual method of accepting increasingly closer approximations of a desired action is called shaping the behavior, and it helps to prevent frustration if your puppy cannot perform the full action right away.

Caution! Keep training sessions short as your puppy's attention span can only cope with a few minutes at a time. Create breaks by playing a game, resting, having a drink and trying a different lesson next time.

Your puppy will learn the desired actions more quickly if you reward him immediately for performing the appropriate behavior.

Guidelines for teaching a new command

- Your puppy should not be not tired or full – never start training him just after a long walk, boisterous game or feeding him a meal.
- Use a location free from distractions – choose a quiet place away from other dogs and people.
- Praise and reward your puppy – with food treats or a game with a favorite toy – for performing the desired action correctly.
- Practice regularly, for a few minutes at a time but not for too long – several short training sessions are more effective than one long one.
- Be friendly and patient – if you are tired or irritable, end the training immediately.

Training sessions should be friendly and fun for both you and your puppy. Get him interested in the process and focusing on you.

Making training fun!

A well-trained dog with good manners is a happy dog and a credit to you, his owner. He will enjoy your training sessions if you keep them short and praise and reward him when he does what you want. He will want to please you, especially if he is rewarded with a tasty tidbit or a special game, making your hard work worthwhile.

Family effort

Work together as a family to use the same training methods, voice commands and hand signals, and understand when and how to reward your puppy. You can agree how to do this in advance. He will respond differently to your various tones of voice, body language, ability to reward and how you play with him. Therefore, some training experience with each member of the family is very important.

If you feel frustrated...

- Take a break – don't persevere with the training session if it's not going well.
- Reassess the training and consider what might be going wrong.
- Be honest about your time and effort.
- Try again later in better conditions.
- Seek professional advice from a puppy class or one-to-one trainer.

Keep it friendly

None of the lessons require you to push or pull your puppy. If he enjoys training, he will learn swiftly. Although punishment has been shown to influence behavior, its timing has to be absolutely accurate if your puppy is to associate it with a particular action. Even then there's the potential that he will become anxious and begin to lose his confidence.

Enjoy yourself

Don't view training as a chore. If you enjoy yourself, this will influence your puppy's attitude, too. This is your first opportunity to see what his potential might be. The basic training commands are just the first step to numerous new adventures with him.

Puppies make mistakes - remain patient and don't use punishment to get results

Sit!

STEP-BY-STEP TRAINING GUIDE

Teaching your puppy the basic training commands may not appear to be an exciting prospect. However, try to think of the simple commands as the groundwork for all your future activities with him. Good habits can form early on if he is given the opportunity. A reliable "Sit" not only encourages good manners but it can also help you to calm him down in certain situations. He can begin his lessons as soon as he has settled in.

Teaching "Sit"

1 Get your puppy's attention and let him see that you have a treat held between your fingers. When he is close, allow him to sniff the treat but do not let him eat it yet.
2 Slowly move the hand holding the treat up and back over his head. He will raise his head to keep his nose close to the treat. As he does this, his bottom will naturally lower toward the floor.
3 Get ready – the second his bottom touches the floor, release the treat and let him eat it. Tell him how good he has been.
4 Repeat the first three steps until he effortlessly sits when your hand begins to rise.

5 Add the verbal cue "Sit," saying it as soon as his bottom touches the floor. Practice will enable him to associate the word with the action.
6 Practice this command while you are standing in different positions.
7 Start to prolong "Sit" by pausing before you release the treat. Gradually build up the time your puppy has to wait before you reward him.
8 As your puppy becomes more proficient at the "Sit," practice this training sequence while he is in different positions and locations with a variety of distractions. He should be able to "Sit" no matter where he is in relation to you.

Step-by-step "Sit"

1 Practice your "Sit" training outdoors as well as inside. Start by showing him a treat in your hand and allow him to sniff it but not eat it.

2 Don't push down on him to make him sit. Move the hand with the treat up and back over his head and his rear end will go down naturally.

3 Be ready to reward him for getting it right. As soon as his bottom touches the ground in the desired "Sit," immediately give him the treat.

Verbal cues

- Introduce the word that you would like to link to an action at the exact moment your puppy performs it. This allows him to link the sound and the action in the fastest way with least confusion.
- Avoid the urge to try to hurry him by repeating the word several times. If he hears the sound "sitsitsitsitsit" every time, he may be less inclined to respond to the individual "Sit" sound.

Hand signal

Your puppy will learn to associate the movement of your hand with the sitting action. With practice he will start to respond by sitting as soon as he sees the gesture, even if you are not holding a treat. It may not be necessary for you to say anything as he will be reacting to your body movements instead.

Caution! Always sit or kneel down on the floor while training really little puppies as leaning over them can be intimidating.

Daily practice

Ask your puppy to "Sit" when:
- Putting his bowl down
- Before giving him chews
- When putting his leash on and taking it off
- Before a friend greets him
- On walks before crossing roads.

Problem solver

- If your puppy rears up during the lesson you are probably holding the treat too high. If this happens, just start again, keeping it close to his nose and using slow movements.
- If he becomes distracted, be patient and don't get irritated. Just attract his attention, using the hand signal and treats to encourage him, or stop and try again later in the day.
- Always begin a new lesson in a quiet, familiar area with few distractions.

If you hold your hand too high when teaching the "Sit" command, your puppy will jump up like this to reach the treat instead of sitting.

Down!

STEP-BY-STEP TRAINING GUIDE

This is a useful command to teach your puppy as it will help him to stay calm and relaxed in some situations, and stop him from jumping up on people.

Teaching "Down"

1 Encourage your puppy into a sitting position when he is standing in front of you. Hold a food treat between your fingers and let him sniff it but do not allow him to eat it.
2 Hold the treat close to his nose and then draw it down toward the floor to a point just between his paws. It is important to do this slowly, so that his nose follows your hand.
3 As your puppy starts to bend to follow the treat in your hand that is descending slowly, he will naturally begin to find the position uncomfortable

and, consequently, he will be inclined to move his body even lower toward the floor, so that he can sniff the treat more easily.
4 Be ready to release the treat and praise him as soon as his chest is on the floor. Do not delay as he must associate the reward with the action.
5 Repeat the first steps until your puppy moves into the "Down" position more swiftly and fluidly.
6 Begin to say the verbal command "Down" as your puppy moves into position.
7 Practice this command in different positions. You might have to do it bending over, then gradually standing taller each time until he recognizes the request even when you are standing naturally.
8 Prolong the "Down" position by pausing briefly before offering the reward. Another useful method is to offer another treat before your puppy has moved, teaching him that the longer he remains down, the more rewards will arrive.

Caution!

Start teaching the "Down" on a soft surface where your puppy feels comfortable.

Verbal cues

Some owners prefer to choose an alternative word to "Down" if they use this cue to mean "Get off the sofa" or "Stop jumping up." The actual verbal command that you use does not matter as long as you are consistent and everyone else in the family uses the same word, too, so as not to confuse your puppy.

Hand signal

The movement of the hand down toward the floor comes naturally to us as we often indicate where we want our puppies to lie down.

Daily practice

Get into the habit of asking your puppy to "Down" when:
- You are about to offer him a chew
- You want him to calm down and settle quietly
- You have secured him into the harness in the car.

Praise and treat your puppy as soon as he goes into the "Down" position

Step-by-step "Down"

1 Get your puppy focused on the treat you are holding when he is in a sitting position in front of you. Hold it close to his nose so he can sniff it, but you must not allow him to grab and eat it.

2 Continue to hold it close to his nose and then slowly lower your hand toward the ground to a point between his front paws. As your hand goes down, your puppy will adjust his position, too.

3 Lying down gives your puppy easiest contact with your hand in this position. At the exact moment his chest touches the ground, praise him and release the treat immediately to reward the behavior.

4 Practice this until you're able to achieve the "Down" while standing up straight. Add the voice cue "Down" as your puppy moves into position, so he associates the command with the action of lying down.

Problem solver

- If your puppy stands up, the treat might be too far away from him.
- If he steps back, you may be holding the treat too close to his body.
- Some puppies raise their bottom instead of lying flat. Stay calm and resist moving the treat around. Let your puppy sniff at it and usually he will tire and naturally drop into a "Down" position. Release the treat and praise him.
- Small or short-legged puppies may not put their chest on the floor as expected. Sit on the floor with a bent leg outstretched in front of you. Lure your puppy under your knee, so he drops low to follow the treat and in doing so will find himself in the "Down" position, which you can reward.
- If he moves around trying to find a way to get the treat, practice in a corner or next to the sofa where his movements will be gently restricted.

Come!

STEP-BY-STEP TRAINING GUIDE

Your puppy is likely to follow you around enthusiastically at first but you shouldn't make this an excuse for not teaching him to come to you when you call him. As he grows in confidence and approaches adolescence, he will be more likely to ignore you in preference to doing his own thing. However, you can minimize the likelihood of this and of any potential future problems by teaching him a reliable recall now.

Teaching "Come"

1 Start at home by calling your puppy from across the room. Crouch down at his level, so that you are even more enticing. Always offer him a tasty treat and praise for running to you.

2 Ask a family member or friend to gently restrain him. Tease him with a treat and then quickly run a few steps away before calling "Come," at which point your helper should release him.

3 Act enthusiastically or crouch down on the floor and spread out your arms to encourage your puppy to rush back directly to you.

4 As he arrives, offer him the treat with one hand while taking hold of his collar with the other. This gives you control over his next movement while teaching him to tolerate being restrained. This is a useful routine when you need to hold him to clip his leash back on.

5 After you have practiced this training command in a variety of quiet locations inside your home and in the yard, try the recall in a variety of more difficult situations, adding distractions as your puppy becomes more reliable and proficient. Keep praising him for coming back to you, and always use big rewards, including "jackpots" for particularly speedy returns or for coming back despite a distraction.

6 When you're in an open space or public place and teaching the recall to your puppy, use a long training line to stay in control (as shown in the photographs opposite).

Useful command: A puppy that can safely be let off his leash in the park or other public spaces will have more opportunity to play and socialize with other dogs than one kept on a short leash, so learning to come when called is very beneficial.

Helpful equipment

A long training line is useful as your puppy can feel free while remaining safely under control. You will probably feel more confident, too. Use the line to stop him running farther away - not to haul him back toward you. Use a happy voice and mannerisms to encourage him to return instead.

Calling your puppy to you

- Avoid getting into the bad habit of calling his name repeatedly when it is clear that he is focusing on something else.
- He is always watching your body language and facial signals when he is deciding how to respond, so behave in a happy, encouraging manner when calling him to you.

Step-by-step "Come"

1 When you're outside, use a training line to teach your puppy recall. As soon as he starts to turn his focus back toward you, respond enthusiastically. Call "Come" and encourage him to run toward you.

2 As soon as your puppy arrives, give him a food treat. While offering him the reward, gently take hold of his collar as this helps to reduce avoidance problems when you try to reattach the leash in the future.

Using the right motivator

Although food is commonly used as a reward, many puppies especially love toys. Recall training with toys is easy and reminds your puppy of how much fun you are. If your puppy has an extra-favorite toy this can be kept especially for walks. Try using:

- Squeaky toys to trigger excitement and get your puppy zooming back to you
- Two toys, so you can always play, even if he is carrying one or if one toy is lost.

Problem solver

- If your puppy returns part of the way but then gets distracted, try to keep his focus on you by calling and interacting as he approaches. Use higher value rewards to really make an impression when he does get close.
- Running the opposite way or playing with a toy often makes a puppy keen to join you.

Never call your puppy over to you to tell him off - next time he will be reluctant to respond

Walking on a leash

STEP-BY-STEP TRAINING GUIDE

All owners would like to own a dog that they can walk easily without him pulling or stopping, and the best way to achieve this is to begin working with your puppy while he is very young, before bad habits develop. In fact, from the moment he is introduced to his leash, he can be encouraged to walk nicely. Teaching him is time consuming but the long-term benefits are worthwhile since walking with a dog that pulls is tiring, stressful, potentially dangerous and likely to result in fewer walks.

Teaching your puppy to walk nicely

1 Decide on which side you would like your puppy to walk. You can teach him to walk on both sides but just using one side is less confusing for him. Get his attention and offer him a treat. Hold the leash and offer treats from the opposite hand. Opt for whichever way around is easiest for you.
2 Keeping your puppy's attention, take a step forward and reward him again. Repeat this part, taking a few more steps and rewarding him for remaining by your side. In a perfect situation you'll see a nice loose leash with no tension at all.
3 If he pulls, stop immediately. Act like an anchor, refusing to move while the leash is tight. If he turns back to you, praise and encourage him to come back into place beside you by luring him with a treat. He will learn that he makes no progress by pulling but paying attention to you is worthwhile.
4 Gradually build up the distance you walk with your puppy beside you.

Maximize training success

- Spend more time training.
- Exercise your puppy before attempting to train.
- Teach him to look to you for fun, even around other people and dogs.
- Pay attention to him while you walk, and praise and reward all good behavior.
- Get his attention focused on you before you near a distraction, so he isn't tempted to pull.

Be relaxed

As a responsible owner, never use any training equipment that causes pain or discomfort to your puppy while he's out on a walk with you. It's important that he always feels happy and relaxed while he's walking if he's to remain confident and sociable.

Problem solver

- If your puppy can see the treat in your hand he may feel it's worthwhile to jump up at you. Keep the treat hidden or use a verbal marker such as "Good" to let him know he's getting it right and then take a treat from your pouch.
- If he is frightened of traffic or busy public places, he may pull more and be less inclined to focus on training. Try to address his fear first and the training will then be much easier.

Step-by-step walking on a leash

1 Choose which side your puppy is going to walk on, hold the leash loosely and encourage him to step into place beside you. You can use a tasty food treat to attract his attention.

2 With your puppy focusing his attention on you, take a step forward and reward him again. Keep moving forward with him walking nicely at your side, encouraging him as you do so.

3 Continue to encourage him and praise him for his good behavior. Notice how loose the leash is – there is no tension in it at all as the puppy continues to walk nicely in position.

4 Offer him a reward while he is walking next to you. He will soon learn what you want him to do and that walking at your side on a loose leash, without pulling, is worth his while.

5 Reward your puppy with a tasty treat while you are still on the move if possible – try not to stop. If he pulls, you must stop walking immediately and lure him back into position with a treat.

6 Continue to practice walking on the leash in this way until your puppy grows in confidence. Keep his attention focused on you and praise and reward his good behavior.

As you walk, keep up the interaction with your puppy or he might become distracted and forget the training

Settle!

STEP-BY-STEP TRAINING GUIDE

Unless a puppy is taught how to settle, he is likely to tear around, flopping down whenever and wherever he wants. Energetic puppies that don't know how to settle are often banished to another room or into their crate. Use the "Settle" to encourage your puppy to relax and quiet down.

Teaching "Settle"

1 Secure a house line to your puppy's collar. Sit in your chair and encourage him to lie by your feet by luring him into the down position with a treat. Step on the house line so he can't walk away.

2 Try to relax, so he is influenced by your own behavior. If he remains relaxed and lying down, say, "Settle! Good dog" and place a treat by his nose for him to eat. If he gets up, ignore him. Just wait for him to lie down again and then praise him as before.

3 It's useful to have a verbal cue, such as "Off you go" to give permission for your puppy to leave when he's ready. Slowly build up the time he settles before giving the release signal.

4 Add the verbal cue "Settle!" just as your puppy begins to lie down.

5 Encourage him to really relax by waiting until he is lying flat on his side and breathing deeply before praising him.

Best and worst times

Best times to teach "Settle":
· Your puppy is already tired
· The room is quiet and peaceful.

Worst times to teach "Settle":
· He hasn't been exercised
· He needs to relieve himself
· Something very exciting is going on.

Always begin training "Settle" at a time when your puppy is already tired to maximize the chance of successful training.

Offering a chew can help your puppy to "settle" in position

Go to bed!

STEP-BY-STEP TRAINING GUIDE

Going to bed should always be enjoyable for your puppy, rather than just something he has to do when under your feet or being reprimanded.

Teaching "Go to bed"

1 Toss a treat onto your puppy's bed to act as a lure. As he steps onto the bed, say "Go to bed!" Toss another treat to him to extend the time he spends there. Repeat this exercise a few times a day for a couple of minutes each time.

2 Gesture as if you are tossing a treat but keep it in your hand. As he moves toward his bed, say "Go to bed!" and then, once he has arrived, toss the treat to him as a reward.

3 If your puppy is not doing so already, encourage him to lie down on his bed in a "settle" before offering him the reward.

4 Build up his skill by practicing this command from various distances, with increased delay before rewarding him and with different distractions.

Useful lesson

This lesson is very useful for those times when you are:

- Eating your dinner
- Watching TV
- Chatting with a visitor or on the phone
- Eating out and have your puppy with you.

Having his own bed to lie on reduces the chance of your puppy getting under your feet or sleeping on the furniture.

Quiet and calm

The "Go to bed" command is different from a specific "Sit" or "Down" as you do not expect your puppy to stay still in exactly the same position throughout. Instead, you just want him to lie down quietly in a relaxed and calm way. Try offering him a treat, edible chew or an interesting toy to keep him busy and contented while he lies in his bed. This is especially useful when you are busy working or sitting down quietly in the evening.

Leave it!

STEP-BY-STEP TRAINING GUIDE

This is useful if you want your puppy to leave an object or stop an undesirable behavior. If you teach him properly, he will know that stopping the behavior, or dropping the item, will bring good results and he will stay relaxed and nondefensive. If he understands "Leave it," he can drop things he has taken, and be prevented from picking up items from the ground and performing inappropriate behaviors.

Teaching "Leave it"

1 Begin in a quiet, low-distraction area. You'll need some basic treats for him to "leave" and some tastier ones for rewards. Sit on the floor with a piece of basic treat in one hand, allowing your puppy to see it on your palm. He will move forward hoping to eat it. As he does so, close your hand around the treat and say "Leave it" just once.

2 Hold your hand still while he sniffs it. Wait for him to turn away or step back and then immediately say "Good! Take it" while offering him the tasty treat from your other hand.

3 Repeat Step 2 several times. Make sure he never eats the "Leave it" treat. He will quickly learn to back away when he hears "Leave it." Some puppies are persistent, especially with higher value items. Try to keep your hand still, raising it slightly out of his reach if he tries chewing.

4 Your puppy is ready to move on. This time, say "Leave it" as you move your hand out toward him. He should stay where he is, not attempting to take the treat. He may look at you instead, which will earn him a "Good! Take it" as you offer him a treat from your other hand. This is an important stage, so practice until he is reliable.

5 He is ready for you to change the variables and extend the command to more complex situations. Begin by practicing the command with:
- The treat on the floor in front of him (be ready to cover it with your hand or foot)
- The treat in your hand at different levels
- The treat on a coffee table or counter.

6 Now practice in different places, with other people or dogs in the room (prevent another dog from rushing in to take the treat), with you standing at various distances from your puppy.

7 Practice this training command with a variety of different items. Start with low-value objects and build up to things that your puppy would really love. Always make sure that you reward him with something that he perceives as more valuable than the item you ask him to leave.

Build up gradually

Some puppies are very greedy and persistent and will try to snatch the treat out of their owner's hand and eat it, even when they are teaching this command with some basic kibble. If your puppy falls into this category, you should begin teaching him the "Leave it" just with pieces of ordinary torn-up cardboard or tissue instead of basic treats. As he starts to understand the command and consistently backs away when you ask him to do so, you can introduce food items and build up gradually to using higher-value treats. As always, be patient and don't rush the training sessions – he will eventually get the message.

Problem solver

One benefit of being able to stop undesirable behaviors with this verbal command is that you won't have to chase, pull or grab your puppy. He's much more likely to remain relaxed and friendly as opposed to distrustful and defensive.

Step-by-step "Leave it"

1 Your puppy will move toward you, knowing that you are holding a treat in your hand. As he approaches, close your hand and say "Leave it."

2 When he realizes that he cannot get at the food treat and eat it, your puppy will eventually turn away or back off.

3 Immediately, offer him a treat from the other hand, saying "Good! Take it." He learns to turn his focus away from the thing he is asked to "Leave."

Perfecting your technique

This command may need considerable practice before your puppy understands what you want of him. Here are some useful training guidelines to make the process easier for you both.

Stay friendly: Your "Leave it" verbal cue must be friendly and should never sound angry. Always remember that teaching this command works best if your puppy is relaxed.

Aim for success

If your puppy is showing any signs of stress at all during this lesson, stop immediately and try again later with another item that he finds less desirable and with a nicer "Take it" reward. Build up gradually to the things that he finds harder to "Leave" and always make sure that the reward that he earns is clearly better than the one he chose to give up.

Easier walks

While you are out on walks with your puppy, try to be observant and preempt any of his attempts to scavenge. Give your "Leave it" command the moment that he lays eyes on something he should not have. Stay friendly throughout and always reward him for choosing to focus on you rather than the temptations that are lying on the ground. Remember that dogs are opportunistic scavengers and that ignoring litter and other interesting items may pose a challenge for them. Always be ready to praise and offer tasty food rewards when your puppy ignores something that would normally present a temptation.

Gradually increase the value of the item over many training sessions

Finding a training class

Attending a group training class can be particularly beneficial for not only your young puppy but for you, too. Getting into good habits early on may reduce the problems you experience later. As soon as your puppy has been vaccinated he will be welcomed into a puppy class. However, good classes are popular so you will need to book early.

Assess the class's suitability

Before you attend the training class with your puppy it is recommended that you arrange a visit to observe it in action and to assess its suitability. Good trainers welcome prospective clients. Training classes are not regulated and anyone can set themselves up to teach a class. Ask your veterinary clinic for their recommendations and search for a trainer with good credentials. You may have to travel to find the right class, but the experience your puppy has there will influence his future behavior, so it's really worthwhile.

What to look for in the class

- Less than eight puppies per class (slightly more if the hall is very large and if there are multiple instructors on hand).
- All puppies should be under 20 weeks when they start training classes to prevent adolescents mixing with very young puppies.
- The class should consist of several short lessons, which are suitable for a puppy's attention span.
- The puppies and owners should be relaxed and enjoying the session.
- Although some puppies might bark when they are excited, there should not be excessive noise if they are genuinely relaxed.
- Any periods of puppy play should be controlled and closely supervised.
- Puppies should ideally begin the course together, so they are all at the same level of training.
- A puppy class should never involve using choke chains, prong collars or punitive methods.

The facilities and training

The location should be spacious for the number of puppies and owners. The floor and facilities

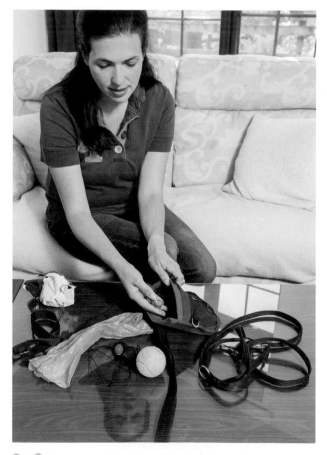

You will need to invest in some basic equipment for training classes, including a treat pouch, toys, a training leash and cleanup bags and wipes.

should be clean and not too slippery. There must be an outdoor area for your puppy to relieve himself and reasonable parking options. Not all training facilities are warm so wrap up. However, a young puppy will feel cold, so outdoor classes are less appropriate for this age range.

A good class will:

- Cover all the basic training commands, using kind and effective methods
- Motivate you
- Adapt to your puppy's personal needs
- Provide positive socialization experiences.

Missed a class? Contact your trainer for handouts, so you can practice before the next lesson.

Be prepared: Arrive at class 15 minutes early. Walk your puppy a little, so he can relieve himself first and still be in class on time. Avoid trying to enter while the previous class is leaving.

Your instructors

Your instructors should be approachable and friendly and build your confidence when working with your puppy. They can advise about problems you may be having at home as well as in the classroom. Never be afraid to ask them for expert advice about any type of inappropriate or undesirable behavior that your puppy may be exhibiting. They will be happy to help you.

Age is important

A puppy class is not suitable for older problem dogs. Younger puppies may be negatively impacted by an older dog's behavior and should not be used to repair social problems.

Checklist

Check that you have the following items before you leave home:

· Your puppy's collar and leash
· Cleanup bags and wipes
· A selection of treats
· A treat pouch
· A travel bowl for water
· Money for the class fees and any other purchases
· A long training leash (optional)

Training classes provide a good opportunity for socializing your puppy with other dogs of different breeds as well as meeting a wide range of people.

Training checklist

There is virtually nothing you cannot train your puppy to do for you. He is like a young child, with a spongelike ability and desire to learn new things and please you. Routine and patience are all you require, and once you have mastered the basics (recall and sit), your puppy will be ready to learn more. If you are consistent and always use the same methods, based on kindness and rewards, you will be successful.

Training guidelines

Make training fun for both of you and always take it slowly and patiently, one step at a time, building on the success of the last session. Your puppy will soon learn that some things he does will please you and will be rewarded, which will make him want to repeat them. Here are some helpful guidelines.

Respect: You must teach your puppy to respect you as the leader in your home. Without proper respect, your training schedule does not matter much as he may learn words and routines but choose not to respond appropriately. Respectful dogs understand and do what you say.

Rewards: Reward-based training is the most effective way of teaching a dog. You can encourage appropriate behavior and good manners by rewarding them when they occur. Use specially formulated dried food treats, dog biscuits or even tiny pieces of cheese or cooked liver as treats and keep them on you in a special training pouch.

Never use punishment: It is always frustrating when your training goes wrong, but a puppy can only take on so much in one session, so never try to teach lots of different commands at the same time – it is better and more effective for him to master them individually. Keep training sessions short and fun – stop immediately if your puppy gets bored or tired. Equally, if you are having a bad day, never get angry with him – just end the session and try again later or on the following day.

Top training tips

- Make training sessions fun – your puppy will learn much faster.
- During the first 2 months, include several sessions per day, but keep them to a maximum of 10 minutes.
- Use hand signals and body language as well as words.
- Never change your commands – once you have decided on the hand signals and words, stick to them.
- Always reward and praise the desired behavior immediately.
- Never reward behaviors that are not correct or the one you want him to perform.
- Use tasty tidbits that will motivate your puppy.
- Never use force when you are training your puppy – it is unnecessary and counterproductive.
- Use the commands in a range of natural situations, so if you see your puppy starting to lie down, say "Down" as he does so.
- Be consistent to avoid confusing him, and make sure that everyone else in the family uses the same commands and cues.
- Always stay in control of the training sessions rather than let your puppy turn them into games – if this happens, stop immediately and just introduce another session later the same day.

Your hand signals and body language are just as important in training your puppy as the voice cues you use.

Training methods and devices

Food rewards	Small pieces of tasty food, such as dog treats or tiny pieces of cheese, can be very effective as a reward for the correct response.
Praise	Kind words, a stroke and a game with a favorite toy will always be regarded as praise by your puppy.
Clicker	Using a clicker as a training aid is what is known as "instrumental conditioning," with the click acting as a positive reinforcer. The dog learns to associate the sound with a treat.
Extinction	This is the act of turning your back on unwanted behavior and completely ignoring it.

Basic training commands

Your puppy should learn the following basic commands. Don't teach them all at once - introduce them slowly.

- Sit!
- Stay!
- Down!
- Come!
- Heel!
- Leave it!
- Settle!
- Fetch!

You can use a combination of a clicker and hand signals to reinforce good behavior by your puppy during training sessions.

Owning a well-behaved, happy dog makes all the hard work of training worthwhile

8 AVOIDING PROBLEMS

Chewing
APPROPRIATELY CHANNELING THE INSTINCT

Owning a puppy is a wonderful experience, but along the way several problems might arise and spoil some of your pleasure. However, by addressing problem behavior in the right way or, better still, preventing it in the first place, your puppy can continue to be a joy to own. After all, there's no such thing as the "perfect" puppy – all puppies make mistakes. It's how you manage them that's important for avoiding problems.

Destructive behavior
Chewing is a common complaint. Puppies explore their environment and use their mouths as a way of finding out about an object. Unfortunately, they may decide that it's fun to play with, or pleasurable to chew on, anything no matter what its suitability. Thankfully, the destructive urge normally decreases with age if you provide suitable alternative outlets.

Why do puppies chew?
• Natural instinct when their teeth are cutting through or moving into place.
• Boredom from having a lack of stimulation.
• Stress.
• Hunger.
• Habit.

When and what?
Recognizing when the chewing is most likely to occur and what your puppy is targeting can help you to determine the trigger for his behavior.

Teething: You may not see puppy teeth dropping out but regular examinations of your puppy's mouth will keep you knowledgeable about his stage of teething. While he is teething, he is more likely to chew to relieve the discomfort and pain. If he's destructive with toys, opt for different, tougher types rather than refusing to give him any at all.

Bored dogs: Puppies with not enough to occupy them often target indiscriminate items that they happen upon, so don't leave shoes and children's toys on the floor. Chewing can occur at any time.

Provide your puppy with an assortment of sturdy, indestructible toys that he can safely chew while he is teething.

Chewing habits often increase during adolescence. As a puppy continues to develop and grow, his larger size and greater strength are likely to lead to more destruction in your home, so take positive steps to prevent this.

Preventing chewing

- Supervise your puppy in high-risk areas.
- Use a suitably sized puppy crate or pen when he is not being supervised.
- Offer him his meals inside a food dispenser to safely utilize his energy and focus.
- Puppy proof more carefully.
- Exercise your puppy regularly.
- Address any fears and anxieties.

Stress-induced chewing: This can be associated with specific triggers. Identifying the cause allows you to remedy it and the symptoms disappear.

Hunger: Chewing may increase around meal times or may be focused on items associated with food or flavor: bowls, or boxes or cupboards containing food. Chewing is less likely after feeding.

Habit: Chewing can be performed just out of habit. It is more likely to occur if your puppy has chewed for long periods for another reason.

Offering chew items

Numerous toys and chews are helpful when addressing a puppy's chew desire. Leave some tempting toys on the floor for him to discover in your absence. Supervision is necessary with new items. Try offering him the following:

- Rubber teething toys
- Tough rubber activity toys
- Cardboard tubes
- Large rawhide chews
- Antler chews
- Rag toys.

Chew deterrents

If your puppy is continuously drawn to chew on objects that cannot be removed, such as table legs, it may be helpful to use a taste deterrent spray. These bitter sprays reduce the attractiveness of the object, making it more likely that he will focus on his tastier toys instead. However, in the absence of alternative chew items, he is likely to tolerate the bad taste since chewing itself makes him feel good.

The act of chewing can release endorphins, which make your puppy feel relaxed and happy

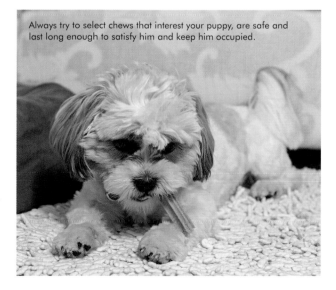
Always try to select chews that interest your puppy, are safe and last long enough to satisfy him and keep him occupied.

Elimination problems

RESOLVING HOUSEBREAKING ISSUES

Many owners have to deal with the occasional housebreaking accident from their puppy inside their home. However, sometimes the incident is more than just a case of being "caught short" or a lack of housebreaking training, and it can be quite difficult to work out why your puppy has started (or continued) to relieve himself at the wrong times or in inappropriate places.

Eliminating indoors

The range of reasons why your puppy might relieve himself indoors include the following:

- His housebreaking was incomplete
- An inability to get outside
- Anxiety, such as when he is left at home alone or a fear of noises
- Submissive urination
- Excitement or illness
- Marking – this is most likely in male dogs from the onset of adolescence.

Old-fashioned methods, such as rubbing your puppy's nose in his mess or smacking him with a rolled-up newspaper, are not effective techniques for resolving an elimination problem.

Submissive urination

This response during a greeting is often a cause for alarm for owners. Typically, this behavior is seen in timid puppies that are attempting to appease the person. They approach, roll over and urinate, or

Training your puppy effectively from an early age to toilet outdoors will help to avoid problems with indoor toileting.

crouch down and urinate. Submissive urination is also likely while being punished.

- Keep greetings low key until your puppy has been let out to empty his bladder.
- Crouch down to greet him rather than bending over him. Avoid excited greetings.
- Stroke his chest rather than moving your hand over his head and neck.
- Ask guests to ignore him until he has settled and then greet him as outlined above.
- Socialize your puppy and try to encourage more confident responses.

Never punish a puppy for submissive urination as you risk reducing his confidence even further, making it more likely that he will urinate.

Sudden change

Any dramatic change in behavior should be discussed with your vet. An underlying infection could cause your puppy to feel unable to hold on, or to urinate much more frequently than usual. Report any urination during sleep, diarrhea or blood in his urine or stools to your vet.

For housebreaking to be successful, it is essential that you always accompany your puppy outside into the yard.

Wait patiently, whatever the weather, for him to perform the required action – praise him afterward.

Excitement urination

Most puppies can get overexcited at times and, in some cases, this can lead to a momentary loss of bladder control. The puppy shows confident body language, so you can distinguish it easily from submissive urination. If this happens, stay calm and follow the advice below to prevent the behavior from becoming ingrained.

- Try to observe your puppy so you can start to recognize the triggers for this problem.
- Interrupt situations that are leading to over-excitement and encourage him to stay calm.
- Use low-key greetings and short play sessions if these are problematic times.
- Don't respond angrily if he has an accident; this could easily trigger submissive urination.

Adolescent females

Some females experience an upset to their housebreaking as they approach their first season. Encourage your puppy to go outside more often in order to prevent this usually short-term problem from becoming established.

Adolescent males

Marking behavior is exhibited by maturing males (and sometimes females, too). It can sometimes be performed indoors, which is frustrating for an owner who may feel that they have only recently completed housebreaking their dog. If your dog marks when a female in season is nearby or around his territory, neutering can help, but if the marking occurs when your dog is worried or frustrated, you will need to address those triggers instead.

Stealing and scavenging

MANAGING THE PROBLEM APPROPRIATELY

A puppy that learns to take items (often for play or chewing) or to search areas, such as the garbage and cupboards, for food is likely to resort to similar behavior in the future when he is hungry or bored. Before you become angry at your puppy, remind yourself that he does not understand our human social rules of not taking what doesn't belong to you.

Careful management

Dogs are opportunistic, so careful management, along with appropriate responses from you, should reduce the incidence of stealing and scavenging problems. Remember that hiding or cringing is not a sign of guilt in your puppy – more likely, he's responding to your angry response.

Why was your puppy tempted?

There are several possible explanations for why your puppy might perform these behaviors, including the following reasons.

Hunger: Your rapidly growing puppy has a high requirement for regular meals. Check that:

- He is getting enough food for his age, size and activity level and also that the number of meals you are feeding per day is correct
- His worming schedule is up to date.
- Talk to your vet if he is constantly ravenous.

Exploration: If items are left within reach of your puppy, or if he can easily break into or chew through food boxes or bags, don't be surprised if you come home and discover that he has done just that. Work hard to keep surfaces clear, cupboards secured and containers closed while he is young, so he never learns to expect "hidden treasures." Then the problem will become less likely as he matures.

Lack of stimulation: Puppies like to be occupied but their attention span is very short. Make sure that your puppy has plenty of toys and safe chews to keep him busy when you are distracted with work, household chores or other things or while you are out. Otherwise he might begin to search for things of interest. Food dispensers and activity toys are great solutions for distracting bored dogs.

Don't leave food items or things you do not wish your puppy to chew in containers at his level.

The "Leave it" command is very useful for when you see your puppy getting into something he shouldn't

Responding appropriately

The way you react when you discover that your puppy has taken something of yours or has raided the garbage will influence his future behavior. By responding inappropriately you could create much more serious behavioral problems.

- Always stay calm – don't get angry.
- Call your puppy to you and trade the item for his toy or a treat. Praise him for returning it.
- Check items for damage or toxins in case he has ingested something he shouldn't.
- Put him outside in the yard or in another room while you clean up any mess.
- Promise yourself not to leave things within his reach again.
- Review your puppy-proofing measures and make improvements.

Anxiety

Anxious puppies will sometimes take personal items that hold your smell and lie on them, or shred them around themselves as a way of coping. Having your scent close by often gives them more security.

- Address your puppy's fears or discuss them with a behaviorist before the problem escalates.
- Consider using a calming diffuser to help settle your puppy.

Don't leave shoes and items you value lying around within your puppy's reach. Teach him to trade them for an interesting toy or treat.

Counterproductive responses

Chasing your puppy and grabbing items from him is counterproductive and more likely to make him feel worried about you getting close rather than about taking the item in the first place. This common and instinctive response by many dog owners can often be a trigger for aggression over possessions by their pets, which leads, in turn, to further behavior problems.

Problems out walking

HOW TO RESOLVE THEM

Owners report different problem behaviors while they are out walking their puppy. Although pulling is a common problem (see page 196 for a step-by-step guide to walking nicely on a loose leash), it's not the only bad habit to occur. Tackle these problems before they become ingrained.

Biting the leash

Grabbing, holding, tugging, shaking and chewing can all be directed at the leash during walks. This behavior often occurs when a puppy feels anxious or frustrated, but it can quickly become a learned habit and a form of attention seeking. Your options for dealing with this include the following:

- Work hard to alleviate your puppy's fears through extra socialization and habituation
- Stay calm and practice your obedience training
- Walk briskly and work to keep his focus on you
- Reward and praise nonbiting behavior

Practicing walking briskly while talking and reassuring your puppy will help him get used to the leash and stop his attempts to unleash himself.

- Offer him a toy to carry instead
- Redirect his attention upon the first sign that these problems are starting
- Consider a harness where the leash is attached at the back, well out of temptation's way.

Lunging at cars

This reaction can be extremely dangerous for the puppy and motorist. Herding and driving breeds are particularly prone to lunging. The reaction usually stems from a fear of the vehicle itself.

- Practice in areas where vehicles are at such a distance away, or going so slowly, that you can easily attract your puppy's attention.

Walk your puppy in an area where he feels safe and confident, and gradually introduce more challenging situations if necessary.

Exhaustion

When a puppy is overtired you will have to allow him to rest or lift him up. Some breeds, such as the English Bulldog, tire and overheat easily and may require gradual introduction to lengthier walks.

Refusing to walk

Occasionally a puppy may refuse to move during walks. This frustrating reaction often happens with very young puppies. Reasons for halting include:

- Fear of being outdoors (may be specifically fearful of vehicles, other dogs or people)
- Feeling tired
- Fear of noise and weight of a chain leash
- Being in pain or discomfort while walking.

Solutions

- Never force your puppy to face things of which he is frightened.
- Stop and wait, allowing time for the scary thing to move away and for your puppy to recover.
- Praise and reward him as soon as he relaxes.
- Don't drag him along the ground. Keep the leash loose, stand still, and wait.
- Try bouncing his favorite ball or rustling his treats. When he shows interest and steps forward, praise and encourage him.
- Where this is not possible, for example while walking along a busy road, pick him up and take him to a quieter location. Avoid busy areas on walks until he has found some confidence and then gradually revisit the areas that are more challenging for him.
- If you are concerned about pain or discomfort, urgently seek veterinary advice.

- Before the car gets close, get his attention and show him a tasty reward. Use your body to block his view of the traffic, if turning him away doesn't work. Stay calm throughout and concentrate on keeping him focused.
- Gradually reduce the distance to the road, or start to walk along slightly busier ones.

Caution! If your puppy persistently jumps out and lunges at passing cars, despite your efforts to prevent this, you must seek professional help.

Carrying your puppy is not a pattern you want to develop but if he is exhausted or terrified, it may be the best option

Damage to yard and home
DEALING WITH A DESTRUCTIVE PUPPY

There are many reasons for destructive behavior by puppies. Some are natural behaviors as a result of breeding, as in the case of terriers that enjoy digging, whereas others include boredom in understimulated dogs or being left alone for long periods, often without interesting toys or chews.

Digging

Many puppies will perform digging behavior at some point in their physical and behavioral development. Although their owners often view this as a problem, for dogs it is natural as it is an innate behavior that used to help them to:

• Dig dens and shelter
• Hide extra food
• Pursue prey.

A puppy that likes digging can create a surprisingly deep and large hole in a relatively short period of time.

Although your puppy does not need these skills now, he may instinctively dig if he is:

• Lacking stimulation
• Trying to hide a special treat or toy
• Trying to escape
• Hunting vermin.

Solutions: Rather than prevent this behavior (which is very difficult) it is better to redirect it to an appropriate location. Create a digging pit with sand and dirt, or you can use a cardboard box filled with shredded paper if indoors.

• Partially bury some large treats or toys and then encourage your puppy to investigate.
• As he pulls out a "prize," praise him lavishly.
• Reward him each time he digs in this location.
• If he makes a mistake ask him to "Leave it" and then redirect him to his digging pit instead. After enough practice, his digging events will mainly focus in this area.

Carpet digging

This may occur when your puppy is overexcited, frustrated, playing, escaping or if he's attracted to lights or shadows. Dogs scrape around in their bed before circling and lying down. This natural behavior creates a flattened hollow for resting in.

Door scratching

Puppies often learn that scratching at the door results in their owner letting them out, or back inside the house, and this is not necessarily a problem. However, a particularly strong dog or enthusiastic scratcher can cause damage to woodwork or plastic frames, and muddy paws will leave their mark, too. Scratching may be:

• A signal to indicate a need to relieve himself
• An attention-seeking activity
• An attempt to reunite with a person or animal on the other side.

Solutions: If your puppy has recently relieved himself and is attention seeking, ignore him. When he stops, praise him and encourage him to do something else. If he asks to go out by scratching, train him to ring, or "target," a bell hanging from, or beside, the door instead. Targeting in this way involves teaching him to touch an item, or area, with a part of his body. It's widely used, particularly alongside clicker training (see page 184).

Ringing a bell is a clever way to signal to you that your puppy needs to go outside.

Target training

1 Teach your puppy to target your hand on cue, with a nose or paw. Hold a treat in your hand and wait for him to approach. The moment contact is made, praise and offer a treat from your other hand (or click and treat if you are using a clicker). Repeat until he approaches and touches your hand, no matter whether it's high, low, left or right.
2 Repeat this procedure until he knows that a touch brings rewards.
3 Add in your cue "Touch" as contact is made.
4 Hold your bell toy and encourage your puppy to "Touch." Reward him for correct responses and then repeat.
5 Start to say the cue "Bell touch" as your puppy approaches. After enough practice, you'll be able to just say "Bell" as the cue.
6 Encourage your puppy to touch the bell hanging from your hand and then place it against the wall or door.
7 Encourage increasingly harder touches, so that the bell alerts you.
8 Begin to request that your puppy rings before you open the door, so he learns that this gives him access to the yard.

Destructive behavior may stem from natural instincts and selective breeding or from boredom

Vocalizing

TARGET THE CAUSE TO SOLVE THE PROBLEM

Frequent barking can lead to neighborhood noise complaints. You must identify the cause and not just focus on punishing the action itself. Without determining why your puppy is so vocal, you are unlikely to resolve the problem. The Yorkshire Terrier, Miniature Schnauzer and West Highland White Terrier are among the breeds most likely to bark excessively.

Common barking triggers

- **Learned behavior:** Barking is often a demand for food or attention. If you respond, your puppy can quickly learn to bark persistently.
- **Excitement:** When an enthusiastic puppy is playing, or meeting people he loves, he can emit bursts of noise as he bounces around.
- **Anxiety:** Barking can be used as a "stay away" signal. These puppies typically bark at the thing that is causing concern while backing away or displaying other fearful posturing.

- **Social facilitation:** As a social animal, a puppy will quickly join in if others in his pack are barking, whether he knows the reason why or not.
- **Pack cohesion:** Canines will vocalize to keep their group together. A puppy left alone will howl or bark in order to communicate and reunite with his "missing" pack members. Usually there are noticeable pauses between barking sessions during which he listens for their response.

Barking can quickly become an unwanted habit if not addressed early on.

Types of vocalization

These range from an affectionate murmur (often directed at owners when greeting them) through to a whine (when a dog wants you to fulfill a need or wish), a pleading bark, a warning bark or aggressive bark, an attention-seeking bark, a low growl or a very deep intense growl, and a muted howl, ranging in intensity over several notes.

Solutions

- Address any fear issues your puppy may have that trigger the barking. Although this could take considerable time and patience, it will eventually be worthwhile.
- If you have several dogs, you must identify which one is triggering the noise. Control this dog and the rest are likely to improve.
- Work on any overattachment issues if your puppy barks when he is left alone.
- Always exercise him properly and provide plenty of stimulation at home.
- Distract him and then provide an alternative task to occupy him.

Managing the environment

You may have to change specific things in your home or your routine, so that your puppy has less opportunity to practice being noisy. For instance, this might involve moving your mailbox, preventing him from sitting in the window, or putting him away to calm down before greeting guests.

Verbal cues

It is useful to have a verbal cue that means "stop barking," such as "Quiet."
1 Trigger the bark yourself, perhaps by ringing the doorbell. Calmly wait for your puppy to pause.
2 Immediately say "Quiet" and reward him.

Lots of practice will be necessary before your puppy associates the verbal cue with silence. Once he has made the association you can begin to give the cue while he is barking.

Pheromone therapy

Puppies that are tense and unable to relax are more prone to vocal reactions. The calming effects from products using canine pheromone therapy can reduce anxiety-based barking.

What you should not do

Don't	Why?
Become agitated and shout	By shouting it may appear that you are joining in.
Smack or chase your puppy	An anxious barker will worsen; it risks creating extra problems.
Respond to noisy demands	Responding to your puppy's barks will make him more likely to demand this way again.
Use an antibark collar	Risks creating severe anxiety problems.

Make the effort to reinforce calm, quiet behavior rather than only reacting when your dog barks.

A house line will prevent your puppy from running around barking

Coprophagia
CONTROLLING THIS BEHAVIOR

The eating of feces evokes very strong reactions in most owners, but it is actually a relatively common behavior among canines. The mother consumes her puppies' feces, and young dogs will eat some during natural exploration. However, there are several reasons why it might continue occurring, even causing a puppy to become unwell.

Check with your vet

If the consumption of feces is becoming urgent and repeated, talk to your vet as this can be a sign of an underlying medical disorder, such as pancreatic problems (even borderline), intestinal infections and malabsorption problems.

Behavioral reasons

Reason	Signs
Normal exploration	Puppy may eat feces during play and investigation.
Attention seeking	Owners usually react when they see their puppy eating feces, and thus the behavior becomes a way of getting attention.
Appetitive behavior	If a puppy is hungry or not being fed often enough to satisfy his needs; it is suggested that overfeeding on high-fat foods can increase coprophagia.
Stimulation	Something about the actual consumption of the feces encourages the behavior, e.g., stimulation resulting from play.
Observation	A puppy may observe his mother eating feces or see his owner urgently picking it up – both actions may draw his attention to it.

Solutions

- Teach the "Leave it" command (see page 200), so you can easily stop your puppy from approaching and picking up the feces.
- Pick up all feces from the yard. Supervise your puppy while he is out relieving himself and distract him when he has finished (to prevent him from consuming his own feces). Once he is distracted or inside the house, remove all traces.
- Make sure that you feed your puppy a high-quality, easily digested diet.
- Satisfy his appetitive drive by placing his food inside an activity toy. This way it will take longer to consume it, using up time and energy.
- Applying an aversive substance onto the feces to deter your puppy from sniffing it can also be helpful. Pepper is commonly used, although you

Keep your yard area clean to reduce any chances of your puppy practicing the habit.

must be diligent when administering it. Ideally, only do this prior to a training session at which you intend to teach him to ignore feces (the "pretend doggy-do" kind is better for this purpose).
• Praise and reward him every time he ignores or walks away from the feces without eating it.

Shouting

Most owners shout and run at their puppy when they see him starting to eat feces. Unfortunately, this is usually counterproductive and only results in him gulping it down and running away. Instead, the best course of action is to take your time training your puppy and keep him on a long training leash when you're out in areas that are frequented by other dogs where the risk is high.

Deterrents

You can buy deterrents to solve this problem. Many commercial products are now available to add to your puppy's diet to make his feces less enticing. However, the results are varied since a puppy relies so little on his "taste" – scent is a far more powerful sense for him. The best results come from using a combination of different methods.

Diet additions

You might like to consider tackling this problem in a dietary way, although (as noted above) taste is not generally an important sense for most dogs and thus its effectiveness is questionable. Pineapple and grated zucchini may be helpful additions to your puppy's diet. They appear to reduce the appeal of feces for some dogs.

Be scrupulous about picking up feces – you can use a special long-handled scooper to make the job easier.

A puppy may observe his owner picking up feces and learn to show interest this way

Bad manners

REWARDING GOOD BEHAVIOR

Your puppy is not born knowing which behaviors humans like and which ones they dislike, so you must help him to learn this. Just as with more formal training, be prepared to reward reactions and decisions that you would like to encourage, and prevent him from making as many mistakes as possible. Remember that he will repeat any action he finds rewarding, so try to make the options you prefer most attractive to him.

Excitable puppies often struggle to contain themselves and they make regular mistakes, especially during training.

Jumping up

Unfortunately, puppies are often encouraged to jump up inadvertently as people bend over to greet them. Habits can form quickly, so it is confusing for your puppy when people suddenly change their minds and reprimand him. They do this when:

- He grows larger
- He is wet or muddy
- They are wearing nice clothes
- They are worried by dogs.

Solutions: As a family it is really important that you all work together to deal with this problem and encourage good manners in your puppy.

- Agree to turn away if your puppy jumps up and interact only when all four paws are on the floor
- Practice asking him to "Sit" before he is petted and ask guests to do this too
- Always be sure to praise him for not jumping up
- Avoid raising your voice or pushing him off as these reactions will excite him further
- Practice these new habits while out on walks.

Training tool: A house line is helpful as you can subtly prevent your puppy from leaping up by stepping on the line or holding it. This allows you to remain calm and avoids causing further excitement.

Caution! If your puppy tends to jump up at you in particular circumstances, such as when you are out walking beside traffic or when he is around new people, he may be unsure of himself and seeking comfort. Work on building his confidence and the jumping up should soon diminish.

Mounting

This embarrassing habit can come as a surprise since even very young puppies may do it during play. Many young dogs will mount when they are overexcited or even a little stressed – it is a normal activity designed to prepare a puppy for adult life. Mounting can be directed toward you, another pet, toward cushions, soft toys or his own bed.

When your puppy first mounts, it may make people laugh or get their attention but as he grows or the habit becomes more frequent, we become less tolerant, although there is still a big response. This pattern can lead to a learned behavior, which he performs whenever he wants you to focus on him – often when guests are visiting and are drawing your attention away from him.

Solutions

- Ignore all mounting attempts.
- Turn and walk away if necessary.
- The withdrawal of contact will reduce the attractiveness of mounting.

Adult instincts

As your puppy enters adolescence, mounting behavior can be triggered by his changing hormonal state. There is often a peak of activity during this time, which causes owners to worry.

Neutering can help to resolve sexually driven mounting behavior. However, after the initial peak in adolescence, it normally settles as long as care has been taken not to encourage it. Therefore, if you do not believe your puppy is ready for neutering it would be advisable to wait.

Turn away until your puppy calms down and offers a more desirable response and then be prepared to praise and reward his behavior.

Help your puppy to learn which behaviors are appropriate and acceptable

Getting up on furniture

BUILD GOOD HABITS EARLY ON

Inevitably, your puppy will seek out comfortable places to rest, and your sofas, armchairs and beds will appear extremely attractive to him. Building good habits from the start is the ideal scenario. Different members of the family are often unable to remain consistent in their approach, which causes confusion as well as problems in the future.

Supervision needed

If your puppy is left alone with uninhibited access to your furniture, you should not be surprised if you find him on it when you return. This type of training should be viewed in a similar way to housebreaking; without supervision, mistakes are likely.

Do...

• While he is still tiny, lift your puppy and carefully place him on the floor or in his own bed. Later on, lure him off the furniture if it's low. Once he's in the right place offer praise and rewards. This teaches him that being in his bed is preferable.

• Teach him to "Go to bed" (see page 199) on cue and always praise him for using his own bed.

• If you don't really mind him being on the furniture, use throws to protect it or encourage him to use only one particular chair or sofa. He will try to use the others initially, so repeatedly place him back where you want him to be. Remember that he only wants to be close by you.

• Prevent access to certain rooms while you are not present. Shut the door or use a child safety gate.

Take the time to encourage your puppy to use his bed as this will help to make it a more desirable resting place.

Don't...

The worst reaction is to shout and drag your puppy off. He will not understand why you are angry and he may become anxious when you approach him. This can lead to defensive aggression on furniture.

Caution! If your puppy displays any signs of aggression while he is on the furniture, expert advice should be sought. Many owners are bitten while they are trying to get their dog off a chair or sofa or attempting to sit on it beside them, and children are at risk since being on the furniture brings the puppy to face height. The earlier you seek professional help, the easier it will be to resolve the situation quickly.

Encourage your puppy off the sofa without scaring him or you could create an even worse problem.

Solutions

- Teach your puppy to sleep in his own bed.
- Invite him up if you wish, once he has matured and is housebroken.
- Teach him "Off" and reward him for complying.
- Ensure he is regularly wormed and treated with flea preventatives.

Sleeping on the bed

Owners often feel very guilty about allowing their puppy to sleep with them on their bed. There is no right or wrong decision about this, but each case should be considered carefully before you let bad habits develop in the future.

Sleeping on the bed is not directly associated with poor temperaments as was once advised, but dogs that do exhibit aggression, or have physical problems that cause them pain, are best kept off your bed as you will be in a particularly vulnerable position if they do react. Remember also that a small cute puppy may be a welcome visitor but if he grows into a large adult dog he will take up a lot of room and there will be less space for you.

Encouraging good habits

Give your puppy time to learn about sleeping in his own bed. Otherwise he may never be able to cope, causing problems if you want to go on vacation or your situation changes, such as if you meet a new partner who does not relish the prospect of sleeping next to a dog.

Make sure your puppy has a comfortable bed in a place where he can relax

Home alone

PREVENTING SEPARATION ANXIETY

All puppies should be taught how to cope by themselves when they are left alone. It is unreasonable to believe that your puppy will never be left on his own. Even owners who don't work or who are retired will need to leave their puppy sometimes, so the earlier this lesson begins the better.

Useful equipment

It's important that your puppy has plenty to occupy him during your absence. Activity toys stuffed with food are usually recommended because they are so interesting and draw his focus much better than his regular toys. Your aim is to build a positive association between being alone and the exciting entertainment you've left for him.

The lesson plan

1 It's helpful to introduce the activity toy before you begin leaving your puppy alone.
2 Start off in the room that is most familiar to him.
3 Once he is preoccupied with his toy, quietly step out of the room and close the door.
4 Go back into the room after just a few minutes' absence without making any fuss.
5 Repeat this exercise several times. Eventually end the lesson by taking your puppy out to do something else.
6 Accustom him to the signs that you are leaving, such as putting your coat on, and picking up your bag and keys. Prepare this way before you leave the room, and then, eventually, the house.

This useful lesson is best taught when your puppy is tired or has just been exercised.

Failure to cope: If your puppy becomes distressed, continue practicing but reduce the time he is left on his own until it's at a duration he can cope with.

Avoid alone time

Until your puppy can relax while he's alone, you should avoid leaving him. This may require taking a few days off work and the help of family, friends, neighbors or a professional puppy sitter to help you through the early weeks. Although he has constant supervision available, your helpers should also make a point of leaving him alone for a few minutes at a time, as per your lesson plan.

Don't leave the room until your puppy is engrossed in his toys, or he may wait at the door and whine until you return.

Departure routine

Don't leave your puppy in total silence – it's helpful to have some background noise. Turning on the radio is an easy option and will prevent the house from suddenly becoming very quiet for him.

Quiet goodbyes: You do your puppy no favours when you make a dramatic, noisy exit. Leaving quietly without fuss draws no attention to the fact that he is about to be left alone.

Calm hellos

You don't leap up and hug your family members every time you return to the room or come home after a quick trip to the shops, so there's no reason why you should respond in this way toward your

puppy. Instead, try to keep your arrival as low-key as possible – just come in quietly, get settled and then say hello to him.

Signs of a potential problem

- Your puppy is like your shadow, unable to let you leave the room without him.
- When he is left by himself, he vocalizes and scratches at the door.
- There is evidence of sweating, drooling, destruction and/or urination when you return.
- He chews, usually around the exit or a window.
- He is very happy to see you and the anxiety stops once you are there.

Provide a variety of interesting toys and chews to keep your puppy calm and occupied while you are out.

Daily practice is important and will allow you to build up the time your puppy is left alone

Neutering

CONSIDER YOUR OPTIONS

As your puppy gets older and embarks on adolescence, you may find that you are faced with increased challenges with regards to his behavior. At this age, he will be getting more confident and trying new responses, which make it appear (in the short term) as though your training has all come to nothing. It is at this stage that you may be advised to have your dog neutered in order to calm him down or to resolve some of his issues, but before you do, take a moment to consider whether castration or spaying is going to have the desired result.

Behavioral benefits of spaying

Female dogs tend to be neutered less often than males in an attempt to resolve behavioral issues. However, there are some areas of their behavior that are affected (see the table below).

Behavioral benefits of neutering

One of the most common reasons for castrating a young male dog is the hope that his behavior will become easier to manage. However, castration will only change behavior patterns that are influenced by testosterone, the male hormone. Even those behaviors that are positively influenced by castration may still occur to some degree, so it is not a "cure" for undesirable behaviors or a replacement for consistent training. Behaviors that will not be affected by neutering include:

• Destroying toys
• Separation anxiety
• Pulling on the leash
• Fear aggression
• High activity levels
• Predatory and chase behavior
• Territorial reactivity
• Barking.

Females

Behavior	Reasons
Inter-female aggression	Two or more non-neutered females can cause significant injury to one another. Spaying reduces the chances of this problem significantly although once a problem exists it is likely that further methods will also be required to resolve the issue.
Reduced likelihood of erratic mood changes	During a season, the hormonal fluctuations and cramping can cause a female to feel irritable and, therefore, more likely to respond aggressively or in an unusually anxious way.
Aggression toward male suitors	While in heat, your female will attract a great deal of unwanted male attention. This can be stressful for her and can result in aggressive responses.

A neutered male dog will be less inclined to urine mark as a response to the presence of other males and non-neutered females.

Males

Behavior	Reasons
Mounting	Sexually driven mounting will cease, although if another motivation exists, such as attention seeking, it will continue to occur.
Roaming	A non-neutered dog can detect a female in heat for miles and may go to great lengths to get to her. Studies have shown up to 90 percent reduction of this post-castration. This makes walking more relaxing and escape from home less likely.
Marking	Neutered males urine mark much less frequently than non-neutered males, unless the marking is caused by insecurity.
Inter-male competitive aggression	This has been shown to be reduced by castration in up to 60 percent of cases. Most appropriate where the problem is specifically directed only toward non-neutered males.
Frustration aggression	A male that is aroused by the scent of a female in heat may become irritable and frustrated. In some cases this causes reactive behavior when he is handled or toward other household pets. Neutering reduces this problem.

Affected behaviors

Some behaviors are likely to be affected by the removal of testosterone via castration (see above).

Neutering does not delete learned behavior, so an older dog with a long history of behaving in a certain way may continue to do so. Before deciding whether to neuter your dog, do your research and see your vet who can advise on the advantages and disadvantages as well as what it involves.

Seek professional help

If you are considering neutering your puppy as a way of solving a behavior problem, you need to ask your vet's advice and possibly consult a professional pet behaviorist before making your final decision. There may be other preferable options.

Fear-based problems

Castration can be a disadvantage for some young males with fear-based behavior problems. The problem, particularly fear aggression, can escalate in some cases. Seek professional advice before making any decision.

Neutering a male puppy can sometimes solve the problem of sexually driven mounting and aggressive behaviors but not if it is done too late.

9 DAILY CARE

Coat care
ENSURING TIP-TOP CONDITION

Looking after your puppy requires daily care and attention. This will help to keep him fit and well while maintaining a strong social bond. Although caring for him may take a lot of initial planning and preparation, the results are worthwhile when he remains healthy and friendly and can travel with you safely as part of your family. Your puppy has much denser hair than a human being because, compared to our single hair growing from each pore, he has a bundle of seven to 20 hairs. The hair and follicles are part of his outer skin layers and are therefore highly representative of his nutritional status.

Coat types
Many different coat types and variations exist, but the main divisions are into three types: short-haired, medium-haired and long-haired. These divisions

A clean, glossy coat is a sign of a healthy animal. The Cavalier King Charles Spaniel's long-haired coat requires regular grooming.

can be subdivided into smooth, rough, wiry and curly coats, which can be soft, medium or harsh. The different types of coat require special grooming and handling.

- **Short-haired dogs:** Their hair is usually smooth with a very fine undercoat, making it easy to care for and groom. All they need is a quick brush to get rid of any dead hairs and the occasional polish with a chamois leather.
- **Medium-haired dogs:** These dogs usually have a double coat and require grooming two or three times a week.
- **Long-haired dogs:** These coats need daily grooming to remove tangles and keep them in good condition.

Double coat: In this sort of coat, coarser primary, or "guard," hairs overlay a softer undercoat of secondary hairs. This coat provides warmth and waterproofing.

Single coat: In this type of coat, which lacks an undercoat, only the primary "guard" hairs are present. This is much cooler than a double coat.

Hair growth

During an active stage called anagen, a hair grows from a follicle, which, after a while, enters a dormant phase (catagen) in which it stops growing and is pulled out easily. Synchronization of the hair growth cycles involves often significant shedding at particular times of the year. Molting cycles depend on:

• The breed of dog
• His health and hormone status
• His age
• His living environment
• The day length.

Coat changes

Your puppy's coat is different from the one he will grow as an adult. All puppies grow softer and shorter hair initially. During adolescence, there may be a noticeable change in the balance between primary and secondary hair as well as a dramatic period of shedding. Your puppy may suddenly look scruffy and extra grooming is required to address

his "blown coat." Don't panic – this is entirely normal. With the appropriate attention and good nutrition, his coat will be in top condition again.

Hypoallergenic coats

If you're allergic to dog hair, you should choose a breed that's less likely to trigger a reaction. These breeds shed less but they can still cause a problem since most people react to the dander on the coat rather than the hair itself. Examples of breeds with hypoallergenic coats include the Labradoodle and Maltese.

Hairless breeds

If you opt for a hairless breed, you must use sun protection on your puppy's exposed skin. Ask your vet for advice. It is also important to limit contact with potential irritants. Examples of hairless breeds include the Chinese Crested and Mexican and Peruvian Hairless Dogs.

Grooming schedules

Coat length	Grooming schedule	Breed example
Short	Biweekly attention, other than during molting when daily attention is needed.*	Hungarian Vizsla
Medium	Weekly attention to remove knots and to prevent mats.*	Golden Retriever
Long	Daily attention to prevent mats and knots.	Lhasa Apso

* Even if your puppy does not require a full groom, a daily tidy up is important and will get him used to being groomed.

A short coat, such as that of a Staffordshire Bull Terrier, is easy to maintain but it does require regular attention to look at its best.

Common grooming tools

Type	Suitable for	Benefit
Bristle brush	Any coat type	Good for dirt removal and shine
Wire pin brush	Medium to long hair	Untangling and tidying up
Slicker brush	Longer and curly coats	For smoothing and detangling
Rubber brush and grooming mitt	Short coats and puppies	Dead hair removal and massage
De-shedding brush	Most coat types	Removes dead and loose hair
Shedding blade	Thick-coated, short-haired dogs	Strips out dead and loose hair
Combs	Medium to long hair	Useful to remove knots and tidy tail
Scissors and clippers	Medium and long hair	Removes and tidies hair
Rakes (undercoat)	Double-coated dogs	Removes dead hair from undercoat

Grooming your puppy

Your puppy should feel very comfortable in the place you choose to groom him, although you may select a room where hair can easily be swept up or vacuumed. A professional groomer is likely to use a grooming table but many owners prefer to do it on the floor at their dog's level or outside in the yard where it's easy to clean up afterward. If you are using a table, cover it with a nonslip mat or a towel and get your puppy accustomed to being up there before grooming begins.

- Start a grooming session when you have plenty of time to focus on your puppy.
- Spend time petting and talking to him first.

You will need...

- A rubber or puppy bristle brush will be all you need initially, as these are gentle and massage without scraping or tugging. When your puppy can tolerate a brush, a soft slicker will probably be appropriate. You can follow up with a comb to tidy up specific areas.
- Treats, a chew or toy for distraction and reward.

Caution! If your puppy becomes quite wriggly or mouthy, don't tell him off as he may be feeling anxious. Instead, slow your movements down and try to occupy him with a tempting chew.

Allow your puppy to get used to the grooming table and to the sensation of being handled.

Step-by-step guide to grooming

1 Before you start using a brush or grooming tools, get your puppy accustomed to you running your hands gently over his body.
2 Focus on your puppy's back to start with, as this is less sensitive than his face or legs.
3 Go slowly and gently as this will keep him calm and will minimize any mouthing.
4 Praise him often and always end the session after just a minute or two.
5 Build up the sessions every day by a few minutes.
6 Once he is very comfortable with you running the brush over his back, extend your attention to his tummy, head, tail and rear.
7 Always reward him as this is the best way to keep grooming sessions positive and enjoyable.
8 When he is comfortable with being groomed, practice going faster. This is very important if you want to use a grooming parlor in the future.

Additional techniques

Stripping: Some dog breeds, including many terriers, have a nonshedding coat, so the dead hair must be pulled out with a tool called a stripping knife or with your fingers. It should be painless if done correctly. Accustom your puppy to having his hair gently pulled in preparation.

Ear hair removal: Some breeds have hair in their inner ears, which, in order to keep the ear canal clean and healthy, need to be kept hair free. The hair in the canals can be pulled out. A puppy must get used to this treatment slowly.

Above: Routinely check inside your puppy's ears to identify any potential problems and thereby minimize their development.

Left: A regular comb-through will help to tease out knots or tangles that could become problematic and keep your dog's coat healthy and shiny.

Sensitivities vary, so always proceed at your puppy's pace

Bath time and nail care

MAKE THEM BOTH AN ENJOYABLE EXPERIENCE

Dogs don't require regular bathing. In fact, doing so causes the loss of natural oils and may even create coat and skin problems. It's helpful for a puppy to get accustomed to being bathed in preparation for the future, but as an adult he should need no more than two to three full baths per year. It's normally sufficient to target dirty parts, such as the feet.

Equipment

Get prepared before you start. You will need the following items to bathe your puppy:

- A shower basin, bath, sink or a large basin
- A nonslip mat
- A plastic jug or shower attachment
- Several old towels
- Puppy shampoo.

Step-by-step guide to bathing

1 Pour a few inches of warm water into the basin, sink or bath – it should not be too hot nor too cold. Always test it with your hand before placing your puppy in it.

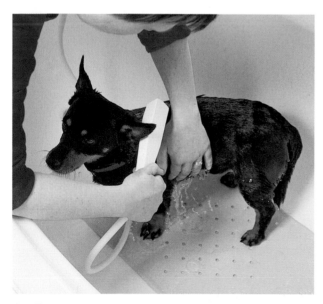

2 Wet your puppy's body all over, taking special care to avoid his face and ears.
3 Talk to him reassuringly and praise him for good behavior and staying calm, and periodically offer him treats.
4 Shampoo him, according to the manufacturer's directions on the container – always check. Be careful to avoid his eyes and ears.
5 Rinse off all the lather thoroughly and remove as much water as possible.
6 Lift your puppy out of the basin, sink or bath onto an old towel laid on the floor. Use another clean dry towel to dry him. Make sure the room is warm to prevent him from becoming cold.
7 Let him have a good shake. (Close the doors to other rooms to prevent him rubbing himself down on the carpets or sofas.)
8 Keep your puppy in the warm room until he has thoroughly dried.

Caution! Take care with antiparasitic shampoos. The chemicals must be administered in controlled amounts on a schedule; overdosing can be dangerous. Do not bathe your puppy too often or you will strip away his coat's natural oils. Once a month is sufficient, and some dogs only need bathing a couple of times a year.

Nail care

Your puppy's nails will grow continuously. If they are left untrimmed, they might curl under, making it

Use a nonslip rubber mat in the bath and take care not to get water and shampoo in your puppy's eyes and ears.

increasingly difficult for him to walk – an ingrown nail can cause pain and infection. While some dogs have little trouble with their nails, having the physique to wear them down while walking on hard ground, most need some attention. You may wish to cut the nails yourself or ask your groomer or vet to do it for you. Use guillotine, scissor-type or grinder nail clippers.

Step-by-step guide to clipping nails

Your puppy must learn to trust you handling his feet as it does not occur naturally between dogs.

1 Spend time touching and holding his feet during petting sessions.
2 Gently run your fingers between his toes to get him accustomed to the sensation.
3 When he is comfortable with paw handling, hold a paw so that the nails are in a position to cut.
4 Aim to cut only the tip of the nail, avoiding the inner quick, which can bleed profusely. Just trim small slivers off the tip if you are unsure.

Facial hair

Excess hair around the eyes may not only irritate your puppy but it can also prevent him from clearly seeing the world around him, increasing the chance of being startled. Tie any long hair back or consider clipping it off, so that he can see clearly.

The "quick"

The inner part of the nail, called the "quick," has a rich blood supply. It's visible through white nails and, sometimes, by looking at the underside of dark nails. Take care not to nick this area during clipping. The more often you trim your puppy's nails the better, as the "quick" can grow further down the nail if left for too long.

Clean matted hair and staining under the eyes with some moistened cotton balls or special eye wipes formulated for this purpose.

Eye care

Some dog breeds require daily cleaning of the eye area to prevent the buildup of matter and staining of the facial hair. Use a soft cotton pad to gently wipe the eye with clean water. Moist eye wipes are also available.

Get your puppy accustomed to being handled from an early age

Dental care

LOOKING AFTER YOUR PUPPY'S TEETH

Dental hygiene is an important but often neglected area of puppy care. Mouth examinations can be a struggle, but if your puppy gets used to this as part of his regular routine right from the beginning, it will be easier for both of you when you want to clean his teeth or examine him.

Your puppy's teeth

Your puppy will have 28 deciduous teeth (commonly known as milk or puppy teeth). They first appear at about 4 weeks and gradually start to fall out to make way for 42 permanent adult teeth, which appear at between 14 and 30 weeks.

Tooth care

Even though the milk teeth don't last for long, it's helpful for your puppy to become accustomed to you checking and cleaning his teeth in preparation for the future. This makes you aware of any wear,

damage or buildup of plaque or calculus before they become a problem. Periodontal disease can lead to tooth loss and even serious infection. The resulting pain can cause inadequate feeding and may impact negatively on your puppy's behavior.

Your puppy's tongue does a good job of cleaning the inner surfaces of his teeth, so you can focus most of your attention on the outsides.

Equipment

There are several different tools available to make it easier for you to clean your puppy's teeth.

- **Finger brush:** This is a rubber fingertip with soft bristles on it.
- **Baby toothbrush:** The bristles are soft enough for your puppy's tender gums.
- **Your finger wrapped in a cloth:** This method is accepted more easily by some puppies while they get used to the sensation.
- **Canine toothbrush:** This must always be angled for maximum contact with the teeth.

Check your puppy's teeth while he's relaxed during your normal petting sessions. Get him accustomed to having his mouth touched.

Canine toothpaste

Never use human toothpaste to clean your puppy's teeth as this could cause him to feel very unwell. Canine toothpaste is available, often in meat flavor, to make the experience more pleasurable. A gel product, distributed around the mouth by the saliva, will target problem areas. Ask your vet if you have any concerns.

Getting started

1 Every day, while you are petting your puppy, gently run your fingers over his muzzle and lift his lip to expose his teeth. Briefly rub your finger over his teeth and gums, then praise and reward him. practice on both sides. Gradually build up the time that the teeth are exposed.

2 Gently introduce the toothbrush and toothpaste and rub against his teeth at a 45-degree angle. Cleaning the molars (at the side) is often tolerated more than the incisors (at the front).

Teething

While he is teething, your puppy's mouth will feel sensitive. He may appear off his food at this time, although the chewing desire typically intensifies. To prevent him from damaging your possessions, make sure that he has constant access to a variety of different chew toys.

A canine toothbrush combined with a suitable cleaning paste or gel can help maintain tooth health if you use it regularly.

Dry foods

Feeding a dry diet can boost dental health as the abrasive action of the kibble helps to prevent some buildup of problem-causing tartar - a veterinary dental diet is designed to be particularly effective.

In combination with regular cleaning and annual veterinary checks, this will help you to keep your puppy's mouth fresh and healthy.

Chew toys promote good dental health by increasing the flow of saliva, flossing and removing food debris

Seek advice

If one of your puppy's adult teeth comes through but the correlated milk tooth is still present, you must seek advice and make an appointment to see your vet. Occasionally milk teeth need to be removed to prevent problems.

Your puppy's diet
ENCOURAGING GOOD FEEDING HABITS

Exactly when you feed your puppy will depend on your schedule and lifestyle. Since he should not be fed prior to walks, this is often a factor that influences feeding times. If you like routines, feed him at the exact same times daily. His internal body clock will soon learn the pattern, and he will begin to prepare for mealtimes as the clock ticks around. However, if you don't want a dog that insists on being fed the moment your regular evening TV show or news program ends, vary his mealtimes.

Monitor his intake

Monitor the amount you feed your puppy as he grows. The amount of calories he needs is very difficult to calculate accurately since his metabolism varies, depending on his age, reproductive status, size, amount of fatty tissue and activity levels.

How many calories?

Surprisingly, a small dog needs more calories in proportion to his size than a large dog.

Feeding guide

Puppy age	Energy requirement compared to a similar-weight adult dog
8 weeks – 4 months	Twice as much.
4 months – 7 months	1.6 times as much.
7 months – adult	1.2 times as much.

Considering costs

It can be tempting to select cheaper food brands, although the apparent savings can be deceptive. Premium brands of dog food appear more costly, but, since the quality of the products is higher, your puppy should find it easier to digest and, therefore, you will need to feed less than other apparently cheaper brands. Another bonus is that food that is easier to digest results in fewer stools, which can aid your housebreaking.

Avoiding problems

Traditionally, owners would claim ownership of food by taking the food bowl away repeatedly during meal times. Unfortunately, this puts a great deal of strain on a puppy. Imagine your irritation if your plate was pulled away as you tried to eat, especially if you were unsure about whether you would ever get to finish your meal. If one dog tries to take food from another there is often a confrontation, and this is something you want to avoid with your puppy. Try tossing in some extra kibble or a treat instead to build up positive associations and to reduce the likelihood of aggression.

Early feeding experience will influence how relaxed your puppy feels, and therefore how likely he is to develop food-related problems.

Using play to feed

Utilizing a puppy's natural instincts is a great way to provide stimulation. His ancestors had to work to get food by searching for prey – stalking, chasing, capturing, killing and dismembering it. Of course, your lucky puppy has food provided by you, but the basic instincts are retained. By adapting the way in which you feed him, you can provide stimulation in an easy, time-effective manner.

- Choose from one of the many food-dispensing or activity toys on the market and place a portion of his food inside, so he has to spend time rolling and pawing at it in order to eat.
- Initially, he might get a little frustrated since he hasn't yet learned what he has to do. Encourage him and, if possible, initially set the toy to the easiest setting.
- Once he understands the concept of being active to earn his food, he will be keen to play.
- Remember to deduct the food portion from his daily allowance.

Eating from a bowl may be convenient but provides little stimulation for a puppy – try putting his food in a dispenser so he has to work to get it .

If you like routines, feed your puppy at exactly the same times every day

Your puppy will learn to anticipate his mealtime if you follow a set routine. Teach him good manners, so he waits patiently for his food.

Eating habits

Different puppies' appetites will naturally vary. Some are happy to consume as much food as they are given, whereas others are more selective and take their daily intake over a longer period of time. There are also noticeable differences between the dietary habits of various breeds.

Picky puppy

Some puppies appear to eat only because they have to. Encourage your puppy to eat by:

• Warming up his meal slightly to increase its odor and interest
• Mixing a little wet food or some meat scraps into the food
• Feeding him in a quiet place away from the hustle and bustle where he feels relaxed
• Keeping your children or other pets away from him while he eats.

Worried owners can accidentally create fussy eating habits if they panic and offer alternative foods too quickly.

Always hungry puppy

All dogs should be able to self-regulate the amount of food they eat, but problems do sometimes occur, usually as a result of their lifestyle and commercial diets. Your puppy may overeat because:

• His diet is particularly palatable and contains calorie-rich food
• He has low amounts of exercise, an illness, a parasite burden or he is bored.
• He just needs some time to learn that food will arrive regularly.

Eating too quickly

If your puppy gulps his food down very quickly, he may swallow air, which can cause extreme discomfort. Rapid eating may occur if you feed him on wet meat or other highly palatable foods. If so, you should consider changing him to a dry diet, adding a little water to his kibble just as you serve them, or feeding him from a special bowl with mounds and grooves that are designed to prevent large mouthfuls of food from being eaten. Another reason for rapid eating may be social pressure from another household pet. In this case, make sure you feed the animals separately (different times or places) and try to address any problems occurring between the pets.

Consult your vet

If your puppy seems either too hungry or he has no appetite and his body condition has changed, you should always make an appointment to discuss the situation with your vet who can check him over, reassure you and give you further dietary advice.

Messy puppy

Like children when they are learning to eat, a puppy can create a great deal of mess. For this reason, the place where you choose to feed your dog should be easy to clean. If he grabs mouthfuls of food to take elsewhere to eat, you should reconsider where he is being fed. There may be something about the environment that is causing him to feel tense; perhaps he needs to stay close to you, or maybe he prefers to eat alone. Once you have identified the problem, you can try feeding him in an alternative place and can begin to slowly help him to adjust.

Ceramic feeding bowls are preferable to metal ones for some puppies that do not like reflective metal surfaces when they are eating.

Food guarding

You must not allow your puppy to snap or growl at you when he is eating. He needs to feel safe and to know that you will not remove the food before he finishes it. This is an extension of the lesson whereby young puppies learn that human hands provide nice experiences rather than taking them away. You may have to seek professional help if your puppy does guard his food aggressively.

Digging in the water bowl

This messy game can become a habit. It may be helpful to ensure that your puppy has lots of other activities to entertain him (things that he really likes doing, not just access to things you would like him to do) as well as other ways of staying cool, or try changing his bowl.

- Exchange a reflective metal water bowl for a plastic or ceramic one.
- Travel bowls and spaniel bowls are narrower, making digging and splashing more difficult.
- A raised water bowl stand can be helpful in some cases.

Resist offering your puppy more food if he already eats the recommended amount

Feeding checklist

By the time your puppy has settled into a feeding routine and any dietary problems have been addressed, he should show all the signs of being healthy. A nutritious diet is key to his mental as well as his physical health, and making the right choices is critical to his development. Here are some checklists, tips and guidelines to help you.

Food hygiene and safety

It is important to observe some basic and sensible hygiene and safety rules when feeding your puppy.

- Keep half-full cans of dog food covered in the fridge – remove and warm to room temperature before feeding.
- Make sure you clean his food and water bowls regularly.
- Don't use strong detergents – just hot water and a clean cloth.
- If your puppy is teething, he can easily destroy plastic food dishes.
- Ceramic food bowls can break and shatter, which can be dangerous.
- Stainless steel bowls are sturdy, unbreakable and teeth-resistant but more expensive.

What not to feed

- Reduce the risk of food poisoning by thoroughly cooking fresh meat (without adding salt) to kill bacteria.
- Watch out for small pieces of bone, especially brittle chicken and fish bones, as they can damage teeth and cause obstructions in the gut.
- If you feed bones, only offer raw marrow bones rather than cooked ones, which can splinter.
- Never feed your puppy human chocolate, onions, garlic, grapes or raisins as all these foods can be highly toxic for dogs.
- You may be a vegetarian but your puppy is not, and a meat-free diet is not recommended. Dogs are natural carnivores, and a meat-free diet can lead to nutritional deficiencies.

Raw diets

Nowadays some canine nutritionists recommend a raw food diet as it has no preservatives and it is closer to a dog's natural diet. Only use good-quality raw meat from a well-respected source. Initially, introduce only one protein source at a time. Feed chicken for a week, then beef for a week, and so on, to introduce these foods gradually to your puppy's system. Once all the foods have been introduced, you can vary the meat daily. Here are some foods you can feed:

Chicken	Whole or any parts (backs, necks, wings, etc.).
Turkey	Whole or any parts (wings, necks, etc.).
Beef	Any cuts as well as oxtail.
Pork	Neck, ribs and any cuts.
Rabbit	Dogs love this.
Organ meats	Liver and kidney are nutritious but quite rich and may upset some dogs' digestive systems, so never make them more than 10 percent of your puppy's total diet.
Fish	Oily and white fish.
Vegetables	Most vegetables are suitable but avoid garlic and onions, which can be toxic to dogs.

Where to feed your puppy

- Place his food bowl in a quiet place away from the hustle and bustle.
- Choose a surface that can be cleaned easily: a tiled floor or feeding mat.
- Prevent children from teasing or playing with the puppy while he is eating.
- If you have other dogs, feed them separately to avoid any bullying and fighting.

Top feeding tips

- Clean, fresh water should always be available.
- If you feed your puppy a dry food diet, offer him plenty of water.
- If your puppy eats wet food (canned) he will require less water.
- Never refill half-empty bowls – discard uneaten food and wash the bowls thoroughly.
- Provide fresh food at every meal, especially in hot weather.
- Don't feed table scraps, which can upset the balance of nutrients provided by commercially prepared dog foods and encourage begging.
- Use treats to reward good behavior and bond with your dog, but only healthy or specially-formulated dog ones.
- Avoid any sudden change in your puppy's diet. Introduce new foods gradually, increasing them slowly over a number of days.
- Follow the same guidelines when you are switching from one brand to another – any sudden change may upset your puppy's digestive system.
- Don't worry about lack of variety in your dog's diet – puppies are happy to eat the same food every day, so ensure that it is good quality and well balanced nutritionally.

Your puppy needs a balanced diet with nutrients from different sources

Prevent food aggression by occasionally lifting your puppy's bowl when he is eating and adding a few tasty treats – return it to him immediately.

Exercise and fitness

KEEPING YOUR PUPPY FIT AND HEALTHY

Regular exercise is an important part of every dog's life. However, your puppy's immature body needs time to grow and develop without the stress and impact that heavy exercise may cause to his joints. Just as some physical activity is not appropriate for children, some things are best avoided until your puppy has grown to his full adult size.

How much exercise?

It's not possible to state exactly how much exercise is safe for a puppy because different breeds will require and cope with various amounts. The concern arises from the fact that his bones are not at full strength during his first year, and any hard wear and tear could cause physical problems. A rough guide is to walk 5 minutes per month of age, twice a day. However, variable needs mean that it's probably sensible to start with these short walks and then, if your vet is happy, to increase the length of your walks very gradually. Your exercise routine should be tailored to suit your puppy's breed, age and physical health.

Benefits of different activities

Activity	Benefits
Walks on flat grass and pavement	Builds your puppy's strength and stamina, burns energy and allows socialization while minimizing stress to his bones and joints.
Controlled walks on a leash	Continues to steadily build strength while he encounters new areas.
Off leash on flat grassy areas	Energy release and socialization without excessive strain on joints.
Off leash on rough ground	Opens up new locations for puppy walks and exploration – often more interesting areas.

Leash work on flat areas combined with shorter off-leash sessions is a safe way to begin teaching your puppy to walk nicely at your side.

Steps

Always take care and carry your puppy up and down steps while he is small. However, as he grows and gets heavier, this may become dangerous for you. Minimize the risk of falling by keeping him on his leash and make sure he goes slowly and steadily.

A sensible approach

The fear of physical injury causes some owners to excuse themselves from walking their puppy or from socializing him during the early months. Missing out on early socialization is likely to cause behavior problems, so make an effort not to do this. Staying at home to play in the yard is not an acceptable alternative. If you have any concerns, discuss them with your vet, who will be able to advise you on the best course of action for your puppy.

Your puppy's needs

Although particular breeds have specific exercise requirements, variances create particularly low-energy or high-energy individuals. Long walks are not the only way to tire a dog – mental exercise is also very important. A combination of physical and mental stimulation is needed to satisfy most dogs. Too much exercise can overtire a puppy and cause behavioral changes. Whereas some puppies will become naturally sleepy, others get hyperactive, appearing "naughty" and unable to relax. These puppies do not necessarily need increased exercise and will often respond well to focused training and lessons to encourage them to settle quietly.

Even small breeds of dog, like this Cavalier King Charles Spaniel, need regular exercise and will enjoy free running as well as leash walking.

Bloat

A painful and potentially fatal condition called bloat can affect dogs, particularly the larger breeds. You should always avoid exercising your puppy just after he has eaten a meal, and do not feed him immediately after exercise.

Multiple dogs

You wouldn't expect a small child to walk as far as you, so don't expect your puppy to walk the same distances as an adult dog. If you have more than one dog, be prepared to walk them separately and limit the time your puppy spends playing with larger, boisterous dogs to a few minutes at a time in order to minimize bumps and jars to his body.

Giant-breed puppies will require less exercise than smaller ones - ask your vet for advice

Games and play

HAVE FUN WITH YOUR PUPPY

Every day your puppy will wake up full of energy and raring to go but, depending on your lifestyle and commitments, some days you will have more time to spend playing with him than others. Even if you only have a short time free for play after you have fulfilled all his other needs, you can still occupy him in so many ways and find something to keep him busy and interested, both physically and mentally.

Fun while you're busy at home

Provide your puppy with activities to keep him out of trouble when you're busy doing other things.

- Fill a cardboard box with shredded paper and some larger treats for your puppy to find.
- Scatter some kibble on the floor or grass, so he has to search and sniff to find each piece.
- Fill different shapes of activity toys and let him play and work out how to remove the food.

Even a plastic water bottle can be used as a plaything for a puppy. He will enjoy chasing it, jumping on it and chewing it.

Interactive games

Puppies love playing social games. You can play together while you're alone or with your family – inside the house or outside in the yard.

Fetch!

Although we traditionally think of a dog retrieving a toy as the most natural game, not all puppies will do this without a little help and training from you.

1 Get your puppy interested in a toy, then roll or toss it a short distance away.
2 As he runs forward and grabs the toy, praise him enthusiastically and say "Fetch, good boy!" in an excited way to encourage him to want to come close to you again.
3 When he gets close to you, don't grab the toy from his mouth. Pet and praise him for returning. Then bring a treat out in one hand and show it to him, while gently cupping the toy with your other hand. He will let go in order to take the treat, and therefore will be rewarded for releasing it.
4 As he gets the hang of this fun game you can throw the toy further and he will be able to reliably return it to you.
5 Eventually the game itself will reward your puppy for returning the toy, so you can phase out the stage where you trade it for a treat.

Playing games with your puppy will be rewarding and fun for both of you

Step-by-step "Fetch"

1 Get your puppy interested in one of his favorite toys, then throw it and encourage him to chase after it and "Fetch!"

2 Ensure that your body language is welcoming as your puppy gets close to encourage him to approach you.

3 Don't grab the toy off your puppy – instead, praise him and trade it immediately for a tasty treat to encourage him to release it.

Performing tricks

Most owners enjoy teaching their puppy a range of actions beyond the basic obedience commands. More advanced obedience is wonderful in itself, but if you have the time, it can be great fun to teach your puppy some tricks. A trick should never be demeaning or risk hurting him. If it is taught with fair and rewarding techniques, it can be useful as a basic command.

Some common examples of puppy tricks: These include simple actions, such as shaking paws, high fives, rolling over and twirling around.

Roll over!

1 Place your puppy in a "Down" (see page 192). Hold a treat close to his nose, then slowly move it toward his shoulder, so he has to turn his head to follow it. Release the treat.
2 Repeat, luring him further around each time until he rolls onto his back.
3 You can divide the movement up into smaller parts if necessary but always take care to reward any improvements.
4 Begin to say "Roll" or "Over" as he performs the movement. With practice, he should be able to respond when he hears this verbal cue.

Problem solver

If your puppy does a celebratory lap of the yard after picking up a toy, resist chasing him to get it.

- Instead, run in the opposite direction as this will encourage your puppy to run with you, rather than running away from you.
- Play with a second toy as this will tempt him to come close, especially if he is not particularly interested in treats.
- Crouch down and turn away from your puppy if you suspect that he lacks the confidence to approach directly.

Keeping your dog safe

YOUR RESPONSIBILITY AS AN OWNER

Protecting your puppy is obviously your priority and there are some very easy ways whereby you can minimize any day-to-day risks. For example, making sure that he can be identified increases the chances that he will be returned to you if he should go missing.

Collar and tag

You are legally obliged to ensure that your puppy wears a collar and identification tag. The tag should include your name and address. A telephone number is particularly helpful if your puppy goes missing and is subsequently found.

Microchipping

This permanent method of identification is likely to become compulsory for all dogs. The microchip is a tiny, rice-sized electronic device that is inserted via a sharp, sterile needle. It is positioned under the skin between the shoulder blades during a simple procedure that takes just seconds and is hardly noticed by most puppies. The microchip contains a unique code, which is linked to your contact details in a national database. It can be read by a special scanner, making it easier for you to be contacted and reunited with your dog if he gets lost. Scanners are held by most veterinary clinics, local authorities, dog pounds, rescue centers and the police. Although it is more reliable, a microchip is not a substitute for a collar and ID tag, which must always be worn. If you move to a new house or change your contact details, you must inform your microchip company.

Microchipping is a simple and painless procedure: a microchip is injected into your dog's skin by your breeder or vet.

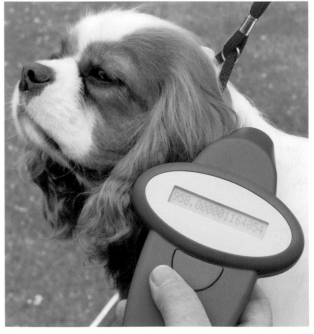

A scanner can be passed over the dog's shoulders during routine health checks to make sure that the microchip is working.

Use a leash by roads

Not having to use a leash while walking your puppy is sometimes seen as a sign of a well-trained pet. However, all puppies and adult dogs can make mistakes, no matter how well trained they appear to be. And just one mistake may cause your puppy to run across the road while chasing a cat or to greet a dog or person. Many dogs are killed in this way every day – as well as causing traffic accidents.

Legally, your puppy must always be under your control and this means using a leash by public roads. Teach him to walk nicely on his leash (see page 196) and to be sociable, and he is sure to receive admiration for his good behavior.

Never assume that your puppy has "road sense." Always keep him on a leash and desensitize him initially to the noise of passing traffic.

Photo ID

If you are ever traveling away from home, it is useful to carry a clear photograph of your puppy, plus ones of any unique identifying markings. This will make it much faster and easier for people to search for him if he should go missing.

Home security

It's extremely important that you keep your puppy safe at all times. Having a secure yard is essential, not only to prevent him from roaming but also, unfortunately, to prevent theft. Avoid leaving him outside in the yard unsupervised for long periods,

and make sure that gates are locked securely from the inside. Always close the front door and gate behind you.

If your puppy goes missing...

You should immediately telephone the following:
- Your local dog pound
- Local rescue centers
- Local veterinary clinics
- Your microchip and insurance companies.

Recall training

You can reduce the chances of your puppy getting lost by taking the time to teach him to return when you call (see page 194). During adolescence, recall training often fails, so you must work extremely hard at reinforcing this lesson while using a long line, especially in areas of high distraction or where your puppy is likely to go out of sight.

Your puppy should wear a collar
and ID tag at all times

Traveling with your puppy

MAKING CAR TRAVEL STRESS-FREE

Most dogs will travel in a car sometimes with their owners, whether it's on short trips to the local park or the vet, or longer trips to holiday destinations. Wherever you are going, always plan ahead to help your puppy feel relaxed while he travels. A puppy that can travel well is far more likely to be taken to new and exciting places – one-third of owners would include their dog more on trips if he were a better traveler.

Stay safe

There are many different ways to keep your puppy safe in the car while you are traveling. He must never be free to move around at will.

Restraint: This is important as a loose puppy can cause a distraction, and during an accident is likely to be flung forward, injuring or killing himself and hurting you or your passengers. He is more likely to escape from a damaged car, too. The range of safety methods you can use include the following:

- Pet seatbelt/car harness
- Car travel crate/kennel
- Wire guards.

A car travel crate will keep your puppy safe and comfortable if it is equipped with a blanket or fleece for him to lie on and some toys or chews.

Comfort: This is also an important consideration and you should think about the different options when you are planning to transport your puppy.

- Window mesh allows air in while keeping the puppy's head and body inside the car.
- Access to water – a thermos will keep a supply cool for your puppy.
- Avoid unnecessary journeys with your dog when the weather is either very hot or cold.
- Avoid smoking in the car.

Signs of stress or motion sickness

Many puppies are unwell during their first journey by car, and some continue to dislike the experience. Always look out for the following signs:

- Panting and/or trembling
- Leaping around
- Failure to settle
- Barking
- Drooling excessively
- Vomiting or retching
- Repeated swallowing
- Relieving himself.

Good habits

You can actively encourage good habits and stress-free car travel by going on short trips around your neighborhood as often as possible during your puppy's early months. Get him accustomed to wearing a car harness or being crated inside the house, separately from the car.

Resolving problems

If your puppy has an intense fear reaction or shows signs of anxiety before and during car travel, you must address this as soon as possible.

- Never force him into the car. He will relax more quickly if you can avoid any journeys until some progress has been made with his training. (However, avoidance combined with no training at all will have negative consequences.)
- Fill a pouch with some small and tasty treats. Clip your puppy's leash on to his collar and walk toward your car. Be enthusiastic while offering him rewards.
- Walk up to and around the car and practice his "Sit," offering rewards all the while to encourage positive associations with the car. After a couple of minutes, stop offering him treats and walk back into the house.
- Repeat until he shows no sign of reluctance.
- Open the car door and encourage him inside. Reward him immediately.
- Sit in the front seat and offer praise and tidbits to your puppy.
- When he has relaxed, sit in the car with the engine running until he settles.
- When you start to move the car, begin with short journeys. Praise and continue rewarding.
- Giving your puppy a toy stuffed with food just before you set off is a useful distraction.

Never allow your dog to move around unrestrained in the car – secure a wire guard behind the back seat or use a car crate or pet seatbelt.

Travel to fun places – the park, or woods – rather than just the vet's office

Traveling longer distances

If you intend to cover long distances with your puppy, ensure that you are prepared and have planned for regular rest breaks to allow him to relieve himself and to eat and drink.

Going by public transportation

Dogs can travel on certain buses, trains, ferries and airplanes. If your lifestyle will involve bus or train rides, begin as early as possible and expose him to these types of environments gradually. If you are unsure whether or not he will be allowed to travel with you, contact the company beforehand.

Be prepared

Let your puppy become familiar with the crate or container he will be transported in. Check that he has room to move around, lie flat and stand up. This will improve his comfort and ability to relax, making the journey much less stressful for him.

Public transportation

Buses and trains	Travel is often at the discretion of the driver although you are more likely to have a problem during rush hour. A friendly, well-trained dog is most likely to be welcomed although he must never be allowed on a seat and must not get in the way of other passengers.
Ferries	Your puppy is likely to have to remain in your car at all times. Depending upon the journey you may be allowed to check on him. Ensure that he is safely confined throughout and has access to water and air, and will not overheat.
By air	You must check with your intended airline to find out their exact policy on shipping a dog. Your puppy will need to feel happy spending time in an approved crate. Tiny puppies may be allowed to travel with you in a carrier while larger ones will be placed either with other "excess baggage" items or as cargo. This form of travel can be intensive due to the noise, isolation and duration so consider your puppy's age, personality and prior experience before making your reservation.

A special seatbelt/car harness is an excellent way to restrain your puppy when he is traveling in your car and will prevent him from jumping around.

Avoiding heatstroke

During warm weather never leave your puppy inside the car, even if the window is open a crack. A car heats up very quickly, more than doubling its temperature within an hour on a hot day, and a sunshade or even a bowl of water will not keep him sufficiently cool. If he overheats, he will lose the ability to control his internal body temperature and will become distressed and pant rapidly. In just a short space of time a dog can go into a coma and die, so don't take any chances. Instead of leaving your puppy in the car, you could do the following:

• When you stop for a break at a rest station, take turns to go inside rather than leave your puppy locked inside the car. Give him some water and let him out for a short walk and to relieve himself.
• Picnic outside together or eat inside the car.

Some travel may require special documentation. Discuss this with your vet who can advise you on the correct and current protocol. Be aware that it can take time to make proper arrangements and you must plan ahead and allow several months for this.

Your vet can advise you of recommended treatments required before you travel.

Health issues for traveling dogs

Talk to your vet about medicinal help for motion sickness before planning long journeys or taking public transportation. Your puppy must be fully vaccinated and treated for parasites before you leave home – the risk of disease may be greater in other areas and it is important that he is parasite-free before traveling. The treatment should continue when you return home to keep him healthy. Tell your vet where you will be traveling as there may be particular risks that are not covered by your usual treatment choices.

Ticks	May carry Lyme disease or *babesiosis* parasite.
Mosquitos	Risk of heartworm.
Sandflies	Spread the *Leishmania* parasite.

Checklist for the trip

- Feed your puppy a light meal a few hours before traveling to quell hunger.
- Take him out to relieve himself before you depart.
- Give him access to water and a small amount of food during the journey.
- Place a familiar-smelling blanket or a toy in his container to help him relax.
- Double-check that you have all his relevant paperwork safely with you.

Before you set off on a road trip with your puppy, check that your automobile association will transport him, too

Vacations with your puppy

MAKING THE EXPERIENCE STRESS-FREE

If you decide to take your puppy on vacation with you, it is essential that you plan it carefully to choose the appropriate accommodation and transportation and what to do in case of emergencies. Taking him with you is a wonderful experience for you both, but he must be friendly, housebroken and well behaved, so you can relax together in public places.

Choosing a vacation

Choices of vacations with your pet can be almost as diverse as those without a dog. Depending on your available time, personal preferences and budget, you can take a vacation in a tent, an RV or motorhome, a cottage, or even stay in a bed-and-breakfast or dog-friendly hotel.

Check first: Never assume that your puppy will be accepted – always check first. Some establishments won't allow puppies in bedrooms, while others have limitations regarding the rest of their facilities. Some hotels will charge extra for a puppy.

Considerations: Be sensible and choose a vacation that you both can manage. It would be unwise to travel to another state or province before your puppy has experienced car travel at home. If his house training is still problematic, don't book into a nice hotel, cottage or apartment. Before booking check the following:

- Are ground floor rooms available?
- Where will he relieve himself and walk?
- Can he stay in your room while you have meals in the hotel or go out to eat?

Packing for your puppy

You will require an extra bag to accommodate all your puppy's essential items as well as a few useful extras. Here's a handy list for you to check off.

Essentials

- Your puppy's own bed as it's familiar and comforting.
- A selection of his favorite toys and perhaps some new ones to keep him occupied.
- Puppy food – buying food may be possible but pack enough for your trip.
- Food and water bowls.
- A large water bottle.
- Puppy pads and bags for picking up feces.
- First-aid kit and any medications.
- Towels for cleaning and drying your puppy.

Your puppy will love play time on the beach, but check in advance since many beaches are dog-free during peak seasons.

Always carry a clear photograph of your puppy (in case he gets lost) and make sure he wears an ID tag engraved with your contact details.

- Sunshades, sunscreen and car fans.
- Dog coat for colder camping trips and rainy days.
- ID tag with your cell or vacation contact details.
- A backpack or similar bag to carry your puppy's essentials on day trips.

Useful extras

- Can opener for canned food.
- Tick remover.
- Stain remover.
- Cloths and paper towels.
- Protective sheets for furniture.
- Hair remover roller.
- Extra leash and collar.
- Long line and ground peg.

Documentation

While you are traveling with your puppy internationally, all the documentation relating to him (his vaccinations, etc.) should be kept together and carried safely with you at all times just in case the authorities request that you produce it.

Safety first

In unfamiliar locations, keep your puppy on his leash until you know the area is free of hazards and are confident that his recall is reliable.

- **Veterinary care:** Look up details of veterinary clinics close to your vacation destination in case your puppy becomes ill or injured. Check your insurance coverage.
- **Water:** In hot weather he must stay hydrated. Water is essential for survival and is lost through panting and sweating as well as most biological processes. Take a supply everywhere and carry a travel bowl for regular drinks.
- **Beaches:** Be careful on beaches where the tidal activity is unknown to you. Afterward, carefully rinse off sand and salt water from your puppy's coat to avoid skin irritations.

Vacations on your own

ARRANGING FOR YOUR PUPPY'S CARE

Leaving your puppy can cause anxiety because his early months and experiences are so important. Whether you go away just overnight or for several weeks, it is essential that you have confidence in the caregiver who is responsible for looking after him.

Potential options

- Family member, friend or neighbor.
- Professional home boarder/pet sitter.
- Boarding kennels.
- Your puppy's breeder.
- Veterinary clinic.

Family member, friend or neighbor

This person is likely to be familiar to your puppy and a less expensive option. They may have to find time for him and should puppy-proof their home and yard unless they move into your home.

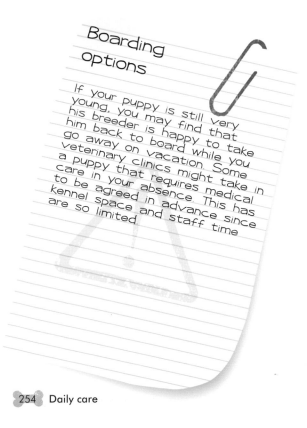

Boarding options

If your puppy is still very young, you may find that his breeder is happy to take him back to board while you go away on vacation. Some veterinary clinics might take in a puppy that requires medical care in your absence. This has to be agreed in advance since kennel space and staff time are so limited.

Professional home boarder/pet sitter

There are professionals who can either stay in your home or take your puppy into theirs during your absence. Your choice will be influenced by availability, budget and the age and temperament of your puppy. Plan the arrangements in advance and seek recommendations. Meet with prospective sitters to assess their suitability. They should:

- Be friendly toward you and your puppy
- Be knowledgeable about puppy care and health
- Have time to care for your puppy properly
- Meet with you in advance to discuss all your requirements in detail
- Provide references and a police check report
- Hold professional insurance
- Be able to administer any medications that have been prescribed by your vet.

Boarding kennels

This is a common choice due to availability and cost, although the quality of kennels varies. Take the time to ensure that your puppy spends his holiday in a comfortable and caring environment. A noisy kennel where he feels isolated or encounters an aggressive dog could trigger problems that you will have to deal with on your return. Check that:

- The staff are friendly and not overstretched
- They are knowledgeable about specific puppy care and behavior
- The kennels are clean and well-maintained
- You are free to look around
- The kennels are not excessively noisy
- Your puppy's kennel is spacious with a choice of inner chamber and separate run

Vaccinations

To stay in boarding kennels, your puppy must have completed his vaccinations and will also require the kennel cough vaccine. He will need certification to this effect from your vet. There is also usually a minimum age of acceptance.

Checklist for leaving your puppy

- A plentiful supply of food, measuring cup and clear written instructions.
- Vaccination certificate, relevant health records and written consent for veterinary treatment.
- Full contact details of your veterinary clinic.
- A familiar blanket from your puppy's bed.
- Several toys and safe chews.
- Grooming equipment.
- A list of medications and clear instructions.
- An ID tag with the contact number of the temporary caregiver.
- A leash, collar and other equipment.

- The staff follow a strict health and safety policy
- Your puppy will be exercised appropriately
- He will not mix with any unknown dogs without your permission
- The staff will adhere strictly to your diet plan.

Caution! Try an overnight stay first to get your puppy used to the environment.

Some breeders are able to welcome a puppy back while you are away on vacation – check with your breeder if this is an option.

Professional pet sitters can come to your home to provide care and company for your puppy during your absence.

Examining your puppy

IDENTIFYING POTENTIAL HEALTH PROBLEMS

Throughout his life, your dog will rely on you to watch out for telltale signs of physical problems. If you get into good routines right from the start, you will be more likely to notice any changes before they become a real problem. Early intervention almost always makes treatment easier, so your attention and regular examinations are worthwhile. By getting into the habit of checking your puppy daily, during routine grooming and petting sessions, you will become very familiar with his body.

Body
While stroking your puppy, run your hands over him, feeling for lumps, swellings, cysts or scratches. Assess whether he is gaining or losing weight.

Skin and coat
Their condition is often a reflection of a puppy's underlying health. They should be free from:

- Signs of dryness
- Excess oils
- Sores or cuts
- Rashes
- Dirt
- Grass seeds
- Parasites.

His coat should be shiny and clean with no bare patches or mats. It's normal for it to change as he matures, but if grooming does not improve it, or you are concerned, seek veterinary advice.

Mouth
When examining your puppy's mouth, look for sore areas or growths on the soft tissues. Healthy gums are pink or black if pigmented. If you notice redness around the teeth, bleeding, or the gums are very pale, always seek professional advice from your vet. Tooth damage will require urgent attention as does:

- Unexplained drooling
- Unpleasant breath
- Yellowish tartar along the gum line
- Unwillingness to eat
- Coughing or retching.

Your puppy's teeth should be clean and the gums free from any redness or inflammation.

Nose

A healthy puppy's nose is wet to maximize his olfactory ability – a dry nose may indicate a problem. The nose should be free from discharge and he should not sneeze repeatedly or scratch it.

Eyes

Your puppy's eyes should be bright and clear with no signs of any discharge (see below).

Ears

Puppy ears can be vulnerable to problems. Seek advice if you notice any of the following:

- An unwillingness to be touched on or around the ear area
- Redness or inflammation
- Odor
- Discharge or wax
- Unusual heat in the area

Healthy eyes

Area of eye	Sign of health
White area	Free from redness or yellowing
Pupils	Free from cloudiness or discoloration
	Should adapt well to changing light
	Both eyes should appear similar
Eyelids	Free from entropion (inward rolling of the eyelid)
	Free from ectropion (outward rolling of the eyelid)
	Able to blink freely without eye irritation
	Free from growths
	Not watery

Note: Some breeds, such as Pugs, experience a little discharge or watering from the eye, but a sudden change, or heavy discharge, should be checked out urgently.

- Repeated shaking of the head
- Rubbing or pawing at the ear
- Swelling of the ear flap
- The head being held to the side.

Grass seeds

After walking in fields or long grass, check your puppy over for grass seeds. They can penetrate his body, causing pain and infection, and may require surgery. Vulnerable areas include the ears, eyes, nose and between the toes. They can also pierce the skin, and small seeds can be inhaled. Some dog breeds, particularly Spaniels, are susceptible to grass and hay seeds becoming embedded in the pads of their feet.

An enjoyable walk in the countryside can involve unexpected irritations, so check for errant grass seeds, thorns or other debris upon your return.

Nails

The nails should not be split, brittle or bleeding. Check the dew claws as they can quickly grow too long and curl back on themselves or become caught. Nails can get torn and will require removal by your vet, followed by a course of antibiotics.

The inner quick is clearly visible through white nails but is less easy to discern in dark ones. Take care when cutting your puppy's nails to ensure that you do not cut into the quick, which can bleed profusely.

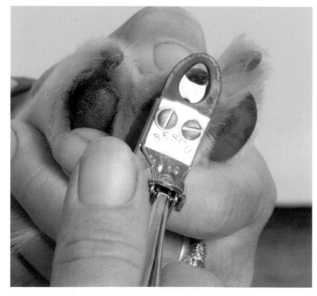

Use a special pair of nail clippers to keep your puppy's nails trimmed and short. They should end level with the pad and not be too long.

Toes and pads

The pads on your puppy's feet are important and when problems occur they can negatively impact on the way he moves. Examine them regularly and look for signs of licking his paws excessively, chewing, limping or refusing to bear weight. Healthy pads act as shock absorbers for energetic maneuvres and they are relatively tough. However, they can get injured and therefore you should check them on a regular basis for the following:

- Cuts
- Cracks
- Scratches
- Splinters
- Grass seeds, thorns and burrs
- Stings
- Swelling
- Hot spots
- Burns or blisters (from hot pavement).

Examine between the toes to check they are free from trapped hay or grass seeds, stones, matted hair, burrs, sand, ice, stings and parasites.

Limbs

Gently run your hands down your puppy's legs and feel carefully for any signs of swelling, hot areas, scratches, cuts or growths.

Anus and anal glands

Check your puppy's bottom and observe him when he is relieving himself, so you can respond quickly to any abnormal signs. Most common problems involve the anal glands, which are positioned on either side of the anus. When these fail to empty properly, infection can set in. Look out for the following:

- Your puppy dragging his bottom on the ground
- Chewing at his bottom, base of his tail or surrounding areas
- Straining to pass feces
- A foul odor
- Sensitivity around the bottom areas
- Swellings
- Discharge
- Bleeding
- A hole near the anus.

Blocked glands: These can be emptied by your vet, or you can do it yourself. Your vet will show you how to perform this task. Regular emptying may be required for some breeds and certain individuals. Another problem is parasitic worms (they often appear as tiny, white rice-shaped flecks) around the anus and on the surrounding coat.

Testicular or mammary lumps

This examination is mainly to get into good practice since problems with young puppies are not particularly frequent. However, some male puppies do experience an undescended testicle. This is not particularly uncommon in very young puppies and will be noted by your vet during his routine checks. As your puppy approaches adolescence, pay attention to whether the testicle can be felt within the scrotum as he may require surgery to remain healthy. Signs of testicular problems include significant disparages in the size and shape of the testes, hard lumps, cysts, redness, swelling or signs of pain.

A female puppy has, on average, 10 mammary glands between her chest and groin. Get into the habit of running your hands down either side of her body to feel for lumps or masses. It is important that any changes are reported to your vet as soon as possible.

Don't panic!

Changes to the mammary area during a season, pregnancy, false pregnancy or raising puppies are normal. Ask your vet if you are unsure.

While you're sitting quietly with your dog, take the opportunity to check his paws, especially the nails and between the toes.

Examinations can be relaxed and under the guise of offering fuss and attention.

Physical development

HOW YOUR PUPPY GROWS

When your puppy was born it would have been difficult to confidently determine to which breed he belonged – all puppies look incredibly similar during the early days. Over the following months, however, they change significantly as their varying genetics orchestrate differences in development, allowing them to gradually take on their adult form.

Growth stages of a puppy

Months	Type of growth
0–1	Growth rate between different breeds differs dramatically. Growth occurs during sleep and your puppy will spend approximately 90 percent of his time sleeping.
1–3	Growth and development during this stage are at their most rapid. Your puppy's shape is very different from his adult form and some of his limbs may appear disproportionate at times.
4–12	Isometric growth stage where growth patterns across the breeds stabilizes and the body parts grow at approximately the same rate. Proportions between adult and juvenile do not differ significantly although younger dogs are lighter in size and stature.
12–36	Giant breeds may take a full 3 years to complete their growth.

Very young puppies are visibly infantile and this often triggers our nurturing instincts and helps us to bond with our dogs.

Growth influences

Females have slower growth rates than males. They reach their full height at between 8 months and a year, but muscular development continues. The influences on the development of your puppy are:

• Nutrition
• Hormones and metabolic changes
• Environmental factors.

Bone and limb development

Growth plates are soft areas at the end of your puppy's bones. This is where growth takes place. When the growth plates finally "close" by hardening with calcium, significant growth is complete. On average, this is at about one year of age. Before this stage the soft areas of the bone are susceptible to certain types of stress, which is one reason why excessive physical activity is not advisable.

Sex hormones: The growth of your puppy's limbs is influenced by the sex hormones that are responsible for closing the growth plates during puberty. A male or female dog that has been neutered before this stage will continue growing, making them typically taller and leaner, with a slightly narrower chest and skull.

Growing pains

Medium to giant breeds sometimes exhibit short periods of lameness, often shifting between limbs, during periods of rapid growth. Usually, growing pains will disappear as the puppy's growth slows, but you should ask your vet, who will check that he is growing as he should. He may benefit from analgesics during this time.

Muscular changes

While your puppy matures, his muscle mass will increase. This is very noticeable from adolescence onward when increasing muscle mass causes the dog to appear to be "filling out."

Puppies are naturally boisterous and exuberant but take care not to overexercise your dog while he is still growing.

Genetic influences

Your puppy's inherited genetic codes will be the most powerful influence on his overall growth and development. Selecting physically sound and psychologically stable parents is vital.

Your puppy's DNA will determine his overall shape as it controls how much the body grows and when it stops. You may be surprised to know that a small dog has a shorter growth period than a larger one.

Healthy exercise

Your puppy requires regular exercise throughout his growth period, although some giant breeds may need less than you might imagine (ask your vet for advice). You must customize his exercise routine to meet his individual requirements: his breed, age, size and general state of physical health. His bones are not at full strength until he is a fully grown adult dog, so don't overdo it during the early months and cause potential future health problems.

Find a healthy balance of exercise for your growing puppy to protect his limbs

Visiting the vet

MAKE IT A PLEASANT EXPERIENCE

Trips to the veterinary clinic can be quite stressful for your puppy due to illness or injury. However, providing positive experiences early on in life can reduce the likelihood of fear associations causing later problems.

Find a vet

Ask for recommendations or research nearby vet clinics. The clinic should be reasonably close, allowing you to get there quickly in an emergency. Find out about its services and opening hours by visiting or checking online. You will need to register your puppy.

Book an appointment: Choose a time when the clinic is most likely to be quiet – the receptionist can advise you. The benefits of this include:

- Avoiding too many new people and animals at once, which might overwhelm your puppy
- A reduced risk of cross-infection
- Less chance of long delays.

What to expect

Your puppy's first visit to your local veterinary clinic is likely to consist of a full physical examination:

- A physical check of his eyes, ears, mouth and body condition
- Listening to his heart and lungs
- Weighing him
- His first vaccination
- Microchipping.

Waiting room

These areas may be tiny, forcing owners and their pets to sit very close to one another, or they can be very spacious with separate rooms provided for cats and dogs. If possible, try to avoid sitting next to a noisy, boisterous dog since your puppy may feel overwhelmed. Talk quietly and reassuringly to him but avoid making too much fuss.

Stay calm! Your behavior will influence how your puppy responds. If he thinks you are tense, worried or nervous, he is more likely to feel stressed, too.

Be prepared

Prior to your appointment, gather together the things you'll need to avoid rushing on the day.

- Take along any paperwork relating to your puppy's earlier medical history, including the dates of worming and flea treatments and the names of the products used.
- A selection of his treats, so the staff can make friends with him and also for rewarding him during the examination.
- Cleanup bags and wipes for your journey and for any waiting room accidents.

A visit to the vet should be a pleasurable experience for your puppy.

During the consultation

Puppies are usually examined on the table by the vet, but, if preferred, you can request that he is checked on the floor. Tell your vet briefly about his background, health and diet. This gives your puppy an opportunity to relax. Your vet may offer him some treats periodically throughout the examination or you can do so yourself.

• Talk quietly to your puppy, gently stroking him.
• Don't panic if he gets a little wriggly or upset.
• If possible, distract him while your vet vaccinates or inserts the microchip.
• Offer praise and treats when he stays calm and after any treatment.

Your vet will probably examine your dog on the table.

Physical contact

From the moment you bring your puppy home from the breeder, get him accustomed to being touched and handled from head to toe. Ask your family and friends to get involved, so he learns to tolerate contact with different people.

Before you leave...

• Clarify any instructions.
• Settle your bill.
• Make an appointment for your puppy's next vaccination and make a note of it.

Extra visits

It is good practice to take your puppy to your local veterinary clinic regularly during his first year. Rather than leave him at home or outside in the car, take him in with you while you shop or just to have him weighed. The staff may allow you to go into an empty consulting room to explore and practice lifting him onto the examination table. Praise and treat him for his good behavior and make it a pleasant experience for him. Visiting the clinic without any cause for examinations or treatments will help your puppy to relax and he is less likely to be fearful on future visits to the vet.

Checkups at 6 months and 1 year are recommended

Vaccinations

PROTECTING YOUR PUPPY FROM DISEASE

It is very important to protect your puppy from the diseases that can cause him serious harm, or even death. Although routine vaccination of puppies has reduced the incidence of canine disease, a risk remains since many dogs are not, and never have been, vaccinated. A vaccination contains a small amount of an infectious agent that stimulates the dog's immune system to develop protection against that particular disease.

Routine vaccinations

Vaccination provides protection against the following contagious viruses:

- Rabies
- Canine distemper virus
- Infectious canine hepatitis
- Canine parvovirus
- Parainfluenza
- Leptospirosis.

Additional options

- **Kennel cough vaccine:** This is required for puppies going into boarding kennels and it is normally given intra-nasally.

Vets recommend that your puppy has yearly boosters

Understanding the viruses

Rabies	Attacks nervous system; usually fatal. Transmittable to humans.
Canine distemper virus	Attacks immune system; 90% fatal.
Infectious canine hepatitis	Protects against two forms of virus: • CAV-1 attacks the liver • CAV-2 causes a persistent infectious cough.
Canine parvovirus	Attacks digestive system; weakens heart and immune system. Puppies are particularly vulnerable, especially Rottweilers, Dobermann Pinschers and German Shepherds. Often fatal; requires hospitalization.
Parainfluenza	Infectious respiratory disease.
Leptospirosis	Damages kidneys and liver. Contracted through contact with water contaminated with rat urine. Can be transmitted to humans.
Infectious canine tracheobronchitis (kennel cough)	Respiratory illness.

Timeline

Time	Vaccination type
From 6 weeks	First vaccination
From 10 weeks	Second vaccination
Approximately 16 weeks	A third parvovirus vaccination, if required
14–15 months	Booster vaccination
Each year thereafter	Booster vaccination

A few seconds is all it takes to vaccinate your puppy against the most common contagious canine viruses.

Once immunity has been gained, your puppy is free to socialize with all dogs and to be taken for walks in public places.

Routine vaccination procedure

It takes just seconds to administer the vaccine. The vaccination is given as a combination to cover all the diseases. Puppies rarely react, although some might feel a sting for a few seconds.

Vaccination certificate

A vaccination record card will be provided, and this will be required as evidence if your puppy needs to stay in kennels, is joining a training class or traveling with you. Each year the card will be updated and stamped by your vet.

What happens next?

It is usual for your puppy to wait a week after the second vaccination for full immunity before going out walking. Your vet will advise you according to the brand of vaccine that is used.

Side effects

While problems are very rare, if your puppy has a reaction after being vaccinated, call your vet immediately and explain the symptoms. Usually only minor treatment is required in the form of an antihistamine. Discuss any reactions before giving future boosters but don't let them put you off. They include reduced appetite, a small swelling at the injection site, low-grade fever, muscular aches and altered sleeping patterns. More severe reactions may be a swollen face, hives and vomiting.

You must take care to restrict your puppy to your yard and areas that are free from un-vaccinated dogs until he is fully protected.

Health checklist

Most puppies are very robust and it is highly unlikely that any health problems will arise. Regular and basic observation of your dog will alert you to any changes in his normal health and behavior. It is always better to be aware of and prevent any potential problems before they happen. Most minor ones can be sorted out at home, but if you are concerned about your dog's health, make an appointment with your vet.

Routine care

The most important thing you can do for your puppy's health is to simply practice regular care. Make sure his feeding times are regular (and that his food suits him), and give him regular exercise and grooming. Also make sure that his vaccinations are up to date. Preventative health checks are also a good idea, although there is no need to become obsessed with your puppy's health and you should remember that the key word is "preventative."

Check the following

- Eyes for changes in color or appearance, discharge or staining.
- Feces for frequency and consistency and any abnormalities.
- Ears for discharge, inflammation or soreness.
- Paws for lameness, wounds, cracks, overgrown claws and grass seeds.
- Skin for wounds, sore patches, rashes, scaling or inflammation.
- Body for lumps, swellings, fleas and ticks.
- Mouth for broken teeth, swellings or growths.

Vaccinations

It is important to keep up to date with your dog's vaccinations. Puppies have an immune system of their own from birth and are safeguarded by this for a few weeks via their mother's milk. However, they do need protection from some canine diseases, and there are routine vaccines to guard against rabies, canine distemper, hepatitis, parvovirus, coronavirus, leptospirosis and parainfluenza.

First vaccination: At 6 to 8 weeks.

Second vaccination: At least 2, not more than 4, weeks later; it can't be given before 10 weeks.

Booster: This is required annually following the second vaccination.

Symptoms of intestinal worms
- Loss of appetite
- Coat in poor condition
- A pot belly
- Weight loss
- Diarrhea
- Vomiting
- Lethargy
- Anemia – pale gums
- Worm segments around anal area
- Continual licking of anal area
- Dragging bottom along the floor

From 6 months onward, dogs should be wormed once every 3 months

Health problems and symptoms

Lameness	Problems with mobility, painful areas, swellings and lumps.
Appetite	Variations in appetite can indicate ill health.
Weight loss	Progressive weight loss needs checking out by your vet.
Skin problems	Should feel tight and elastic with no rashes, lumps or bumps.
Eye problems	Signs of veins, ulcers, sores, persistent watering, opacity, inflammation or discharge.
Ear problems	Buildup of wax, matted hair, discharge, scratching ears and shaking head or tilting it to side.
Mouth problems	The gums and roof should look pink and healthy. Teeth should be white with no discoloration.
Constipation	Not passing stools may be due to old age, poor diet or an obstruction.
Vomiting	Could indicate various problems. Take your puppy off his normal food and offer rice and plain chicken for a couple of days. If this does not work, see your vet.
Diarrhea	Bloody or loose stools – offer lots of fluids and cut out solid foods. If it is severe, consult your vet.
Sneezing	Inhaling grass seeds can cause sneezing. Other causes of persistent sneezing or nasal discharge include rhinitis, sinusitis, canine distemper and kennel cough.
Coughing	Constant coughing can indicate an infection, inflammation or irritation. See your vet.
Fleas	Persistent scratching and telltale "coal dust"-like droppings in the coat.
Worms	Bowel upsets, dragging the rear end along the floor and even emaciation and fits.

Parasite control

KEEPING YOUR PUPPY PARASITE-FREE

Your puppy is susceptible to several different types of parasites, external and internal. Protect his health and prevent transmission to other pets and humans with a regular parasite prevention and removal routine.

Fleas

These are the most common external parasite affecting all ages of dog. They feed on blood and reproduce remarkably quickly.

Transmitted by	Contact with infested animals or environment.
Signs include	Scratching, excessive grooming, flea feces (black flecks) in the coat, skin irritation, scabs.
Risk to humans	Fleas can bite and feed from humans.
Control and treatment	Regular application of topical products (available as sprays, powders or liquids), tablets, injections or prescription collar and treatment of the home (sprays, powders, vacuuming).

Caution! Flea control is now required throughout the year, due to central heating.

Effectively controlling fleas

If you notice fleas on your puppy, take urgent action to prevent a serious infestation. For every flea found on your pet there will be many more in your house; repeated vacuuming, washing and powders/sprays are required. Treat all pets with suitable products. Dogs and cats will need different treatments, and dosages will vary depending upon pet weight.

Ticks

Just a few of the North American tick species are problematic to dogs, but while traveling your puppy may encounter other species that pose an increased risk. Ticks are irritating and can also carry and transmit disease, especially Lyme disease (borreliosis).

Transmitted by	Physical contact with infected areas, including woods, forests, swampy areas and grasslands.
Signs include	Often mistaken as small warts, ticks start out tiny, becoming more noticeable while feeding. Engorged females can grow to pea size. Puppy may scratch or have skin irritation around site of bite.
Risk to humans	Ticks can bite and feed from humans with a risk of disease transmission.
Control and treatment	Use a tick remover to detach a tick without breaking off the head, which burrows into skin. Topical treatments can provide protection.

Caution! If your puppy appears unwell during or after a tick bite, seek urgent veterinary advice.

Over-the-counter parasite remedies are not prescription strength

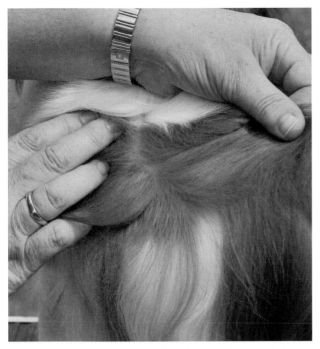

Examine your puppy regularly to check for fleas. Gently part his hair to look for evidence of flea feces (sooty black flecks) or skin irritation.

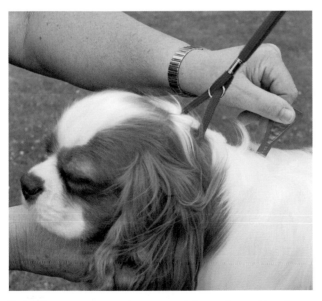

Topical flea treatments come in a measured dose and are quick and simple to administer. Just apply on the back of the neck behind the head.

Mites

The most common and problematic mite infestations cause a condition called mange.

Demodectic mange

Transmitted by	Lives naturally on skin, usually without causing a problem. Inherited low-resistance or stress may leave puppy vulnerable, particularly in first year.
Signs include	Thinning or patchy hair around eyes, mouth, front legs; may spread across body; possible skin irritation and scabs.
Risk to humans	None.
Control and treatment	Many cases recover within 3 months. Use medicated shampoo; relieve stress.

Sarcoptic mange (scabies)

Transmitted by	Contact with shared bedding and furniture.
Signs include	Itching and scratching, scabs on ear tips, hair loss, skin irritation and painful sores.
Risk to humans	Highly contagious but very short-lived.
Control and treatment	Pharmaceutical treatment kills the mite; antibiotics for secondary infections; regular use of medicated shampoo.

Other mite infestations

These include: cheyletiellosis, which causes a short-lived "walking dandruff"; harvest mites, which causes skin irritation, particularly on paws: and ear mites, which live in the ear canal.

Internal parasites

Living inside your puppy's intestines and other organs, internal parasites have complex life cycles involving other hosts and environmental conditions. Transmission between puppies and humans is possible but is not very common. However, infection with roundworm is particularly serious for children, so regular worming is essential.

Worming medications: These are available from your vet, and puppies usually receive their first dose at 3 weeks of age. This should be repeated every 3 weeks until they are 16 weeks old, and then at 6 months and twice a year thereafter.

Roundworm

This is the most common type of internal parasite affecting young puppies.

Transmitted by	Nursing from infected mother; during embryonic development if the mother is infected; eating an infected prey animal, e.g., birds or mice; eating worm eggs from the soil during play or exploration.
Signs include	Pot-bellied appearance, poor coat condition, impaired growth, diarrhea, vomiting, coughing, pneumonia.
Risk of transmission	Children are particularly at risk from roundworm.
Prevention	Good hygiene; regular puppy worming.
Treatment	Routine worming with follow-up treatment is required.

Caution! Thorough parasite treatment of both the mother and her puppies is essential for the continued health of both.

Tapeworm

You may notice this if small sections are passed out in your puppy's feces. They appear as tiny grains of rice on or around the anal region.

Transmitted by	Most commonly via eating an infected flea during grooming; ingesting other intermediate hosts (lice, mice, rats).
Signs include	Appetite loss, lethargy, dull coat, itchy bottom, anemia; can be asymptomatic.
Risk of transmission	Humans are susceptible.
Prevention	Good flea control; pick up feces to prevent eggs infecting the soil; good hygiene around dogs and cats and after contact with soil.
Treatment	Routine worming is required.

Lungworm

This lives in blood vessels supplying the lungs.

Transmitted by	Ingestion of slugs and snails.
Signs include	Coughing, diarrhea, vomiting, lethargy, loss of appetite, poor blood clotting (many dogs are asymptomatic).
Risk of transmission	Not transmissible to humans
Prevention	Pick up feces; control slugs and snails in yard (puppy-safe products only).
Treatment	A specific worming product in topical form and in some worming tablets.

Caution! Routine worming treatment will not necessarily prevent lungworm.

Hookworm and whipworm

Puppies that travel to other countries with their owners may be at increased risk from these blood-feeding worms, which live in the large intestine.

Transmitted by	Ingestion of eggs from environment or mother's milk; physical contact with larvae.
Signs include	Diarrhea, vomiting, weight loss, dehydration, anemia.
Risk of transmission	Transmission to humans in contact with contaminated ground.
Prevention	Regular worming to protect environment: picking up feces.
Treatment	Routine worming, then several follow-up treatments.

Heartworm

Puppies traveling to other countries may also be infected by this parasite.

Transmitted by	Mosquitos.
Signs include	Breathing difficulties, lethargy.
Prevention and treatment	Treatment prior to travel.

The breeder should provide paperwork of your puppy's worming history

Children are especially at risk of roundworm, so ensure that you worm your puppy on a regular basis – write the dates on your calendar.

Talk to your vet

Check which worming products are most suitable for your puppy. Treatment options usually involve a tablet or topical liquid, which you apply on the skin between his shoulders.

Take sensible measures to prevent transmission of parasites to humans. Worm your puppy regularly.

Neutering

WHY AND WHEN

Deciding whether or not to spay or castrate your puppy is a matter of personal choice. However, that choice should always be an informed one and you must consider the benefits and discuss them with your vet.

Should you breed from your puppy?

Rescue shelters and many breeders require you to sign an agreement to neuter your puppy and not to breed. Despite being adored by you, your puppy may not be suitable for breeding if he has physical, genetic or temperament problems.

When do you neuter?

Neutering at 6 months is commonplace. However, considering each case is important since puppies mature physically and emotionally at different rates. Therefore, many owners wait much longer than this until their puppy has physically matured in the hope that any potential problems can thus be avoided.

Choosing whether or not to allow your dog to breed should be a careful and considered decision – always talk to your vet about this.

What happens?

- **Males:** The testes are removed via a small incision across the scrotum.
- **Females:** The ovaries and uterus are removed via abdominal surgery.

Preparing for surgery

Your veterinary clinic's exact procedure will be explained to you in advance of the operation.

- You must not feed your puppy from the evening onward the night before surgery.
- Water can be available until early morning on the day of surgery.

Your puppy will be checked into the clinic early on the day of the operation. You must sign some paperwork, and he will remain an in-patient until he recovers from the anesthetic, usually later that afternoon.

Benefits of neutering

- No unwanted litters.
- Prevents the spread of genetic problems.
- Removes the risk of testicular disease in males.
- Reduces the risk of testosterone-driven diseases in males.
- Almost eliminates the risk of many cancers and pyometra in females if they are spayed before their second season.

The health benefits of neutering are extremely significant for females since one-quarter of non-neutered females will develop mammary tumors.

The right age at which to neuter your puppy will vary, depending to some extent upon his confidence – or lack of it.

Post-operative care

When you bring your puppy home after surgery, try to keep him calm, and avoid any strenuous exercise wherever possible. This can be quite challenging since most puppies revert to their normal exuberant behavior shortly after the operation. If your puppy is licking or scratching at the wound, you may have to use a plastic cone collar to prevent contact with the site. Return to the office for a wound check.

A healthy weight

Although your dog is more inclined to gain weight after neutering, you can avoid this potential side effect by feeding a healthy, nutritious diet in the correct quantities and strictly monitoring his exercise.

Common concerns

Concern	True or false?
A female should have a season	Not necessarily – the risk of cancers increase significantly with each subsequent season.
A female should have a litter	Absolutely not – having puppies puts strain on a dog and there's always a risk. There are too many unwanted puppies to justify having a litter for the experience.
Neutered dogs become fat	Neutering does not cause obesity; over-feeding and under-exercising do. Your neutered pet needs 25 percent fewer calories.
Neutering reduces a dog's working ability	There's no scientific evidence for this as most activities are not testosterone driven.
A male should be allowed to mate	Allowing this could result in puppies and development of unwanted behavior.
A male won't be male after neutering	This human fear is unfounded – your male dog will always be male. The reduction in testosterone may tone down specific behaviors but won't alter his genes.

Neutering during the second fear-imprint stage is not advisable if your puppy appears unusually sensitive or anxious

Weight management
THE RIGHT WEIGHT FOR YOUR PUPPY

While your puppy is small, you may not worry about his weight or the amount he eats, but bad dietary habits now can lead to a range of avoidable conditions. Overfeeding him increases his fat cell numbers, which remain with him throughout his life, making weight gain easier.

Obesity-related health problems

These problems include the following conditions and diseases: breathing difficulties, an increased risk of heat stroke, skin conditions, anal gland problems, high blood pressure, diabetes, heart disease, mammary tumors, bladder cancer, pancreatitis and a compromised immune system.

An active puppy fed a sensible diet is more likely to remain healthy than one that overeats and does not receive sufficient exercise.

Weighing

To ensure that you feed the appropriate amount of food, make sure you weigh your puppy regularly and adjust his portions accordingly. You can weigh him at home or take him into your veterinary clinic. Weighing is free and encouraged by your vet.

Body condition

Although your puppy's physique differs from his adult shape it's still possible to determine whether he is overweight. You should be able to feel his ribcage if you run your hands down his sides. If the ribs are visible, he may be underweight, (even Whippet and Greyhound puppies are rounded while very young). If there is a generous amount of padding over the ribs, making it difficult to feel them, this is a clue that he is carrying too much weight. His stomach should not sag excessively.

Sources of extra calories

Common treats	Human snack foods
Puppy milk bone: 10 kcal	Plain cookie: 80 kcal
Small gravy bone: 34 kcal	Old Cheddar (10 g): 44 kcal
Small dental sticks: 44 kcal	Bacon (1 slice): 64 kcal
Small jumbo bone: 295 kcal	Brown toast (1 slice): 65 kcal
Treat strips: 28 kcal	Chicken breast (whole): 342 kcal

Exercise

Increase your puppy's exercise gradually in line with your vet's recommendations. An additional leash walk around the block will burn calories while putting minimum strain on his limbs. Swimming is also good exercise, although take advice and implement safety measures.

Reasons for excess weight gain

- **Overfeeding:** Puppy food is highly palatable, resulting in overconsumption. Guessing portion sizes often results in inaccuracy. Overfeeding

Weigh out your puppy's food or use a marked measuring cup to prevent accidental overfeeding.

Unexplained weight gain

If you are genuinely at a loss as to why your puppy is gaining weight, it is a good idea to discuss the situation with your vet. Some medical conditions can lead to excess weight gain, including:

- Hypothyroidism
- Hormonal imbalances (more common in adult dogs).

treats, or the wrong kind, can also lead to excess weight gain (see the table opposite).
- **Lack of exercise**: Failure to burn off calories will result in weight gain.
- **Overindulgent owners**: Offering too many treats and scraps from the table will dramatically increase your puppy's calorie intake.

Family meeting

Sit down as a family and discuss how many and which treats you will offer your puppy. It can help to set out his entire daily food allowance in a specific treat container or pouch in the morning. Everyone should use these when they wish to feed, train or reward him until the supply is used up.

Diet choice

High-fiber diets help make a dog feel full, but feed a high-quality puppy diet while he is growing.

At least half of all dogs are overweight - a shocking statistic

Genetics checklist

Most dogs from reputable breeders will come to you with various genetic health checks already in place. Puppies are usually very robust and will grow into adults and lead extremely healthy lives. Unfortunately, some breeds are more inclined to suffer specific hereditary diseases, and it's good practice to know what they are in order to test for them and catch them early.

Inherited diseases

During the development of today's dog breeds, which has taken place over many years or even centuries in some cases, a particular set of physical and behavioral characteristics was achieved, sometimes by inbreeding. These physical traits are passed on to the next generation of dogs through genetic information, which is stored in their DNA. However, intensive breeding has also led to inherited diseases, which are passed on genetically, too, and these are now a matter of concern. You need to find out as much as possible about genetic disorders in the breeds that interest you before buying your puppy if possible, and discuss them with your vet and the breeder. Check that both parents of the puppy you choose are fit, healthy and free of any inherited conditions and that there are none in their bloodlines.

Testing

Many tests are available to determine whether your puppy carries any genes that may lead to health problems. Most reputable breeders will breed only from health-checked parents, but if you have any concerns, the following tests are available:

- prcd-PRA test for progressive retinal atrophy (PRA): Australian Shepherd, Miniature Poodle, Norwegian Elkhound – a group of diseases that cause the retina of the eye to degenerate slowly over time.
- Canine leukocyte adhesion deficiency (CLAD) test: Irish Setter – a devastating condition. Puppies that inherit this usually die early in life from multiple severe infections.
- Collie eye anomaly (CEA): seen most frequently in American Collies, but also Rough and Smooth Collies, Border Collies, Australian Shepherds, Lancashire Heelers and Shetland Sheepdogs.
- Hip dysplasia test: This test uses a system of hip scoring based on X-ray results. The lower the score the better.

There are tests for less common genetic defects. Speak to your vet if you have any concerns.

Warning signs

Females

- Excessive thirst – pyometra or diabetes.
- Mammary glands (breasts) – lumps and changes should be reported to your vet.
- Thickened skin/hair loss – possibly linked to hormonal problems.

Males

- Change in foreskin – discharge or blood could signify severe infection.
- Testicles – lumps need checking out by the vet.
- Feces – excessive straining could signal an enlarged prostate.

Genetic diseases and breeds

Addison's disease	Leonbergers, Rottweiler, Standard Poodle, West Highland White Terrier.
Anemia	American Cocker Spaniel, Miniature Schnauzer.
Atopic dermatitis	Golden Retriever, Labrador, Bull Terrier, Staffordshire Bull Terrier, West Highland White Terrier.
Cataracts	American Cocker Spaniel, Beagle, Golden Retriever, Labrador, Poodle, Pug.
Collie eye	Collie, Shetland Sheepdog.
Deafness	Border Collie, Boston Terrier, Bull Terrier, Dalmatian, English Setter, Old English Sheepdog.
Ectropion	Clumber Spaniel, St. Bernard.
Entropion	Shar-Pei and other breeds.
Glaucoma	American Cocker Spaniel, Poodle.
Hip dysplasia	Labrador, Retriever, German Shepherd, Rottweiler.
Hypothyroidism	Beagle, Dobermann, Golden Retriever.
Lens luxation	Border Collie, Shar-Pei, Fox Terrier, Yorkshire Terrier.
Lymphoma	Rottweiler, Boxer, Cocker Spaniel, German Shepherd.
Mitral valve disease (MVD)	Cavalier King Charles Spaniel, Cocker Spaniel, Dachshund, Irish Setter, Poodle
Osteochondrosis dessicans	Border Collie, Great Dane, Golden Retriever, Labrador.
Patella luxation	Pomeranian, Chow Chow, Labrador, Shar-Pei.
Progressive retinal atrophy	Irish Setter, Springer Spaniel.
Pyometra	Cavalier King Charles Spaniel, Rough Collie, Rottweiler.
Subaortic stenosis	Boxer, German Shepherd, German Shorthaired Pointer, Newfoundland.
Syringomyelia	Cavalier King Charles Spaniel.
Von Willebrand's Disease	Dobermann, German Shepherd, Golden Retriever.

Accidents and first aid

ALWAYS BE PREPARED!

Unfortunately, despite all their owners' care and attention, puppies do sometimes injure themselves. While it's important to seek veterinary attention, sometimes it can be very helpful to know how to manage the situation until you get your puppy to the clinic. Minor problems may just need your attention at home to prevent them worsening.

First-aid kit

Every dog owner needs a well-stocked first-aid kit. Assemble one yourself or purchase a ready-made one. Regularly check that it is fully stocked and dispose of out-of-date or damaged items. Keep one at home and another in your car; injuries can occur while you are out walking your puppy. In addition to the items in the table below, you may also need:

- A blanket or towel that you can use to lift and transport an injured puppy.
- A flashlight, since not all accidents occur in

First-aid kit

Useful items	Purpose
A strong, sealed container	To keep all your items safe, clean and dry.
Contact details of veterinary clinic	Makes contacting them easier if you panic or rely on another person.
Saline solution	Flushing out dirt from eyes and wounds.
Antiseptic ointment	For minor cuts and grazes.
Alcohol-free cleansing wipes	Cleaning wounds.
Sterile, nonstick dressing pads	Protecting wounds.
Flexible bandages, different widths	To wrap around injured area.
Microporous tape	To secure bandages and dressings.
Cotton balls	Wiping and absorbing fluids.
Latex gloves /hand cleaner/sanitizer	Hygiene.
Tweezers	Removal of splinters, glass, grass seeds.
Blunt-ended scissors	Cutting bandages and dressings to size; removing hair.
Foil blanket	Helps maintain body warmth – vital in cases of shock.
Cold pack	To reduce swelling and inflammation.
Tick remover tool	Safe removal of ticks.
Styptic powder	To stop bleeding nails.
Plastic pouch/bags and tape	To cover injured feet.
Muzzle or spare bandage to secure mouth	Pain often leads to aggression, so protect yourself.

daylight; this is also useful for checking inside ears.
- A dog bowl that can be used to offer water or hold a saline solution while cleaning a wound.
- A filled water container for drinking or washing minor cuts and wounds.
- Treats to distract your puppy and reward him for tolerating handling (do not feed him if an operation seems necessary).

Road traffic accidents

Always seek veterinary help, even if the incident seems minor, since internal injuries or even some fractures are not always immediately apparent.

- Take care never to put yourself in danger on the road.
- Lift your puppy onto a towel or a coat to make transportation to the vet easier.
- If he is able to get up, make sure that his leash is attached to prevent him from running away in panic – even injured animals can be surprisingly mobile at first.
- Use a pressure bandage to slow the rate of any heavy bleeding.
- If his legs are injured, carry your puppy by supporting his chest and stomach, allowing the limbs to hang freely.
- If possible, call ahead to the veterinary clinic to prepare them for your arrival.

If your puppy gets injured, you can use a towel, blanket or some clean clothing to pick him up and keep him safe from further damage.

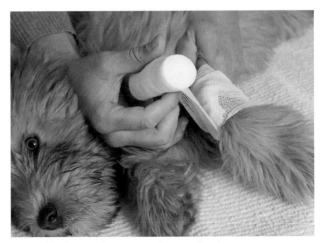

To stem bleeding, apply pressure to the wound and use a temporary dressing and a bandage to keep it in place.

Stay calm - panicking will cause delays and worry your puppy

Open wounds

The sight of blood can cause owners to panic, but you must try to stay calm. Some parts of the body, such as the ears and tail, bleed profusely, even from tiny wounds. Apply pressure and seek help if even small wounds don't stop bleeding.

Cuts and grazes	Clean minor wounds to prevent infection. Bathe with saline solution to flush out dirt before adding a protective dressing. Seek veterinary advice if you are concerned about infection or the wound needs more attention.
Internal bleeding	Any bleeding from nose, ears, mouth or anus should be taken seriously and urgent veterinary care sought. Pale gums are an indicator that something is wrong – get your vet to examine your puppy.
External bleeding	Apply a pressure bandage to slow the bleeding and seek veterinary help.

Accidental ingestion

Your puppy's inquisitive nature might lead him to ingest a dangerous product. Report swallowed nonfood items to your vet; intestinal blockages could be serious.

Poisoning	If you suspect that your puppy has ingested poison in any form, seek urgent veterinary attention. Any delay could prevent treatment being successful. Take the product or a sample of it with you, so the appropriate treatment can be selected.
Choking	Puppies often get twigs or bones wedged in the roof of their mouth. Pull these out carefully, and arrange a veterinary check as splinters may remain. If the airway is completely blocked, a dog will not be able to cough or make a sound. Try to get hold of the object but don't push as you risk forcing it further down. Tip your dog forward or lift him to help the item fall out. Call the vet's emergency line to find out about safe procedures while taking your dog to the clinic.

Using a tie as an emergency muzzle

1 Carefully wrap the tie around your puppy's muzzle to keep his mouth closed.

2 Swivel the tie so that the long ends are positioned below his muzzle.

3 Secure the ends behind the back of the head by tying firmly in a bow.

Bites and stings

Disturbing insects and other animals when out walking can have unintended consequences.

Stings	If your puppy sustains multiple stings, seek veterinary care. Remove single stings with tweezers by scraping them out rather than squeezing, which could force more poison into your puppy. Bathe the wound with diluted vinegar solution for wasp stings; baking soda solution for bee stings. Keep your puppy quiet and seek help if he has trouble breathing or if there's excessive swelling.
Snake bites	Limit movement by carrying the puppy and transporting him directly to a vet. Identify the snake but never put yourself at risk.

If your puppy gets burnt or scalded, immerse the affected area in cold water or apply a cold compress for approximately 10 minutes.

Burns and scalds

It's imperative that you act really quickly. Apply plenty of cold water immediately and then hold an ice pack or a bag of frozen peas on the affected area. For electrical and chemical burns, you must always seek veterinary advice. Don't wait.

Serious conditions

Some problems require emergency attention, so seek veterinary attention if you see or suspect any of the following.

Seizure	Make sure your puppy is not in a dangerous position (near stairs, fires, electrical equipment). Remove his collar to ease breathing. Keep his airways open. Keep the area quiet and dark. Pay attention to details, e.g., duration of the fit, how he appears afterward and how he was before. This will help your vet when you can get there.
Bloated stomach	Any unusual distension requires immediate veterinary attention.
Collapse	Ensure your puppy's airway is open and transport to your vet.
Heat stroke	Veterinary care is critical. During the trip to the vet, try to cool him down with water sprays, air fans or cooling pads (pay attention to foot pads, front armpits and groin).

INDEX

ACKNOWLEDGMENTS

Executive editor: Trevor Davies
Designed and produced by SP Creative Design
Editor: Heather Thomas
Designer: Rolando Ugolini
Special photography: Tom Miles

Picture credits

The publishers would like to thank: Jay Allen and Phlip Taylor, Yvonne Bannister, Ros Beck, Philip Chippindale, Nikki Fowler, Helen and Zoe Gardner, John and Ruth Hopkin, Victoria Judge, Margaret Kempster, Tim Lodge, Claire Martin, Helen Pickering, Heather Pitt, Ann and Trevor Reynolds, Victoria Rock, Donna Rowan-Gold, Lesley Thomson, Julia Wigley, Clare Wilson.

Octopus Publishing Group Limited/Tom Miles 11 bottom left, 33, 37, 51, 53, 55, 61, 65, 67, 69, 73, 80 top right, 81 bottom left, 82, 83, 88, 89 top, 91, 93 right, 94, 98, 100, 103, 105, 108, 109, 110, 111, 112, 119 right, 121, 122, 123, 124, 125, 129 bottom, 131, 133, 134, 143, 146 top, 149 left, 154, 158, 159, 160, 163, 165 top, 169, 170, 171, 172, 175, 179 bottom, 180, 181, 182, 183, 185 bottom, 186, 189, 190, 191, 193, 195, 197, 198, 199, 201, 202, 207, 208, 210, 213, 216, 217, 218, 220, 221, 222, 223, 225, 230, 231, 234, 236, 237 left, 238, 241, 245 255, 256, 257, 259, 271 top, 275,

Octopus Publishing Group Limited 10, 12, 14, 17, 18, 19, 20, 23, 31, 39, 47, 76, 78, 81 top left, 95, 101, 104, 106, 107, 116, 117, 118, 126, 136, 140, 141, 142, 147, 156, 161, 162, 164, 165 bottom, 179 top, 203, 209, 215, 224, 232, 239, 247, 251, 252, 262, 263, 265 top left, 279, 280, 281

Octopus Publishing Group Limited/Mugford 11 top left, 11 bottom right, 13, 15, 21, 49, 57, 59, 63, 71, 75, 77, 79, 86, 114, 115, 135, 139, 145, 146 bottom, 151, 152, 153, 155, 157, 167, 174, 177, 185 top, 187, 188, 205, 211, 212, 219, 227, 244, 249, 261, 274,

SP Creative Design 7, 8, 9, 11 top right, 16, 25, 27, 29, 35, 41, 43, 45, 80 top left, 80 bottom, 81 bottom right, 85, 89 bottom, 90, 93 top left, 96, 97, 99, 113, 119 left, 120, 129 top, 137, 138, 144, 149 right, 150, 166, 176, 206, 214, 226, 228, 229, 233, 235, 237 right, 242, 243, 246, 248, 250, 253, 258, 260, 265 top right, 265 bottom, 269, 271 bottom, 272, 273,

Philip Chippindale 127

Warren Photographic 22, 24, 26, 28, 30, 32, 34, 36, 38, 40, 42, 44, 46, 48, 50, 52, 54, 56, 58, 60, 62, 64, 66, 68, 70, 72, 74,